FUTURES BY DESIGN

THE PRACTICE OF
ECOLOGICAL PLANNING

Edited by
DOUG ABERLEY

THE NEW CATALYST BIOREGIONAL SERIES

NEW SOCIETY PUBLISHERS

Gabriola Island, BC   Philadelphia, PA

Canadian Cataloguing in Publication Data
    Main entry under title:
    Futures by Design

    (The new catalyst bioregional series; 7-8)
    Includes bibliographical references.
    ISBN 1-55092-240-8 (bound). -- ISBN 1-55092-241-6 (pbk.)

    1. Land use -- Planning -- Envirnonmental aspects. 2. Urbanization -- Environmental
aspects. 3. Human ecology. 4 Environmental impact analysis.
    I. Aberley, Doug. II Series.
    GF101.F87 1994   363.7'05   C94-910539-2

Inquiries regarding requests to reprint all or part of *Futures by Design: The Practice of
Ecological Planning* should be addressed to:
    New Society Publishers,
    P.O. Box 189, Gabriola Island, B.C., Canada V0R 1X0,
or
    4527 Springfield Avenue, Philadelphia PA, U.S.A. 19143.

Canada ISBN: 1-55092-241-6 (Paperback)
Canada ISBN: 1-55092-240-8 (Hardback)
USA ISBN: 0-86571-298-0 (Paperback)
USA ISBN: 0-86571-297-2 (Hardback)

Cover design by David Lester.

Printed in the United States of America on partially recycled paper using soy-based ink
 by Capital City Press, of Montpelier, Vermont

To order directly from the publishers, please add $2.50 to the price of the first copy, and
75 cents for each additional copy (plus GST in Canada). Send check or money order to:
    New Society Publishers,
    P.O. Box 189, Gabriola Island, B.C. Canada V0R 1X0
or
    4527 Springfield Avenue, Philadelphia PA, U.S.A. 19143.

New Society Publishers is a project of the Catalyst Education Society, a nonprofit
educational society in Canada, and the New Society Educational Foundation, a non-
profit, tax-exempt public foundation in the U.S. Opinions expressed in this book do not
necessarily reflect positions of the Catalyst Education Society nor the New Society Educational Foundation.

Futures by Design represents numbers 7 & 8 (a double volume) in *The New Catalyst*'s
Bioregional Series of books which is also available by subscription. Write: New Society
Publishers, Canada.

The New Catalyst Bioregional Series

The *New Catalyst* Bioregional Series was begun in 1990, the start of what some were calling "the turnaround decade" in recognition of the warning that humankind had ten years to turn around its present course, or risk such permanent damage to planet Earth that human life would likely become unviable. Unwilling to throw in the towel, *The New Catalyst*'s editorial collective took up the challenge of presenting, in new form, ideas and experiences that might radically influence the future.

As a tabloid, *The New Catalyst* magazine has been published quarterly since 1985. From the beginning, an important aim was to act as a catalyst among the diverse strands of the alternative movement—to break through the overly sharp dividing lines between environmentalists and aboriginal nations; peace activists and permaculturalists; feminists, food co-ops, city-reinhabitants and back-to-the-landers—to promote healthy dialogue among all these tendencies working for progressive change, for a new world. The emerging bioregional movement was itself a catalyst and umbrella for these groups, and so *The New Catalyst* became a bioregional journal for the northwest, consciously attempting to draw together the local efforts of people engaged in both resistance and renewal from as far apart as northern British Columbia, the Great Lakes, and the Ozark mountains, as well as the broader, more global thinking of key people from elsewhere in North America and around the world.

To broaden its readership, *The New Catalyst* changed format, the tabloid reorganized to include primarily material of regional importance, and distributed free, and the more enduring articles of relevance to a wider, continental audience now published twice yearly in *The New Catalyst*'s Bioregional Series—a magazine in book form! Through this new medium, we hope to encourage on-going dialogue among overlapping networks of interest, to solidify our common ground, expand horizons, and provoke deeper analysis of our collective predicament as well as a sharing of those practical, local initiatives that are the cutting edge of more widespread change.

The Bioregional Series aims to inspire and stimulate the building of new, ecologically sustainable cultures and communities in their myriad facets through presenting a broad spectrum of concerns ranging from how we view the world and act within it, through efforts at restoring damaged ecosystems or greening the cities, to the raising of a new and hopeful generation. It is designed not for those content with merely saving what's left, but for those forward-looking folk with abundant energy for life, upon whom the future of Earth depends.

Other volumes in the series include *Turtle Talk: Voices For A Sustainable Future*, (No.1), *Green Business: Hope or Hoax?* (No.2), *Putting Power In Its Place: Create Community Control!* (No.3), *Living With The Land: Communities Restoring The Earth* (No.4), *Circles of Strength: Community Alternatives to Alienation* (No.5) and *Boundaries of Home: Mapping for Local Empowerment* (No.6).

The *Bioregional Series* and *The New Catalyst* magazine are available at a discount by subscription from: Box 189, Gabriola Island, B.C., Canada V0R 1X0.

Table of Contents

Acknowledgments

Publication of this volume would not have been possible without the support of the 19 contributors who freely donated their considerable ecological insight and writing talent. Despite busy schedules, illness, and in one case, family loss, they all demonstrated a dedication that bodes well for the future of the alternative culture we are trying to create.

This is the second volume I have edited in *The New Catalyst*'s Bioregional Series, the first being *Boundaries of Home: Mapping for Local Empowerment*. The idea for these two volumes came from discussions with New Society Publishers about the acute need to demonstrate processes by which bioregional intent could be translated into bioregional action. I am particularly grateful for the support of Chris Plant in this endeavor. Without his transatlantic patience, and shared commitment to the evolution of guides to practical bioregionalism, neither volume would have been completed. Sincere appreciation is also given to my partner, Amandah Lea, who assisted with the complicated logistics of organizing these words.

The discipline of ecological planning does not exist wholly in any textbook, nor can it be found under a convenient heading in any library. It is a pursuit alive in the words of a number of disparate and talented writers, and in the deeds of thousands of individuals. The articles in this volume represent only a highly selective sample of this lore. Because any such compilation is ultimately a personal construct, I take responsiblity for any errors of fact, organization, or omission. I should also make clear that this short book is not intended to be the definitive work on ecological planning. It is more a trail marker, meant to guide a journey rather than to explain fully the destination.

Grateful acknowledgment is made for permission to reprint previously published material from the following sources:

"An Outline for an Ecological Politics" by Murray Bookchin is excerpted with modifications by the author from *Defending The Earth: A Dialogue Between Murray Bookchin and Dave Foreman*, Boston: South End Press, 1991, and is reprinted with permission of the author and South End Press.

"Cerro Gordo: Eco-Village Building and Eco-City Networking" by Christopher Canfield is excerpted from *Sustainable Cities: Concepts and Strategies for Eco-city Development*, Los Angeles: EcoHome Media, 1992, and is reprinted by permission of the author and Eco-Home Media.

"Natural and City Ecosytems: Thoughts on City Ecology" by Jane Jacobs is excerpted with modifications by the author from her foreword to a new (1993) Modern Library edition of her first book, *The Death and Life of Great American Cities*, New York: Doubleday, 1992, and is reprinted by permission of the author and Doubleday.

"If the World Were a Village of 1,000 People," by Donella H. Meadows is reprinted by permission of the author.

"Permaculture" by Bill Mollison is excerpted from *Permaculture: A Designers' Manual*, Tyalgum, New South Wales: Tagari Publications, 1990, and is reprinted by permission of the author and Tyalgum Publications.

"The Wildlands Project: Land Conservation Strategy" by Reed F. Noss is reprinted from *Wild Earth* Special Issue Fall 1992, by permission of Wild Earth.

"Ancient Futures" by Helena Norberg-Hodge is excerpted with modifications by the author from *Ancient Futures: Learning From Ladakh*, Rider Publications, 1991 and is reprinted by permission of the author.

"Coming in to the Watershed" by Gary Snyder is reprinted from *Wild Earth* Special Issue, Fall 1992, by permission of the author and Wild Earth.

"The Living Landscape: An Ecological Approach to Landscape Planning" by Frederick Steiner is excerpted from *The Living Landscape: An Ecological Approach to Landscape Planning*, New York: McGraw-Hill, 1991, by permission of the author and McGraw-Hill.

All remaining articles are adapted from previously unpublished speeches, or are original written works. Illustrations were kindly supplied by the authors of the articles within which they appear.

This book is dedicated to those who kept the regionalist beacon burning throughout a long lonely period: Sophie and Peter Kropotkin, Anna and Patrick Geddes, Sophia and Lewis Mumford, Benton MacKaye, Clarence and Aline Stein, Howard and Anna Odum, Florence and Peter van Dresser, and their colleagues. These people lit the beacon for us. It's our turn, now, to turn that beacon into a wildfire.

Doug Aberley
Edinburgh, Alba

Foreword

David Suzuki

As a biologist, I tend to look at our species the way I look at the fruitfly, an insect that I spent 25 years of my life studying. Viewed as a biological organism, we're not that impressive—a fruitfly can fly on its own, land on the ceiling, and easily give birth to 600 offspring! Humankind is not very strong or fast, nor gifted with sensory acuity or defence mechanisms. The great survival strategy of our species is an immense and complicated brain which has conferred upon us qualities of memory, curiosity, imagination and inventiveness.

Our ability for abstract thinking gives us a sense of a future which no other species has. Because of this, humankind—more than any other species—has deliberately chosen from an array of options to ensure its maximal chances of survival. And it has worked. So it is strange that, today, when we have computers and telecommunications and all of the amplified brainpower of scientists and engineers, we no longer seem able to choose from a range of options based on what the present indicates, as our ancestors did so succesfully in the past.

This century, human societies have undergone explosive change as a result of technological innovation, increased population, higher material demands and consumption, a massive move to cities, and the globalization of economies. Most people alive today have been born since the end of World War II, an interval of unprecedented change and unsustainable growth. The print and electronic media glorify the benefits of greater consumption while fragmenting information into bits and pieces that are disconnected from context or time. Subsequently, people have become increasingly myopic about the past and future, at the same time as being unaware of the setting within which to assess current events.

Following the broadcast of a five-part Canadian Broadcasting Corporation radio series, "It's a Matter of Survival," over 16,000 listeners wrote letters in response. Most agreed with the thesis of the series that the very fabric of the biosphere is being torn apart by human activity. But they ended with the plaintive question, "What can I do?" While humans have access to massive amounts of information describing the state of the

Earth, we seem incapable of acting upon it to influence the future.

In a historically short period of time, we have come to accept that change is a necessary part of our lives, that the global economy must dominate our political and social agendas, that what is newest is best, that bigger is better, and that economic growth is the measure of progress. Each of these erroneous assumptions has enormous consequences while, collectively, they paralyze us with a sense of our own impotence.

Fortunately, another kind of change is already taking place. The environmental movement of the 1970s and '80s has been enormously succesful at sounding the alarm. But now, with massive political and economic restructuring taking place, we need a concrete vision of truly sustainable communities, together with specific strategies to take us toward that vision. Increasingly, the ingredients of such a vision are coming from a wide range of people who have spent considerable time developing an ecological awareness, as well as putting that awareness into practice. The outcome is the rapid development of ecological planning, embraced by professionals and grassroots activists alike, and focusing equally on city and country, North and South. Appropriately, by providing us with the tools for seeing the past and present clearly, and thus being able to actually *plan* for a future of our best choosing, this trend promises to restore to our species the ability to adapt.

Futures by Design brings together some of the leading thinkers who are "doers" as well as theorists. Based on extensive and practical experience, they offer us a chance to reclaim that unique survival protocol of our species: to be able to examine our current state, consider the options that are available, and then select the best paths to a harmonious relationship with our surroundings and communities that provide us the highest possible quality of life.

There is still time to change, and *now* is that time. *Futures by Design* goes a long way to giving tangible directions that each of us can follow.

Trained as a geneticist, David Suzuki is also a well-known broadcaster, and Chairman of the David Suzuki Foundation in Vancouver, British Columbia.

1

Weeds in the Cartesian Garden: The Context of Ecological Planning

Doug Aberley

A visit to any progressive bookstore will reveal shelves full of useful volumes which reflect on aspects of social change. The great majority of these texts fall into predictable categories. They critique the status quo of industrial capitalism, explain ecological processes and warn of their catastophic collapse, or offer methods by which academic disciplines or isolated parts of human society can be transformed. The best current compendium relates that a daunting 3,000+ books on these subjects are currently in print.

A review of this literature reveals that with few exceptions it has three predominant characteristics. Individual titles address only certain aspects of social change, divorcing social from ecological concerns, or explaining development of, say, 'new' economics without explaining how it relates to other parts of life. Authors are often dogmatic, proposing detailed philosophies or strict methods which must be followed to guarantee large or small reform. Taken as a whole, social change literature is waterlogged by supposedly analytical objectivity, and its ability to kindle the spark of practical application is drowned in inaccessible syntax and vocabulary. While these characteristics do not preclude sustained public interest in social change, they do combine to make actualization of social change a game for either disciplinary specialists or disciples. The vast majority of people who understand that change is necessary if social justice and ecological sustainability are to be achieved are essentially left to chart their own paths.

What is missing in the literature of social change are titles which relate processes by which cultures embedded in vastly different social and ecological environments can evolve place-related approaches to wholistic change. The key words here are "process," "place-related," and "wholistic"—terms which, when taken together, imply the need for exploration of a means by which continuous connection between forms of knowledge and forms of action can be achieved in local communities and regions. For purposes of convenience rather than any great necessity, this connective activity can be labelled *ecological planning*—social change as a process of integrated perception and action fundamentally meant to be adopted, adapted, and applied in a great variety of cultural and spatial circumstances.

This book purposefully does not include arcane permutations of academic debate over what ecological planning irrevocably is, nor does it detail a model for a universally applicable ecological utopia. It is of more radical intent. *Futures By Design* is a tool to assist individuals and groups in evolving localized but interrelated approaches to sustainable and just reinhabitation of bioregion habitats. It is a book that has been created to be *used*. To achieve this goal an anthology format has been adopted which brings together the thought and experience of a remarkable group of social change activists. These women and men are from several continents, are from 20 to 70 years of age, have greatly diverse experience, and have never before shared pages of the same text. What they have in common is that they have all helped to pioneer expression and use of the ecological planning process, each contributing an important part of a puzzle whose larger image will emerge in these pages.

The contributions in this book have been grouped to address four critical questions, each of which is concerned with important aspects of the ecological planning process:

- Social change requires an alternative vision of the means by which socially just and ecologically sustainable human societies will be created. How do a variety of successful social change activists express such an ecological world view?

- An ecological world view is actualized within a physical context— primarily in urban settlements and the cultural and biophysical territories which they occupy. How can human settlements be transformed into sustainable eco-villages and eco-cities? How can the territories that associations of human settlements steward—bioregions—be conceptualized and instituted?

- Practical implementation of social change requires the use of highly adaptable processes by which transformation of city and bioregion can occur. What ecological planning processes have been pioneered that are adaptable for wide application?
- Responsibility for the achievement of social change ultimately rests with individuals and communities. What book and journal resources are available for those committed to the adaptation of ecological planning, or related techniques, as personal and place-related approaches to achieving social change?

These questions are answered in six interrelated sections. An introduction defines ecological planning as part of a persistent intellectual tradition which offers a practical alternative to the ruling scientific world view. Three central chapters present ecological planning as philosophical expression, as it relates specifically to the creation of sustainable human settlements, and as it is being applied in a specific bioregion, Cascadia, in northwestern North America. Three concluding sections describe pioneering methodologies by which people can apply ecological planning processes to wild and settled habitats, and a first bibliography of essential ecological planning texts and journals. This structure has been adopted to mix philosophical and practical expression in a manner which should prove useful to social change activists living "in place," as well as students of social and applied sciences who are charting the post-modern futures of their disciplines.

The World as a Machine

Fortunately, human history is no longer confined to the recitation of dates related to male-driven concepts of discovery, conquest, and progress. In our defiantly post-modern era it is possible to reinvent history, allowing the past to be interpreted in terms of what positive and negative impacts the practices of the last centuries have *actually* had on thousands of regions of the planet. While not as flattering to the ruling status quo, our new histories are eminently able to put the purpose of our desire for social change in clear metaphorical perspective.

On the last day of his life Nicolaus Copernicus (1473-1543) received the first copy of a book which summarized the results of over thirty years of his astronomical investigations. In addressing the task of devising a calendar by which the Catholic papacy could control its vast ecclesiastical realm, Copernicus perceived that the Sun, not the Earth, was the center of the solar system. This revolutionary idea was refined in mathematical and philosophical terms over the next 200 years by Bacon (1561-1626), Galileo (1564-1642), Kepler (1571-1630), Descartes (1596-1650) and Newton (1642-1727). The creative, mystery-laden alchemy of the Renaissance came to a forced end. The reality of "life as machine" had been successfully manufactured.

Application of the new scientific world view set off a chain reaction of irrevocable change. A new breed of male scientists had proven that the universe was not a mystical organic entity ruled by spirits or metaphysics, but a collection of parts that ran like a machine. The universal machine was too big to be figured out all at once, but it *could* be divided and understood section by section. Physics, chemistry, biology, engineering, and hundreds of subdisciplines each were invested with control over a part of the machine. Over time, the machine was divided into more and more parts, and observations of these compartments became the factual verification by which parallel strands of scientific reality came to rule the mind of western civilization.

As the scientific world view grew in importance, benefactors were needed to underwrite and protect increasingly complex and expensive observation of the machine. Scientists, fundamentally at odds with religious institutions, turned to those who controlled merchant capital and political power. What could science offer these men? Political leaders needed ever more powerful weapons, and merchant capitalists required means by which wealth could be wrested from human and natural resources. Science began to serve its new masters well. Extraction and conversion of resources achieved ever grander scales of vested monetary wealth, and continuous development of lethal weapon systems allowed the evolution of the nation state. Progress came to be defined as the measure of the degree to which scientists could manipulate their particular part of the machine to distill for their masters the most valued of elixirs—wealth and power.

As we near the end of the second millennium, the cumulative impact of the scientific world view has been wealth and power for a relative few, and naive or purposeful subjugation of all else. Much of the planet's soil is tainted or is blowing away, water sources are depleted or polluted, the air is dirty and pierced by radiation, and animal and plant populations are harried to extinction. Only a fraction of all human cultures that originally inhabited the planet have survived imperialism and disease—the majority of those which remain are impoverished. Human population has risen exponentially, and is concentrated into ever larger urban agglomerations supported by vast networks of exploitative social and ecological subsidy. Any collective quest for the best that human societies could be is denied or forgotten in an orgy of institutionalized and self-destructive consumerism. The cause of this collective calamity is that the scientific world view has missed several essential facts: all the parts of the machine are irrevocably linked together, fiddling with one part of the machine has knock-on impact on its other parts, *and the machine is alive.*

The scientific world view is a paradigm gone wrong. It must be replaced.

The iniquity of the scientific world view is not that it is inherently evil. It is the fact that science, as corrupted by its keepers—industrial capital and centralized government—has been divorced from any consideration of values or interconnection. Science and technology can be forces of good *and* evil. Social justice and environmental quality *cannot* be factored out of human agency. Natural capital is *not* inexhaustible. A fix *cannot* be manufactured for every mistake that large scale technological enterprise is capable of inflicting. The scientific world view is a paradigm gone wrong. It must be replaced.

Weeds

During the last 250 years there has been a continuous harmony of voices which have resisted the paradigm of the machine. So-called "Cartesian" reality has been bravely challenged by resistance against the enclosure of common lands, the tenacious survival of aboriginal and traditional cultures, and the existence of a plethora of revolutionary and social change movements. A centuries' long counterpoint has also come from healers, midwives, and practitioners of spiritual paths who all share the perception that connectedness, not separation, is the most vital of universal forces. Less well understood is that there is an identifiable western intellectual tradition based equally upon resistance against the machine age, and support for the reintegration of human society with ecological processes. It is in the history of this intellectual tradition that ecological planning has its roots.

As the industrial revolution of the mid-1700s gained momentum, many strands of reaction and alternative prescription arose in response. This history is little understood, but five important strands of resistance can initially be identified. Utopian socialists such as Charles Fourier (1772-1837), Robert Owen (1771-1858), and Ebenezer Howard (1850-1928) worked to describe and create new and humane settlements and societies. Geographers led by Vidal de la Blache (1845-1918) and Jean Brunhes (1869-1930) championed stewardship of vital regionbased cultures as the foundation of stable humannature interrelation. Anarchists PierreJoseph Proudhon (1809-1865), Peter Kropotkin (1842-1921), and brothers Elie and Elisée Reclus (1827-1904; 1830-1905) openly confronted forces of centralized political and economic control. The synthetic science of sociology was pioneered by Auguste Comte (1798-1857) and Frederic Le Play (1806-1882), and later evolved into a potent applied human ecology by Patrick Geddes (1854-1932). Ecology itself was formally created by Ernst Haeckel (1834-1919), for whom the belief that humans and nature were inextricably linked became the centerpiece of a unified philosophy, science, arts, theology, and politics.

The unique attribute of these movements was that they did not focus on a reductionist specialty, but on principles which defiantly and diametrically opposed the scientific world view. The main principles of this juxtaposition were:

- systems not isolated things
- patterns not categorical order
- co-operation not competition
- process not prescription
- quality not quantity
- connection not separation
- biocentric not anthropocentric
- decentralization not centralization.

Institutions that controlled the scientific world view overtly and covertly oppressed any individual or group that espoused wholistic alternatives to the ruling status quo. Utopian socialists were labelled as crackpot dreamers, anarchists as dangerous radicals, and regional geographers and ecologists were marginalized for attempting to make impossible connections between separate sciences. The women and men who practiced any of these forms of wholism were denied access to precincts of "legitimate" academia, and in some cases were jailed or exiled. They were not effete poseurs, and suffered greatly for the strength of their convictions.

In reaction against marginalization, those who embraced wholism wove a web of friendship and mutual aid that is remarkable to discover. Proudhon came from the same town as Fourier, was his student and later editor of one of his books. Elisée Reclus contributed to Kropotkin's radical journal *Le Révolté*. Geddes' career turned from the "necrology" of natural sciences to wholistic sociology after a chance meeting with Le Play's disciple Demolins in Paris. Later, Geddes named his activist sociological institute after Le Play. Reclus and Haeckel taught in Edinburgh with Geddes, with Elie Reclus later entrusting Geddes with the care of his exiled son. Kropotkin also visited Edinburgh, playing revolutionary songs long into the night on Geddes' piano.

The five early strands of intellectual resistance against the machine age have continued through more contemporary history on two levels. On one level each continued to maintain its separate activity and evolution. For instance, utopian communities continued to be eloquently proposed by Le Corbusier, Frank Lloyd Wright, Constantinos Doxiadis, Paolo Soleri, and contemporary communitarians. Similarly, ecology was used as a central organizing principle by George Perkins Marsh, Henry David Thoreau, Aldo Leopold, brothers Eugene P. and Howard T. Odum, and many others.

On a second and less well articulated level, all the traditions began to be combined into one overarching approach to social change. This integration was primarily the result of the work of Patrick Geddes, a Scot of varied learning who gained great influence as an observer of nature and a student of regional culture in the early 1900s. Geddes pioneered practical techniques of ecological planning and systematic surveying of bioregions, each designed to assist resident human populations to become self-determining and sustainable. Although Geddes' radical ideas remained obscure due to his Celtic propensity to teach orally, his approach to synthesis and application of ecological knowledge spread through his wide travels, by that most revolutionary of methods— word of mouth.

Lewis Mumford (1895-1990), a North American, discovered obscure pamphlets written by Geddes in 1915, and the two men began a thirty-year correspondence. Mumford, who called Geddes "Master" in their letters, absorbed Geddes' teaching, added his own perspective, and wrote the classics *Technics and Civilization* (1934), *The Culture of Cities* (1938), and *The Myth of the Machine* (two volumes, 1967/1970). Mumford, along with cohorts Benton MacKaye (1879-1975), Clarence Stein (1882-1975), Catherine Bauer Wurster (1905-1964), and Henry Wright (1878-1936), went on to found the Regional Planning Association of America (RPAA), an organization which in the May 1925 edition of *Survey Graphic* described an organic alternative to the metropolitanization juggernaut. Later, the work of Mumford and the RPAA inspired Howard W. Odum (1884-1954), who in 1938 wrote *American Regionalism*, a classic book which remains the single best summary of North American regionalist expression.

In Mumford's later years he often received letters of inquiry and admiration from activists who fermented the social change which occurred in the 1960s and 1970s. Kirkpatrick Sale, Ian McHarg, Steve Bear, Theodore Roszak, Paolo Soleri, Abraham Maslow, Ludwig Von Bertalannfy, just to name a few, were all drawn to Mumford's critique of the machine age, and the wholistic/organic alternative he envisioned to take its place.

Why did this decades' long process of interrelationship not bear greater fruit? It has yet to be fully understood, but it seems that each of these acolytes of wholism only got one part of the big picture. Some could admirably outline their philosophy, but were unable to relate idea to practice. Others prescribed the minute detail of how a new world should be constructed, and were brusque with anyone who would not be a disciple. Yet others were content to use beautiful but ultimately ambiguous literary flourish. There was rarely the means or opportunity for enough of them to work together so that some larger synergy could be achieved.

Bioregionalism

In the early 1970s, a grassroots social change movement emerged in North America that had unique origins in both the five strands of resistance against the scientific world view, and in the regionalism of Geddes, Mumford, and Odum. Described under the awkward title of "bioregionalism," it is arguably the first social change movement which proposes a powerful union of principles which previously had been sympathetic but separated. From a grassroots, non-academic, multicultural, gender-balanced, and highly decentralized crucible, the bioregional ideal expresses a unique blending of tenets, the four primary of which can be summarized as:

1. Biologically and culturally defined regions—bioregions—offer the most opportune spatial scale within which a great variety of forms of human governance and development can be practiced;

2. Human governance within a bioregion should be democratic and responsible to local control, should nurture a high quality of life, and should be judged on its ability to achieve social justice;

3. Economic development within a bioregion should be locally regulated, use appropriate technology, focused on self-reliance with limited, value-added export manufacturing, and should expand only to the extent that resident ecosystems can sustainably support exploitation;

4. The political and economic interdependence of bioregions should be institutionalized at state/provincial, federal, continental and global levels through federation.

Although bioregional tenets are being adopted in a quickly growing number of locales, the success of the integrative alternative that the bioregional movement proposes is not assured. The five strands of resistance against the machine have inspired independent movements, each with its own fiercely loyal constituency. Deep ecologists, social ecologists, systems theorists, conservationists, communitarians, radical environmentalists, ecofeminists, greens, permaculturists, currently compete for pieces of the same intellectual ground. Each does important work, but a lack of allegiance to a common vision defeats the creation of what could be a much stronger force for social change.

How can this division be overcome? First, advocates of bioregionalism could better explain its unifying purpose, making it clear that the philosophical umbrella it offers is fundamentally inclusionary. And second, they can begin to propose a series of processes which allow the strength and creativity of unified action toward social change to become absolutely and clearly apparent. These processes do not have to be invented; they only need to be summarized from the experience of many scores of folk who have evolved working tenets of change—practice rooted deep in the experience of place.

A Tribute to Peter van Dresser

There are many authors, including those whose words appear in this volume, who have admirably expressed the essence of ecological planning. However, if there are individuals whose life and work exemplify the ecological planning ideal, Florence and Peter van Dresser deserve special mention. A 1930s dropout from Cornell University, East Coast marine vagabond, Florida homesteader, respected rocket propulsion scientist, and ardent decentralist, Peter van Dresser immigrated in his middle years with his partner to the uplands of New Mexico. Together they perceived that the path to sustainability was not to be found in utopian isolation, but in achieving an understanding of processes by which the tempermental bounty of their adopted region, and the unique culture it had spawned, could be brought back together in vital reintegration.

Peter van Dresser's *Landscape For Humans* (Albuquerque, New Mexico: Biotechnic Press, 1972) is the written legacy of a bioregional pioneer. In this slim 128-page book are the real goods—ideas which are heartfelt yet unsentimental, learned yet based on the patient faith that an empowered culture, rooted in place, can achieve a vital and sustainable synthesis. The book is built around six tenets, philosophical principles that may well serve as the basis for a similar vision in every region on the planet. Van Dresser's guidelines for bioregional planning include:

1. The redistribution and regrouping of population, of means of production, and of patterns of trade to facilitate greater local and regional self-sufficiency in the production of goods, services, and amenities.

2. The revitalization of smaller "urban places" (villages, towns, provincial cities) as significant elements in the economic and cultural order, with a corresponding diminishment in the relative importance of major cities and metropolitan conglomerations.

3. The channeling of social effort towards the enrichment and diversification of localized production within efficient smaller communities, rather than dependence upon massive mechanized transport of goods and people, as the enlightened solution of the "logistic" problem.

4. The encouragement of production technology which is adapted to the utilization of renewable "flow resources" (vegetative growth, climatic cycles and energies, etc.) on a small-scale, intensive, science, skill, and manpower basis, rather than on a large-scale, extensive machine, and mechanical-energy basis.

5. The development of an ecologically grounded science of community design, to guide the recolonization of vast semi-abandoned and under-used areas on a sustained yield, symbiotic basis with the soil, climatic, and biotic regimens of such regions.

6. The enhancement of communication and education techniques to foster this organic type of population dispersion, renucleation, and regionalization, while maintaining a high level of social and ecological awareness, and a degree of scientific and intellectual competence which will effectively counteract the dangers of parochialism and insularity.

There are perceptions and processes—tools of change— that we don't have to reinvent. We simply need to learn how to use, and further adapt, what others have struggled so hard to create.

Successive generations of social change activists may feel that the thoughts of dead writers hold little that is useful to their cause. Nothing could be farther from the truth. Many important lessons are to be found in the words of van Dresser and others who were long engaged in the struggle against centralization and homogenization. There is inspiration in the commitment made by our forebears. And there are perceptions and processes—tools of change—that we don't have to reinvent. We simply need to learn how to use, and further adapt, what others have struggled so hard to create.

Conclusion

This volume is descriptive rather than prescriptive. Within the wide boundaries of ecological limits and the interests of social justice, human populations in hundreds of different bioregions will evolve greatly varying approaches to governance and development. This concept of social change puts immense responsibility on the shoulders of individuals and communities to chart their individual paths in transforming and stewarding a future. This book is intended to be a reference, a guide, an inspiration to those who are on this path to change. While it does not hold the whole truth, or exact answers to the action that will transform human society, it comes as close to sign-posting these ideals as possible. There are many solutions to the crises and opportunities that confront us. The fundamental challenge is simply to start the process of social change in yourself, in your community, in your bioregion.
—Ready?

2

Bounding Whole Systems: Contemporary Perceptions of Ecological Planning

Introduction

Doug Aberley

As a child I listened to my grandfather's rambling stories about pioneer life in the redwood forests of California. In these same years I lived on the high east rim of San Francisco Bay, unconsciously learning systems and chaos theory by watching the spread of suburbs and freeways, the swirl of Pacific fog sliding in through the Golden Gate, and the pattern of hate-fires burning when the injustice of urban life reached a flashpoint. My youthful diaries are full of reflection on free speech, the death of a president, and the colorful anarchy of Haight-Ashbury. My bookshelf still holds the volumes that were my friends in this time of formation—Rilke's *Letters to a Young Poet*, Muir's *Mountains of California*, and the Russell brothers' *On the Loose*. From this crucible of family history, life-in-place, and reflection came the slow evolution of a world view that committed me to wholism and social change—and resulted in my eventual migration north to a rainforest much like that my grandfather was raised within. It was a totally circumstantial process of growth into ecological awareness that was no doubt shared by many thousands of my peers.

I think that today the world is a much more complicated place. We are more persistently bombarded in a will-destroying manner, anaesthe-

12

tized by narcotics and tricked into insecurities designed to make us docile consumers. Inspiration to understand ecological processes, or to become involved in social change may be much more readily available, but it is often cloaked in jargon, or tied to cults which are eager only to supply the exact details of salvation. What is missing is the simple message that every one of us has the personal ability—the power—to contribute to the reshaping of place and destiny. It is not the job of government, or industry, or church—it is the responsibility of individual, family, community, culture. Without this internal guiding orientation, all the social change theory or ecological planning technique that can ever be explained will fall on sterile ground.

This first section of the book is designed to introduce you to a variety of what can be called ecological world views. The authors that have been brought together have each evolved a personal vision of how life can be led in a manner that respects ecological limits and that engenders social justice. Each approaches her or his vision from a slightly different perspective, demonstrating how much variation can be accommodated within the same broad movement towards transformative change.

Each individual reader of these pages will know people in their home regions who express an equally powerful integration of wholistic philosophy and practice.

Uniquely, these authors do not look for acolytes: they simply introduce tenets which have served them well in a quest for change. They teach by example, their words offering powerful inspiration to take the same type of path yourself. Gary Snyder begins by weaving an understanding of bioregional thought and practice in a style that is perhaps unique to a person who has navigated a Kyoto/Sierra cultural fusion. Donella Meadows distills global systems modelling into statistical poetry giving a powerful perception of collective human identity. Helena Norberg-Hodge ventures into the territory of cross-cultural understanding, broadening knowledge of social change beyond the confines of western perceptions. Jane Jacobs relates her vision of cities as ecosystems, challenging us to see broader patterns of interrelation in our urban environments. A pioneer of contemporary bioregional thought, Raymond Dasmann explains an intensely personal ecological world view based on a lifetime of ecological investigation. Murray Bookchin introduces social ecology, a symbiosis of ecology and libertarian/anarchic politics. And Bill Mollison, who brought the word permaculture into being, explains the world view within which his vision of permanent culture/agriculture is actualized.

A final introductory thought: Each individual reader of these pages will know people in their home regions who express an equally powerful integration of wholistic philosophy and practice. In my own region there are several scores of women and men who innately practice the tenets of an ecological world view. Many of these folk have known each other for decades, sharing inspiration and knowledge, and who together absolutely confound the machine juggernaut. Who are these people in your region? How many thousands of these leaders are there in the hundreds of regions on the planet? It is not hard to sense that, as a decentralized but connected force, we have great potential to go beyond being a non-associated mass of movements. It is time to better understand and expand the power of our shared purpose.

◆

Coming in to the Watershed

Gary Snyder

watershed: 2. The whole region or area contributing to the supply of a river or lake; drainage area. — Webster's *New Collegiate Dictionary*

In February of '92 Jeff Lustig asked me to give the keynote talk for the annual conference of the Center for California Studies based at Sacramento State University. The theme of the conference was "dancing on the edge"—of ecological breakdown, social confrontations, and versions of history. I wanted to look again at the question of engagement with place, and speak of bioregional and watershed organizing as ways to get down, get on the ground, and make "biodiversity" and public lands issues walk, not just talk. Although framed in terms of California, the same points can be made for the whole country. The possibility of watershed councils becoming the building blocks of a continent-wide bioregional/ecosystem governance has broad relevance. Recovering wilderness in North America must start with grassroots (tree roots, sagebrush roots...) people and their communities.

Biological and Cultural Diversity in Our California Habitat

The question of "place" is curiously cogent to our present political, social, and environmental condition. Economically we're in misery, politically we are hopelessly stagnant, educationally we're a disgrace, and socially we are watching the emergence of a multi-racial multi-ethnic population that will radically shape the future direction of the culture of our country. We are also seeing the re-emergence of a crude racism and chauvinism that may destroy us all. As for the land itself, we see fine agricultural soils and orchards being steadily converted by real estate development. The publicly owned forests of the West are being overcut, and the long-range effects of erosion and air pollution raise the very real possibility of their gradual slide from productive forest lands to steady state brushfields. There's a parallel deterioration of grasslands and semi-desert. Yet, at the same time it looks as though non-indigenous North Americans are on the verge of discovering—for the first time—their place. People are slowly coming to the realization that they can become members of the deep old biological communities of the land in a different kind of citizenship.

In February my son Gen and I were visiting friends in Arcata and Crescent City on the north coast of California. We drove north from Marysville—through that soulful winter depth of pearly tule fog—paralleling the Feather and then crossing the Sacramento at Red Bluff. From Red Bluff north the fog began to break, and by Redding we had left it behind. As we crossed the mountains westward from Redding on 299 we paid special attention to the transformations of the landscape and trees, watching to see where the natural boundaries could be roughly ascertained. From the great valley with its tules, grasses, valley oak and blue oak, we swiftly climbed into the steep and dissected Klamath Range with its ponderosa pine, black oak, and manzanita fields. Somewhere past Burnt Ranch we were in the redwood and doug-fir forests—soon it was the Coastal Range. Then we descended past Blue Lake to come out at Arcata.

We drove on north. Just ten or fifteen miles from Arcata, around Trinidad Head, the feel of the landscape subtly changed again—much the same trees, but no open meadows, and a different light. At Crescent City and again Manila we asked friends Jim Dodge (the novelist) and poet Jerry Martien just what the change between Arcata and Crescent City was. They both said (to distill a long discussion), "You leave 'California.' Right around Trinidad Head you cross into the maritime Pacific Northwest." Even though the political boundary is many miles yet to the north.

So we had gone in that one afternoon's drive from the Mediterranean-type Sacramento Valley climate, with its many plant alliances toward the Mexican south, over the interior range with its dry pine forest hills, into a uniquely Californian set of redwood forests, and on into the maritime Pacific Northwest: the edges of four major areas. These boundaries are not hard and clear, though. They are porous, permeable, arguable. They are boundaries of climates, plant-communities, soil-types, styles of life. They change over the millennia, moving a few hundred miles this way or that. A thin line drawn on a map would not do them justice. Yet such are the markers of the natural nations of our planet, and they establish real territories with real differences, to which our economies and our clothing must adapt.

On the way back we stopped at Trinidad Head for a hike and a little birding. Although we knew they wouldn't be there until April, we walked out to look at the cliffs on the Head, where tufted puffins nest. This is virtually the southernmost end of the tufted puffins' range. Their more usual nesting ground is from Southeast Alaska through the Bering Sea and down to northern Japan. In winter they are far out in the open seas of the North Pacific. At this spot, Trinidad, we could not help but feel we touched on the life-realm of the whole North Pacific and Alaska. We spent that whole weekend enjoying "liminality" and dancing on the brink of the continent.

I have taken to watching the subtle changes of plants and climates as I travel over the West. This vast area called "California" is large enough to be beyond any one individual's ability to travel it and take it all into imagination clearly enough to see the whole picture. Michael Barbour, a botanist at the University of California at Davis, is bringing out a book to be called *California's Changing Landscapes*. He writes of the complexity of California: "of the world's 10 major soils, California has all 10.... As many as 375 distinctive natural communities have been recognized in the state.... California has more than 5,000 kinds of native ferns, conifers, and flowering plants. Japan has far fewer species with a similar area. Even with four times California's area, Alaska does not match California's plant diversity, and neither does all of the central and northeastern United States and adjacent Canada combined. Moreover about 30 percent of California's native plants are found nowhere else in the world."

But all this talk of the diversity of California is a trifle misleading. Of what place are we speaking? What is this "California?" It is, after all, a recent human invention with straight line boundaries that were drawn with a ruler on a map and rushed off to an office in DC. This is another illustration of Robert Frost's lines, "The land was ours before we were the land's." The political boundaries of the western states were established in haste and ignorance. Landscapes have their own shapes and structures, centers and edges, which must be respected. If a relationship to a place is like a marriage, then the Yankee establishment of a jurisdiction called California was like a shotgun wedding with six sisters taken as one wife.

If a relationship to a place is like a marriage, then the Yankee establishment of a jurisdiction called California was like a shotgun wedding with six sisters taken as one wife.

California is made up of what I take to be about six regions. (The numbers could be argued, but the main outlines of agreement will remain). They are of respectable size and native beauty, each with its own makeup, its own mix of bird calls and plant smells. Each of these proposes a slightly different lifestyle to the human beings who live there. Each led to different sorts of rural economies—for the regional differences translate into things like raisin grapes, wet rice, timber, and cattle pasture.

The central coast with its little river valleys, beach dunes and marshes, and oak-grass-pine mountains is one region. The Great Central Valley is a second, once dominated by swamps and wide shallow lakes and sweeps of valley oaks following the streams. The long mountain ranges of the Sierra Nevada are a third. From a sort of Sonoran chaparral they rise to arctic tundra. In the middle elevations they have some of the finest mixed conifer forests in the world. The Modoc plateau and volcano country—with its sagebrush and juniper—makes a fourth. Some of the Sacramento waters rise here. The fifth is the northern coast with its deep interior mountains—the Klamath region—reaching (on the coast) as far north as Trinidad Head. The sixth of these six sisters is the coastal valleys and mountains south of the Tehachapis, with natural connections on into Baja. Although today it supports a huge population with water drawn from the Colorado River, the Owens Valley, and the Great Central Valley, it is naturally almost a desert.

One might ask what about the rest? Where are the White Mountains, the Mojave Desert, the Warner Range? They are splendid places, but they do not belong with California. Their watersheds and biological communities belong to the Great Basin or the lower Colorado drainage, and we should let them return to their own families. Almost all of core California has a summer-dry Mediterranean climate, with (usually) fairly abundant winter rain. More than anything else, this rather special type of climate is what gives our place its fragrance of oily aromatic herbs, its olive green drought-resistant shrubs, and its patterns of rolling grass and dark forest.

I am not arguing that we should instantly re-draw the boundaries of the social construction called California, although that could happen some far day. We are becoming aware of certain long-range realities, and this thinking leads toward the next step in the evolution of human citizenship on the North American continent. The usual focus of attention for most Americans is the human society itself with its problems and its successes, its icons and symbols. With the exception of most Native Americans and a few non-natives who have given their hearts to the place, the land we all live on is simply taken for granted—and proper relation to it is not taken as part of "citizenship." But after two centuries of national history, people are beginning to wake up and notice that the United States is located on landscape with a severe, spectacular, spacey, wildly demanding, and ecstatic narrative to be learned. Its natural communities are each unique, and each of us, whether we like it or not—in the city or countryside—live in one of them. When enough people get that picture, our political life will begin to change, and it will be the beginning of the next phase of American life, coming to live on "Turtle Island."

*

Those who work in resource management are accustomed to looking at various maps of the West, each of which addresses a rich set of meanings. Land ownership categories give us (in addition to private land) Bureau of Land Management (BLM) lands, National Forests, National Parks, State Parks, military reserves, and a host of other public holdings. The idea of public domain is descended from the historic institution of the commons in Europe. These lands host much of the water, forest, and wildlife that is left to us. Although they are in the care of all the people, they have been too often managed for special interests.

No single group or agency could keep track of, or take care of grizzly bears, which do not care about park or ranch boundaries and have ancient territories of their own.

Conservationists have been working since the 1930s for the preservation of key blocks of public land as wilderness. There has been some splendid success in this effort, and we are all indebted to the single-minded (and often unpaid) dedication of the people who are behind every present-day Wilderness Area that we and our children walk into, take heart in. Our growing understanding of how natural systems work brought us the realization that an exclusive emphasis on disparate parcels of land ignored the insouciant freeness of wild creatures. Although individual islands of wild land serving as biological refuges are invaluable, they cannot of themselves guarantee the maintenance of natural variety. As biologists, public land managers, and the involved public have all agreed, we need to know more about how natural systems work at larger scales, and find "on the ground" ways to connect wild zone to wild zone wherever possible. Thus the notion of biological corridors or connectors. The Greater Yellowstone Ecosystem concept came out of this sort of recognition. Our understanding of nature and our practice in regard to it have been radically altered by systems theory. Specifically, systems theory as it comes through the science of ecology, and in particular the very cogent sub-disciplines called Island Biogeography and Landscape Ecology. They provide some extraordinary detail to fill out the broader generalization that comes both from John Muir and the 8th century AD Chinese Buddhist philosophers, "Everything is connected."

No single group or agency could keep track of or take care of grizzly bears, which do not care about park or ranch boundaries and have ancient territories of their own. A recognition that habitat flows across private and public land is needed to provide the framework for the "management" of bears, owls, or redwoods. A definition of place unencumbered by the illogical boundaries of states and counties is essential. Such a territory would have its own functional and structural coherence. It often might contain or be a watershed system. It would usually be larger than a county, but smaller than a western U.S. state. One of the names for such a space is "bioregion." The concept is basic and sensible, that of the simple fact of naturally observable regions.

Colors of the Land, Colors of the Skin

The word "bioregion" has thus begun to be common vocabulary in California, but in a context of some dubiousness. A group of California-based federal and state land managers trying to work together on biodiversity problems saw that it must be done in terms of natural regions. Their "memorandum of understanding" calls for us to "move beyond existing efforts focused on the conservation of individual sites, species, and resources...to also protect and manage ecosystems, biological communities, and landscapes." The memorandum goes on to say that "public agencies and private groups must coordinate resource management and environmental protection activities, emphasizing regional solutions to regional issues and needs." The group identified eleven or so such working bioregions within California, making the San Francisco Bay/Delta into one, and dividing both the Sierra and the Valley into northern and southern portions. There are lumpers and there are splitters. It is entirely appropriate that the heads of the BLM, the Forest Service, Fish and Wildlife Service, California Department of Fish and Game, California Department of Forestry, and such should take these issues on: almost 50 percent of California is public domain.

Hearing about this agreement, some county government people, elected officials, and timber and business interests in the mountain counties went into a severe paranoid spasm, fearing—they said—new regulations and more centralized government. An anonymous circular made its way around towns and campuses in northern California under the title "Biodiversity or New Paganism?" It says that "California Resource Secretary Doug Wheeler and his self-appointed bioregional soldiers are out to devalue human life by placing greater emphasis on rocks, trees, fish, plants, and wildlife." It quotes me as having written that "Those of us who are now promoting a bioregional consciousness would, as an ultimate and long-range goal, like to see this continent more sensitively re-defined, and the natural regions of North America—Turtle Island—gradually begin to shape the political entities within which we work. It would be a small step toward the deconstruction of America as a super power into seven or eight natural nations, none of which have a budget big enough to support missiles." I'm pleased to say that I did write that. I'd think it was clear that my statement is not promoting more centralized government, but these gents want both their small town autonomy and the military-industrial state at the same time. Many a would-be Westerner is a "libertarian" in name only, and will scream up a storm if taken too far from the government tit. The real intent of the circular seems to be—as it urges people to write the state Governor—to resist long-range sustainability and the support of biodiversity, and to hold out for maximum resource extraction.

As far as I can see, the intelligent but so far toothless California "bioregional proposal" is simply a basis for further thinking and some degree of cooperation between agencies. The most original part is the call for the formation of "bioregional councils" that would have some stake in decision-making. Who would be on the bioregional councils is not spelled out. Even closer to the roots, the memorandum that started all this furor suggests that "watershed councils" be formed, which would be the truly local bodies that could help design agreements for the preservation of natural variety. Like, let's say, helping to preserve the spawning grounds for the wild salmon that still come (amazingly) into the lower Yuba River gravel wastelands. This effort would have to involve a number of groups and agencies, and would have to include the blessing of the usually development-minded Yuba

County Water Agency

The term "bioregion" was adopted by the signers to the Memorandum on Biological Diversity as a technical term from the field of biogeography. I'm sure they couldn't have known that there were already groups of people around the United States and Canada talking in terms of bioregionally-oriented societies. They could not have known about the first North American Bioregional Congress held in Kansas in the late

80s, and subsequent gatherings right down to a "Shasta Nation" (northern California) gathering held last September in the Napa Valley. (Continent-wide gatherings have dropped the name North America and refer to our larger place as "Turtle Island," after the Native American creation myth.) They had no idea of the twenty-year history of community and ecology-minded dwellers-in-the-land living in places called "Ish" (Puget Sound and lower British Columbia) or "Columbiana" (upper Columbia River) or "Mesechabe" (lower Mississippi), or "Shasta" (northern California), all of whom had periodicals, field trips, gatherings, and were active in local politics.

That "bioregion" was an idea already in circulation was the bad, or good, luck of the biodiversity agreement people, depending on how you look at it. As it happens, the bioregional people are also finding "watershed councils" to be the building blocks of a long-range strategy for social and environmental sustainability.

A watershed is a marvelous thing to consider: this process of rain falling, streams flowing, and oceans evaporating causes every molecule of water on Earth to make a complete trip once every two million years. The surface is carved into watersheds—a kind of familial branching, a chart of relationship, and a definition of place. The watershed is the first and last nation, whose boundaries, though subtly shifting, are unarguable. Races of birds, subspecies of trees, and types of hats or rain gear go by the watershed. The watershed gives us a home, and a place to go upstream, downstream, or across in.

For the watershed, cities and dams are ephemeral, and of no more account than a boulder that falls in the river, or a landslide that temporarily alters the channel. The water will always be there, and it will always find its way down. As constrained and polluted as it is at the moment, it can also be said that in the larger picture the Los Angeles River is alive and well under the city streets, running in giant culverts. It is possibly amused by such diversions. But we who live in terms of centuries rather than millions of years, must hold the watershed and its communities together, that our children might enjoy the clear water and fresh life of this landscape we have chosen. From the tiniest rivulet at the crest of a ridge, to the main trunk of a river approaching the lowlands, the river is all one place, and all one land.

The water cycle is our springs and wells, our Sierra snowpack, our irrigation canals, our carwash, and the spring salmon run. It's the spring peeper in the pond and the acorn woodpecker chattering in a snag. It's where our friends live, it *is* our friends. The watershed is beyond the dichotomies of orderly/disorderly, for its forms are free, but somehow inevitable. And the life that comes to flourish within it constitutes the first kind of community.

The agenda of a watershed council starts in a modest way: like saying, "Let's try to rehabilitate our river to the point that wild salmon can successfully spawn here again." In pursuit of this local agenda, a community might find itself combating clearcut timber sales upstream, water-selling grabs downstream, Taiwanese drift-net practices out in the North Pacific, and a host of other national and international threats to the health of salmon. A small but significant number of watershed councils are already in existence, fully awake and conscious, with some strong views about what should be done. These include the Friends of the Los Angeles River, the Putah Creek Council, the Yuba Watershed Institute, The Greenwood Watershed Association, The Redwood Coast Watersheds Alliance, and the Mattole Restoration Council.

The water cycle is our springs and wells, our Sierra snowpack, our irrigation canals, our carwash, and the spring salmon run. ... It's where our friends live, it *is* our f riends.

They are ready and willing to play ball with the California BLM, the State of California, the Pacific Southwest Region office of the Forest Service, and the others who signed the 1991 Agreement for a "coordinated regional strategy for saving biological diversity in California." If a wide range of people join this effort—people from timber and tourism, settled ranchers and farmers, fly-fishing retirees, the businesses and the forest-dwelling new settlers—something might come of it. But if this joint agreement is implemented as a top-down prescription it will go nowhere. Only a grassroots engagement with long-term land issues can provide the political and social stability needed to keep the biological richness of California's regions intact.

All public land ownership is ultimately written in sand. The boundaries and the management-categories were created by Congress, and Congress can take them away. The only "jurisdiction" that will last in the world of nature is the watershed, and even that changes over time.

If public lands come under greater and greater pressure to be opened for exploitation and use in the 21st century, the local people, the watershed people, will prove to be the last and possibly most effective line of defense. Let us hope it never comes to that.

The mandate of the public land managers and the Fish and Wildlife people inevitably directs them to resource concerns. They are proposing to do what could be called "ecological bioregionalism." The other movement could be called "cultural bioregionalism." I would like to turn my attention now to cultural bioregionalism and to what practical promise these ideas hold for the *fin de millennium* America.

Living in a place

The notion has been around for decades, and has usually been dismissed as provincial, backward, dull, and possibly reactionary. But new dynamics are at work. The mobility that has characterized American life is coming to a close. As Americans begin to stay put, it may give us the first opening in over a century to give participatory democracy another try.

Daniel Kemmis, the mayor of Missoula, Montana, has written a fine little book called *Community and the Politics of Place*. Mr. Kemmis points out that in the 18th century the word *republican* meant a politics of community engagement. Early republican thought was set against the federalist theories which would govern by balancing competing interests, devise sets of legalistic procedures, maintain checks and balances (leading to hearings held before putative experts) in place of direct discussion between adversarial parties.

Kemmis quotes Rousseau: "Keeping citizens apart has become the first maxim of modern politics." So what organizing principle will get citizens back together? There are many and each in its way has its use. People have organized themselves by ethnic background, religion, race, class, employment, gender, language, and age. In a highly mobile society where few people stay put, thematic organizing is entirely understandable. But place, that oldest of organizing principles (next to kinship), is a novel idea in the United States.

"What holds people together long enough to discover their power as citizens is their common inhabiting of a single place," Kemmis argues. Being so placed, people will volunteer for community projects, join school boards, and accept nominations and appointments. Good minds, which are often forced by company or agency policy to keep moving, will make notable contributions to the neighborhood if allowed to stay put. And since local elections deal with immediate issues, more people will turn out to vote. There will be a return of civic life.

"What holds people together long enough to discover their power as citizens is their common inhabiting of a single place," Kemmis argues.

This will not be "nationalism" with all its dangers as long as sense of of *place* is not entirely conflated with the idea of a nation. Bioregional concerns go beyond those of any ephemeral (and often brutal and dangerous) politically designated space. They give us the imagination of "citizenship" in a place called (for example) the Great Central Valley, which has valley oaks and migratory waterfowl as well as humans among its members. A place (with a climate, with bugs), as Kemmis says, "develops practices, creates culture."

Another fruit of the enlarged sense of nature that systems ecology and bioregional thought have given us is the realization that cities and suburbs are parts of the system. Unlike the ecological bioregionalists, the cultural practice of urban bioregionalism ("Green Cities") has made a good start in San Francisco. One can learn and live deeply in regards to wild systems in any sort of neighborhood—from the urban to a big sugarbeet farm. The birds are migrating, the wild plants are looking for a way to slip in, the insects live an untrammeled life, the raccoons are padding through the crosswalks at 2 a.m., and the nursery trees are trying to figure out who they are. These are exciting, convivial, and somewhat radical knowledges.

An economics of scale can be seen in the watershed/bioregion/city-state model. Imagine a Renaissance style city-state facing out on the Pacific, with its bioregional hinterland reaching to the headwaters of all the streams that flow through its bay. The San Francisco/Valley Rivers/Shasta headwaters bio-city-region! I take some ideas along these lines from Jane Jacobs' tantalizing book, *The Wealth of Cities*, in which she argues that the city, not the nation state, is the proper locus of an economy, and then that the city is always to be understood being one with the hinterland.

Such a non-nationalistic idea of community, in which commitment to pure place is paramount, cannot be ethnic or racist. Here is perhaps the most delicious turn that comes out of thinking about politics from the standpoint of place: anyone of any race, language, religion, or origin is welcome, as long as they live well on the land. The Great Central Valley region does not prefer English over Spanish or Japanese or Hmong. If it had any preferences at all, it might best like the languages heard for thousands of years such as Maidu or Miwok. Mythically speaking, the region will welcome whoever chooses to observe the etiquette, express the gratitude, grasp the tools, and learn the songs that it takes to live there.

The Great Central Valley region does not prefer English over Spanish or Japanese or Hmong. If it had any preferences at all, it might best like the languages heard for thousands of years such as Maidu or Miwok.

This sort of future culture is available to whoever makes the choice, regardless of background. It need not require that a person drop his or her Buddhist, Voudun, Jewish, or Lutheran beliefs, but simply add to his or her faith or philosophy a sincere nod in the direction of the deep value of the natural world, and the subjecthood of non-human things. A culture of place will be created that will include the "United States," and go beyond that to an affirmation of the continent, the land itself, Turtle Island. We could be showing Cambodian and Vietnamese newcomers the patterns of the rivers, the distant hills, saying "It is not only that you are now living in the United States. You are living in this great landscape. Please get to know these rivers and mountains, and be welcome here." Euro-Americans, Asian-Americans, African-Americans, can—if they wish—become "born again" natives of Turtle Island. In doing so, we also might even (eventually) win some respect from our Native American predecessors, who are still here and still trying to teach us where we are.

Watershed consciousness and bioregionalism are not just environmentalism, not just a means toward resolution of social and economic problems, but a move toward a profound citizenship in both the natural and the social worlds. If the ground can be our common ground, we can begin to talk to each other (human and non-human) once again.

*

California is gold-tan grasses, silver gray tule fog,
olive-green redwood, blue-gray chaparral,
silver-hue serpentine hills.
Blinding white granite,
blue-black rock sea cliffs.
—blue summer sky, chestnut brown slough water,
steep purple city streets—hot cream towns.
Many colors of the land, many colors of the skin.

♦

If the World Were a Village of 1,000 People

Donella H. Meadows

If the world were a village of 1,000 people, it would include:

- 584 Asians
- 124 Africans
- 95 East and West Europeans
- 84 Latin Americans
- 55 Former Soviets (including Lithuanians, Latvians, Estonians, and other national groups)
- 52 North Americans
- 6 Australians and New Zealanders.

The people of the village would have considerable difficulty in communicating:

- 165 people speak Mandarin
- 86 English
- 83 Hindi/Urdu

- 64 Spanish
- 58 Russian
- 37 Arabic.

That list accounts for the mother tongues of only half the villagers. The other half speak (in descending order of frequency) Bengali, Portuguese, Indonesian, Japanese, German, French, and 200 other languages. In this village of 1,000 there are:

- 329 Christians (among them 187 Catholics, 84 Protestants, 31 Orthodox)
- 178 Moslems
- 167 "non-religious"
- 132 Hindus
- 60 Buddhists
- 45 atheists
- 3 Jews
- 86 all other religions.

One-third (330) of the 1,000 people in the world village are children and only 60 are over the age of 65. Half the children are immunized against preventable infectious diseases such as measles and polio.

Just under half of the married women in the village have access to and use modern contraceptives.

This year 28 babies will be born. Ten people will die, 3 of them for lack of food, 1 from cancer, 2 of the deaths are of babies born within the year. One person of the 1,000 in the village is infected with the HIV virus; that person most likely has not yet developed a full-blown case of AIDS.

With the 28 births and 10 deaths, the population of the village in the second year is 1,018.

In this 1,000-person community, 200 people receive 75 percent of the income; another 200 receive only two percent of the income.

Only 70 people of the 1,000 own an automobile (although some of the 70 own more than one automobile).

About one-third have access to clean, safe drinking water.

Of the 670 adults in the village, half are illiterate.

The village has six acres of land per person, 6,000 acres in all, of which:

- 700 acres are cropland
- 1,400 acres pasture
- 1,900 acres woodland
- 2,000 acres desert, tundra, pavement, and other wasteland.

The woodland is declining rapidly; the wasteland is increasing. The other land categories are roughly stable.

The village allocates 83 percent of its fertilizer to 40 percent of its cropland—that owned by the richest and best-fed 270 people. Excess fertilizer running off this land causes pollution in lakes and wells. The remaining 60 percent of the land, with its 17 percent of the fertilizer, produces 28 percent of the food grains and feeds 73 percent of the people. The average grain yield on that land is one third the harvest achieved by the richer villagers.

In the village of 1,000 people, there are:

- 5 soldiers
- 7 teachers
- 1 doctor
- 3 refugees driven from home by war or drought.

The village has a total budget each year, public and private, of over $3 million—$3,000 per person if it is distributed evenly (which, we have already seen, it isn't).

Of the total $3 million:

- $181,000 goes to weapons and warfare
- $159,000 for education
- $132,000 for health care.

The village has buried beneath it enough explosive power in nuclear weapons to blow itself to smithereens many times over. These weapons are under the control of just 100 of the people. The other 900 are watching them with deep anxiety, wondering whether they can learn to get along together; and if they do, whether they might set off the weapons anyway through inattention or technical bungling; and if they ever decide to dismantle the weapons, where in the world village would they dispose of the radioactive materials of which the weapons are made?

◆

Ancient Futures

Helena Norberg-Hodge

Before I went to Ladakh, the northernmost Tibetan Plateau territory of India, I used to assume that the direction of "progress" was somehow inevitable, not to be questioned. As a consequence, I passively accepted a new road through the middle of the park, a steel-and-glass bank where the two-hundred year old church had stood, a supermarket instead of the corner shop, and the fact that life seemed to get harder and faster with each day. I do not accept that any more. Ladakh has convinced me that there is more than one path into the future and given me tremendous strength and hope.

In Ladakh I have had the privilege to experience another, saner way of life and to see my own culture from the outside. I have lived in a society based on fundamentally different principles and witnessed the impact of the modern world on that culture. When I arrived as one of the first outsiders in several decades, Ladakh was still essentially unaffected by the West. But change came swiftly. The collision between the two cultures has been particularly dramatic, providing stark and vivid comparisons. I have learned something about the psychology, values, and social and technological structures that support our industrialized society and about those that support an ancient, nature-based society. It has been a rare opportunity to compare our socio-economic system with another, more fundamental, pattern of existence—a pattern based on co-evolution between human beings and the earth.

Counter-development

At the moment, an increasingly narrow view prevents us from seeing the roots of many of our many problems; we cannot see the forest for the trees. Western culture depends on experts whose focus of attention grows more and more specialized and immediate at the expense of a broader, long-term perspective. Economic forces are pulling the world rapidly toward ever-greater specialization and centralization and an ever more capital and energy-intensive pattern of life. A concerted information campaign is urgently required if we want to avoid further destruction in the name of development and progress: an education program to correct the incomplete and misleading images of the industrial system that is propelling the world toward social and ecological breakdown. Rather than more development, we need what I call "counter-development."

The primary goal of "counter-development" would be to provide people with the means to make fully informed choices about their own future. Using every possible form of communication, from satellite television to storytelling, we need to publicize the fact that today's capital- and energy-intensive trends are simply unsustainable. Ultimately, the aim would be to promote self-respect and self-reliance, thereby protecting life-sustaining diversity and creating the conditions for locally based, truly sustainable development.

Using every possible form of communication, from satellite television to storytelling, we need to publicize the fact that today's capital- and energy-intensive trends are simply unsustainable.

One of the most critical failings of conventional development is its reliance on a narrow, short-term perspective dominated by quantitative analysis. Counter-development would move beyond specialization and fragmented expertise to reveal the systemic underpinnings of industrial society. It would draw attention to family and community breakup; it would show up the hidden subsidies of a society based on fossil fuels; it would place environmental damage on the debit side of the economic balance sheet. In short, it would expose the escalating costs of our industrial way of life.

At the same time, counter-development would promote and popularize a new, wider, and more humane definition of progress. It would highlight some of the innumerable local initiatives around the world that are exploring more sustainable alternatives. It would point to the viability of traditional systems as well as bringing information about new trends in agriculture: about permaculture, biodynamics, and the booming movement toward organic methods of cultivation. It would report on bioregionalism and local economic systems, on the new, wholistic approach to physics, it would publicize the windmills in Denmark and California, and the growing demand for acupuncture, homeopathy, and other nature-based systems of health care. It would make more visible the enormous interest around the world in environmental protection, soil conservation, and air and water quality.

Truly effective counter-development is a necessary prerequisite to finding sustainable solutions to today's problems. Unless the consumer monoculture is halted there is no hope of preventing ever-greater poverty, social divisiveness, and ecological degradation. But counter-development is not itself enough. In addition to opposing technological uniformity, we need to actively support ecological and cultural diversity, by encouraging the fullest possible use of local resources, knowledge, and skills. In "developed" and "developing" parts of the world alike, agricultural self-reliance should be given a central role in the economy. Equal weight should be given to female perspectives and values; family and community ties should be nourished.

If our starting point is a respect for nature and people, diversity is an inevitable consequence. If technology and the needs of the economy are our starting point, then we have what we are faced with today—a model of development that is dangerously distanced from the needs of particular peoples and places and rigidly imposed from the top down.

We need to regain a balance between the local and the global. Even though the phrase "think globally, act locally" is mouthed frequently these days, the thrust of modernization is entirely in the direction of globalization. Local cultures and economies are disappearing at an alarming rate and taking plant and animal species with them. Finding a sustainable middle path would necessarily involve active steps towards decentralization. Since extreme dependence has already been created on both international and national levels, it would be irresponsible to "delink" economies and cut off assistance from one day to the next. We cannot, for example, suddenly halt our purchase of coffee or cotton from countries in the Third World whose economies totally depend on such trade. But we *can* immediately begin supporting aid programs that will enable farmers to return to growing food for local consumption, rather that cash crops for export to the West.

Parallel to economic decentralization we need to decentralize the production of energy. Again, this ought to happen both in the West and in the Third World, but because the energy infrastructure of most developing countries is still relatively limited, the widespread application of solar, wind, biomass, and hydropower technologies in these regions would be comparatively easy. Until now, however, it simply has not happened. Instead, the West has pushed its own industrial model, based on large-scale, centralized power production. One of the most effective ways of turning destructive development into genuine aid would be to lobby for widespread support and subsidies for decentralized applications of renewable energy.

Just as brick-making in Ladakh varies from region to region, depending on the type of mud available, so small-scale installations adapted to local conditions are required if we are to make optimum use of available resources.

Truly appropriate technology would be far less costly that "high" technology—not just in purely economic terms, but very importantly, in its impact on society and the environment. It would be born of research in specific social and geographic settings, and be tailored to them, rather than vice versa. As anyone who has been close to the land knows, variations in wind, water, sun, soil, and temperature are significant even within very short distances. Just as brick-making in Ladakh varies from region to region, depending on the type of mud available, so small-scale installations adapted to local conditions are required if we are to make optimum use of available resources. This would entail a listening, intimate knowledge of nature—a very different approach from the heavy-handed ways of industrial society.

Wholistic Education

If development is to be based on local resources, knowledge about these resources obviously needs to be nurtured and supported. Instead of memorizing a standard universal knowledge, children need to be given the tools to understand their own environment. In the process, the narrow specialization and urban orientation of Western-style education would give way to a broader, more contextual and ecological perspective. Location-specific knowledge of this kind would be wholistic and specific at the same time. Such an approach would seek to perpetuate or rediscover traditional knowledge. It would build on centuries of empathetic interaction and experience with the web of life in a particular place.

Support for local knowledge ought to extend to all areas of education, including the natural sciences. To get beyond the Eurocentricity of modern-day science we need to promote research that is less centralized and more accessible to a broader section of the population. Instead of isolating variables under artificial laboratory conditions, emphasis would be placed on experimentation by local researchers in diverse cultural and ecological environments. Rather than maintaining elaborate high-tech seed banks, for instance, farmers would be encouraged to grow rare indigenous varieties, thus perpetuating living reservoirs of biological diversity.

Honoring Agriculture

Farming provides the most basic of all human needs and is the direct source of livelihood for the majority of the people in the Third World. Yet the status of the farmer has never been lower. At international economic summits, agriculture tends to be viewed as merely a "stumbling block" to agreement on more important issues. In fact, if present trends continue, the small farmer may well be extinct in another generation. It is imperative that we reverse these trends by giving agriculture the prominence it deserves and actively seeking to raise the status of farming as an occupation. A decentralized development path would offer immense benefits for small-scale agriculture. Small farmers would be better off if emphasis were placed on food production for local consumption, rather than on crops for export; if their products did not have to compete with products shipped great distances via subsidized transportation networks; and if support were given to developing agricultural technologies appropriate for local conditions, rather than capital-intensive farm equipment suited to large plantations and agribusiness. They would also benefit if support were shifted away from the use of pesticides and chemical fertilizers to more ecologically sound methods.

Many of these shifts are already underway. Farmers' markets, which shorten the distance between producer and consumer, are springing up, while around the world thousands of individuals and organizations are exploring locally based, sustainable alternatives, often inspired by the proven success of traditional agricultural systems. Official support, however, still lags a long way behind. Although there are encouraging signs that governments are recognizing the need for a move toward organic agriculture, economic incentives continue to favor biotechnology and large-scale agribusiness. We urgently need to put support for small-scale, diversified agriculture at the top of the list of national priorities.

Decentralization

A decentralized development path would inevitably strengthen the position of women and help to reinstate a balance between male and female values. In industrial culture, power is vested almost exclusively in men. Science, technology, and economics—the cornerstones of this culture—have been male-dominated from their very inception. Development has had the effect of leaving women behind—both literally and figuratively—as their men go off to urban centers in search of paid employment. And even within the farming economy, women have universally been marginalized as a result of mechanization. A decentralized economy, by strengthening local ties, would make it easier for women's voices to be heard. Women would then no longer be at the periphery of decision making and economic activity, but at the center of it.

In much of the Third World today, families are still whole and strong. Children and the elderly live and grow side by side, providing mutual support and security. Even family bonds, however, are under attack from the powerful forces of Western-style progress, which are causing ever-greater divisions between generations. In order to reverse this trend we need to support the strong community ties on which emotionally healthy families and individuals depend. This in turn means supporting strong local economies.

Such economies are much more than utopian ideals; they have served admirably in many parts of the world for millennia. They tend toward a more equitable distribution of wealth than growth-oriented centralized systems, and are more responsive to the needs of people and the limitations of natural resources. By supporting their revival, we also would be helping to maintain cultural and ecological diversity.

We urgently need to steer toward a sustainable balance—a balance between urban and rural, male and female, culture and nature. Ladakh can help to show the way, by giving us a deeper understanding of the interrelated forces that are shaping our society. This wider perspective is, I believe, an essential step in learning how to heal ourselves and the planet.

◆

Some Thoughts on Ecological Planning

Raymond F. Dasmann

E cology is a science with a long history. For much of its intellectual life it was disguised under other names: natural history, geography, taxonomy, and so on. As a recognized discipline and field of study it had difficulty gaining a foothold in academia. Fortunately, by the time I arrived at the University of California as a student in 1946, it was beginning to achieve academic status. I was able to specialize in wildlife ecology in the zoology department, and to take related courses in botany, forestry and geography. I had the good fortune to have Starker Leopold, son of Aldo Leopold, as my major professor. He had inherited his father's philosophy along with a keen interest in the scientific study of wildlife.

My concern for wildlife and wild country goes back to my childhood when I pursued a passion for bird study. But one's life as a graduate student is often shaped by the availability of funds. It was not birds that finally took my time and attention (and paid my way), but deer. This was because deer had become a "problem" for the California Department of Fish and Game, not because they were endangered, but because they had become over-abundant. The Department was under constant pressure from, on one side, the deer-hunting public, who believed there could never be too many deer and, on the other, the gardeners, farmers, ranchers and foresters who complained that hordes of deer were eating up their livelihoods. So following the usual route of a government department when faced with public pressure, the Department funded a deer study to be undertaken under the leadership of Starker Leopold, which then involved me. My first project was a state-wide survey to determine where the deer were, how abundant they were, the adequacy of their habitat to support their numbers, and the extent of "problems" associated with their presence.

In what I have come to see as an ecologically "ideal world," human settlements form an archipelago of urban or agricultural islands, connected by transportation and communication routes, but set within a matrix of wild country.

I did not fully appreciate at the time how fortunate I was to be paid to travel all over California looking for deer, evaluating deer habitat, and talking to local "experts" about the issues that were of concern to them. As a result I developed a familiarity with the state that most people would have had to pay dearly to achieve. That, among other things, made it possible to write *The Destruction of California*, a book that was not about deer, but people and land use. That, in turn, in some devious manner, led me into the field of planning.

It was not my intention at any time to pursue a career in planning. I considered myself to be a wildlife ecologist at that time, although now I find the label conservation biologist more appropriate to my interests. Nevertheless I found myself in charge of environmental planning for the Conservation Foundation in Washington, D.C. during part of the 1960s, working with such distinguished planners as Ian McHarg, who was then writing his *Design With Nature* or with a team from Harvard who were developing what was later to become the GIS system of ecological and landscape mapping and evaluation, or with Florida planners working on environmentally sound urban development for a region of mangroves and lagoons.

Planners must necessarily look to the future, and at least have some alternative scenarios concerning the form of the communities they are working with. In what I have come to see as an ecologically "ideal world," human settlements form an archipelago of urban or agricultural islands, connected by transportation and communication routes, but set within a matrix of wild country. By wild country I mean landscapes in which natural vegetation and animal life can continue to thrive without dependence on human assistance or interference. This surrounding wild matrix could be used in part to provide materials for human use, from fodder for livestock, lumber for housing, or minerals for industrial use, so long as these uses were not so intensive as to interfere with the wild character of the countryside—meaning its ability to maintain and reproduce its natural character. In some parts of the world this pattern of human settlement persists today. Not very long ago it was the predominant pattern. Its sustainability has been tested through centuries or millennia of human use. It is probable that it could continue indefinitely if not destroyed by outside human pressures.

Regrettably, in many parts of the world, because of increases in human population and technological advances, the opposite pattern prevails. Such wild country as still exists consists of islands set within a matrix of urbanized or intensively used agricultural land, usually without connecting corridors over which wild species can move. The pattern is obvious when seen from the air over the American middle west, and even more extreme in western Europe and much of eastern Asia. The sustainability of such a pattern of human settlement is in doubt. The ability of wild species to survive in such a pattern is even more in doubt. Rather, such wild islands seem destined to go through a period of ecosystem deterioration until only the most hardy and adaptable species survive—those able to get by with limited space, to move by air from one wild island to another, or to adapt to using the urban and agricultural areas, as do blackbirds, starlings, crows, raccoons, and possums.

To the extent that I have been engaged in ecological planning, it has been to seek a return to, or the maintenance of, what I consider to be a sustainable pattern of human existence—one that permits the continued existence of all those species that have, in one way or another, provided the background and support for human occupancy of the planet. It is apparent today that the human species is taking up too much space.

One of the greatest obstacles to ecological planning is the time scale involved. Those who seek to maintain old-growth redwood forests for the future need a time horizon of up to 1,000 years. Government agencies don't expect to have a thousand-year life span. Politicians have notably short public lives. Most humans work to survive through the day, week, month, or single year. Some fortunate few may look decades ahead and plan for their retirement; others fear they may be permanently "retired" tomorrow.

After working in the Douglas fir forests of Oregon, Larry Harris, in his book *The Fragmented Forest*, has proposed a sound 300-year rotation by which timber could be cut on a regular basis while maintaining the integrity of old-growth forest. Neither the Forest Service nor private industry has rushed to adopt his scheme. Who dares to really plan 300 years ahead? Regrettably many who do long-range planning ignore the ecological realities on which human survival depends. It is dangerous to project trends far into the future. It is almost certain that present trends in population, urbanization, transportation, etc., will not continue, since the ecological basis for their continuance is being eroded away. Desertification, deforestation, soil erosion, overuse of aquifers, and pollution all continue to make less and less land capable of future support for human enterprise.

Certainly one of the worst barriers to sound ecological planning is unrestrained human population growth. With a sizable majority of the world's people living at best on the edge of serious physical deprivation, and the growing inability of governments to alleviate the problem, it is difficult to see a future that is not marked by starvation, revolution terrorism, and warfare. Planning, if it is to have meaning, must have the support and participation of those likely to be affected by the plan. This is impossible to achieve where communities are being torn apart by aggression and strife, and there is no safe ground on which to build. It is difficult enough to plan when any community is likely to be over-run by refugees or simply swamped by the burgeoning growth of human numbers. Without control of human reproduction we leave only the alternative of massive mortality.

Since the early 1970s I have believed that the best way to build a sustainable human society was through *ecodevelopment*. The term ecodevelopment was first used internationally by the United Nations Environment Program. It has now been largely displaced by the term *sustainable development* popularized by the World Commission on Environment and Development in the book *Our Common Future* and later by the United Nations Conference on Environment and Development held in Rio de Janeiro. However the original meaning of ecodevelopment has been lost in the transition. Ecodevelopment means that development must first of all plan to meet the *basic needs* of all the people before it pays attention to the *wants* of the privileged sectors of society. It must aim, furthermore, at developing local *self-reliance*, the ability of a community to survive on its own resources. Both of these goals must be achieved without disruption of the *ecological support base* on which the future of the community will depend. The three essentials lead to considering the *ecoregion*, however delineated, as the basic unit in development planning, since it provides the support base for the community.

Ecodevelopment means that development must first of all plan to meet the *basic needs* of all the people...without disruption of the *ecological support base* on which the future of the community will depend.

To say that the world today is moving in a direction almost diametrically opposite to ecodevelopment would not be too much of an overstatement. The International Monetary Fund, the Global Agreement on Tariffs and Trade (GATT), the North American Free Trade Agreement (NAFTA), and the activities of international banks all aim at destroying local self-reliance in favor of developing a global network of total economic interdependence—a New World Order. In so doing they almost guarantee that more and more people will be unable to obtain their basic needs, which in turn will lead to greater instability and strife. Meanwhile the ecological base for future survival is eroded as emphasis is placed on producing export crops and converting biotic resources into items for world trade. I see no way of combating this trend. It seems we must wait for things to get much worse before there is real hope possible that we can move toward sustainable human societies.

The world seemed a more hopeful place when I was sitting on a hillside pondering the intricacies of deer population dynamics and behavior. But deer must have suitable habitat, and that involves land and water and the uses that people make of these resources. This unfortunately leads to a consideration of the future of habitat for deer and people, and that leads to consideration of political, economic, and social factors that determine the uses made of land and water. Which is where planning comes in, often accompanied by feelings of frustration and desperation.

I find that I can no longer do wildlife research without considering its relationship to the planetary crises that threaten all species. Like Shakespeare's Hamlet my "native hue of resolution / Is sicklied o'er with the pale cast of thought." Perhaps I should envy the deer whose worries and concerns extend no further than the nose can smell or the eyes can see.

♦

Natural and City Ecosystems: Thoughts on City Ecology

Jane Jacobs

When I began writing about cities, I expected merely to describe the civilizing and enjoyable services that good city street life casually provides—and to deplore planning fads and architectural fashions that were expunging these necessities and charms instead of helping to strengthen them. But learning and thinking about city streets and the trickiness of city parks launched me into an unexpected treasure hunt. I quickly found that the valuables in plain sight—streets and parks—were intimately mingled with clues and keys to other peculiarities of cities. Thus one discovery led to another, then another.

At some point along the trail I realized that I engaged in studying the ecology of cities. Off hand, this sounds like taking note that raccoons nourish themselves from city backyard gardens and garbage bags (in my own city, Toronto, they do, sometimes even downtown), that hawks can possibly reduce pigeon populations among skyscrapers, and so on. But by city ecology I mean something different from, yet similar to, natural ecology as students of wilderness address the subject. A natural ecosystem is defined as "composed of physical-chemical-biological processes active within a space-time unit of any magnitude." A city ecosystem is composed of physical-economic-ethical processes active at a given time within a city and its close dependencies. I've made up this definition, by analogy.

The two sorts of ecosystems—one created by nature, the other by human beings—have fundamental principles in common. For instance, both types of ecosystems, assuming they are not barren, require much diversity to sustain themselves. In both cases, the diversity develops organically over time, and the varied components are interdependent in complex ways. The more niches for diversity of life and livelihoods in either kind of ecosystem, the greater its carrying capacity for life. In both types of ecosystem, many small and obscure components—easily overlooked by superficial observation—can be vital to the whole, far out of proportion to their own tininess of scale or aggregate quantities. In natural ecosystems, gene pools are fundamental treasures. In city ecosystems, kinds of work are fundamental treasures; furthermore, forms of work not only reproduce themselves in newly created proliferating organizations, they also hybridize, and even mutate into unprecedented kinds of work. And because of their complex interdependencies of components, both kinds of ecosystems are vulnerable and fragile, easily disrupted or destroyed.

A city ecosystem is composed of physical-economic-ethical processes active at a given time within a city and its close dependencies.

If not fatally disrupted, however, they are tough and resilient. And when their processes are working well, ecosystems appear stable. But in a profound sense, the stability is an illusion. As a Greek philosopher, Heraclitus, observed long ago, everything in the natural world is in flux. When we suppose we see static situations, we actually see processes of beginning and processes of ending occurring simultaneously. Nothing is static. It is the same with cities. Thus, to investigate either natural or city ecosystems demands the same kind of thinking. It does not do to focus on "things" and expect them to explain much in themselves. Processes are always of the essence; things have significances as participants in processes, for better or worse.

This way of seeing is fairly young and new, which is perhaps why the hunt for knowledge to understand either natural or city ecology seems so inexhaustible. Little is known; so much yet to know.

We human beings are the only city-building creatures in the world. The hives of social insects are fundamentally different in how they develop, what they do, and their potentialities. Cities are in a sense natural ecosystems too—for us. They are not disposable. Whenever and wherever societies have flourished and prospered rather than stagnated and decayed, creative and workable cities have been at the core of the phenomenon; they have pulled their weight and more. It is the same still. Decaying cities, declining economies, and mounting social troubles travel together. The combination is not coincidental.

It is urgent that human beings understand as much as we can about city ecology—starting at any point in city processes. The humble, vital services performed by grace of good city streets and neighborhoods are probably as good a starting point as any. I hope new generations of observers and thinkers will become interested in city ecology, respect its marvels, discover more. An important caveat here. Just as persons who despise nature are destructive when they meddle with natural ecosystems, so are persons who despise cities destructive prescribers for cities. But in both cases, so too are enthusiasts who proceed to meddle without respect, caution, and a wholesome bit of awe.

◆

An Outline for an Ecological Politics

Murray Bookchin

S ocial ecology is neither "biocentric"nor "anthropocentric." Rather, it is *naturalistic*. Because of this naturalistic orientation, social ecology is no less concerned with issues like the integrity of wild areas and wildlife than are "biocentrists." As a hiker, an ecologist, and above all a naturalist who devoutly believes in freedom, I can talk passionately about the trails I have followed, the vistas I have gazed at, or the soaring hawks I have watched for hours from cliffs and mountain peaks. Yet social ecology is also naturalistic in the very important sense that it stresses humanity's and society's profound roots in natural evolution. Hence my use of the term "second *nature*" to emphasize the development of human social life out of the natural world.

This second aspect of social ecology's naturalistic perspective not only challenges misanthropy, it challenges conventional social theory as well. The philosophy of social ecology denies that there can be a complete separation—let alone a desirable opposition—between human and non-human evolution. As naturalists, we respect the fact that human beings have evolved out of first or non-human nature as mammals and primates to form a new domain composed of mutable institutions, technologies, values, forms of communication. Social ecology recognizes that we are both biological *and* social beings. Indeed, social ecologists go so far as to analyze carefully the important social history that has pitted humanity not only against itself but, very significantly, against non-human nature as well.

Over the centuries social conflicts have fostered the development of hierarchies and classes based on domination and exploitation in which the great majority of human beings have been as ruthlessly abused as the natural world itself. Social ecology carefully focuses on this social history and reveals that the very *idea* of dominating nature stems from the domination of human by human. This hierarchical mentality and system has been extended from the social domination of people—particularly the young, women, people of color, and yes, males generally as workers, and subjects into the realm of non-human nature. Thus, social ecologists understand that until we undertake the project of liberating human beings from domination and hierarchy—economic exploitation and class rule, as orthodox socialists would have it—our chances of saving the wild areas of the planet and wildlife are remote at best.

This means that the radical ecology movement must have programs for removing the oppressions that people suffer even while some of us are primarily focused on the damage this society is inflicting on wild areas and wildlife. We should never lose sight of the fact that the project of human liberation is always an ecological project as well, just as, conversely, the project of defending the Earth has also become a social project. Social ecology as a form of eco-anarchism weaves these two projects together, first by means of an organic way of thinking that I call *dialectical naturalism*; second, by means of a mutualistic social and ecological ethics that I call the *ethics of complementarity*; third, by means of a new technics that I call *eco-technology*; and last, by means of new forms of human association that I call *eco-communities*. It is not accidental that I have written works on cities as well as ecology, on utopias as well as pollution, on a new politics as well as new technologies; on a new economy as well as a new ecological sensibility. A coherent ecological philosophy must address *all* of these questions.

We need to create an ecologically oriented society out of the present anti-ecological one. If we can change the direction of our civilization's social evolution, human beings can assist in the creation of a truly "free nature," where all of our human traits—intellectual, communicative, and social—are placed at the service of natural evolution in order to consciously increase biotic diversity, diminish suffering, foster the further evolution of new and ecologically valuable lifeforms, and reduce the impact of disastrous accidents or the harsh effects of harmful change. Our species, gifted by the creativity of natural evolution itself, could play the role of nature rendered self-conscious.

Our species, gifted by the creativity of natural evolution itself, could play the role of nature rendered self-conscious.

One of our chief goals must be to radically decentralize our industrialized urban areas into humanly-scaled cities and towns artfully tailored to the carrying capacities of the eco-communities in which they are located. We need to transform the current pattern of densely populated urban sprawl into federations of much smaller cities and towns surrounded by small farms that practice diversified, organic agriculture for the local area and are linked to each other by tree belts, pastures and meadows. In rolling, hilly, or mountainous country, land with sharp gradients should be left covered by timber to prevent erosion, conserve water, and support wildlife. Furthermore, each city and town should contain many vegetable and flower gardens, attractive arbors, park land, and streams and ponds which support fish and aquatic birds. In this way, the countryside would not only constitute the immediate environs of the city but would also directly infuse the city. Relatively close by, sizable wilderness areas would safely coexist with human habitats and would be carefully "managed" to enhance and preserve their evolutionary integrity, diversity, and stability.

By decentralizing our communities, we would also be able to eliminate the present society's horribly destructive addiction to fossil fuels and nuclear energy. One of the fundamental reasons that giant urban areas and industries are unsustainable is because of their inherent dependency on huge quantities of dangerous and non-renewable energy resources. To maintain a large, densely populated city requires immense quantities of coal, petroleum, or nuclear energy. It seems likely that safe and renewable energy sources such as wind, water, and solar power can probably not fully meet the needs of giant urban areas, even if careful energy conservation is practiced and automobile use and socially unnecessary production is curtailed. In contrast to coal, oil, and nuclear energy, alternative energy sources reach us mainly in small "packets," as it were. Yet while solar devices, wind turbines, and hydroelectric resources can probably not provide enough electricity to illuminate Manhattan Island today, such energy sources, pieced together in an organic energy pattern developed from the potentialities of a particular region, could amply meet the vital needs of small, decentralized cities and towns.

As with agriculture, the industrial economy must also be decentralized and its technology radically reworked to creatively utilize local resources in small-scale, multi-use facilities with production processes that reduce arduous toil, recycle raw materials, and eliminate pollution and toxic wastes. In this way, the *relatively* self-sufficient community, visibly dependent on its environment for its means of life, would likely gain a new respect for the organic interrelationships that sustain it. In the long run, the attempt to approximate local, or at least regional self-sufficiency would prove more efficient than the wasteful and neo-colonial global division of labor that prevails today. Although there would doubtless be many duplications of small manufacturing and craft facilities from community to community, the familiarity of each group with its local environment and its ecological roots would make for a more intelligent and loving use of its environment. These proposals, as well as those which follow, were advanced in great detail in my essays, "Ecology and Revolutionary Thought" and "Towards a Liberating Technology" written in 1964 and available in *Post Scarcity Anarchism*, a collection of my sixties' writing published by Black Rose Books in 1972.

Such a vision appears quite radical on the face of it. Yet I have to stress that my calls for decentralization and "alternative" technologies are, by themselves, insufficient to create a humane, ecological society. We should not delude ourselves into the belief that a mere change in demographics, logistics, design, or scale automatically yields a real change in social life or spiritual sensibility. Decentralization and a sophisticated *alternative* technology can help, of course. The kind of decentralized communities and eco-technologies that I've described here could help open up a new era of direct democracy by providing the free time and social comprehensibility that would make it possible for ordinary people to manage the affairs of society without the mediation of ruling classes, giant bureaucracies, or élitist professional political functionaries. However, a genuine ecological vision ultimately needs to answer directly such nagging questions as "who owns what?" and "who runs what?" The answers we give to these questions will have enormous power to shape our future.

I would argue that the best form of government in an ecological society would be direct democratic self-government; that the best form of ownership of productive enterprises and resources would be neither corporate nor state but communal at the municipal level; and that the best form of economic management would be community self-management. In such a vision, broad policies and concrete decisions that deal with community life, agriculture, and industrial production would be made, whenever possible, by active citizens in face-to-face assemblies. Among the many benefits of such a democratic, cooperative commonwealth is the encouragement of a non-hierarchical, non-domineering sensibility within the human community that would ultimately influence human society's view of its relationship with the rest of the natural world.

To be sure, moving from today's capitalist society—based on giant industrial and urban belts, a highly chemical agribusiness, centralized and bureaucratic power, a staggering armaments economy, massive pollution, and exploited labor—towards the ecological society that I have only begun to describe here will require a complex and difficult transition strategy. I have no pat formulas for making such a revolution. A few things seem clear, however. A new politics must be created that eschews the snares of co-optation within the system that is destroying social and ecological life. We need a social movement that can effectively resist and ultimately replace the nation state and corporate capitalism, not one that limits its sights to "improving" the current system.

Direct nonviolent resistance is clearly an important element of this new politics. The marvelous genius of the anti-nuke alliances of the 1970s was that they intuitively sensed the need to break away from the "system" and form a strong independent opposition. To a large extent, to be sure, they adopted a direct action strategy because earlier attempts to stop nuclear power plants by working within the system had failed. Endless months or years of litigation, hearings, the adoption of local ordinances, petitions, and letter writing campaigns to congress people had all essentially failed to stop the construction of new nuclear power plants. Stronger measures were required in order to finally stop new construction. Yet I believe that an even more important feature of direct action is that it forms a decisive step toward recovering the community power over social life that the centralized, overbearing bureaucracies have usurped from the people. It provides an experiential bridge to a possible future society based on direct grassroots democracy.

Community gardens, block clubs, land trusts, housing cooperatives, parent-run daycare centers, barter networks, alternative schools, consumer and producer cooperatives, community theatres, study groups, neighborhood newspapers, public access television stations—all of these meet immediate and usually neglected community needs.

Thus, community organizing is a key element of a radical new politics, particularly those forms of association where people meet face-to-face, identify their common problems, and solve them through mutual aid and volunteer community service. Such community organizations encourage social solidarity, community self-reliance, and individual initiative. Community gardens, block clubs, land trusts, housing cooperatives, parent-run daycare centers, barter networks, alternative schools, consumer and producer cooperatives, community theatres, study groups, neighborhood newspapers, public access television stations—all of these meet immediate and usually neglected community needs. Simultaneously, they serve, to greater or lesser degrees, as schools for democratic citizenship. Through participation in such efforts we can become more socially responsible and more skilled at democratically discussing and deciding important social questions.

However—and this may shock most conventional anarchists—I also think we need to explore the possibilities of grassroots electoral politics. While it cannot be denied that most ways of participating in the electoral arena only serve to legitimize the nation-state, with its standing bureaucracy and limited citizen involvement, I think it is important and possible for grassroots activists to intervene in local politics and create *new* kinds of local structures such as ballot initiatives, community assemblies, town meetings, and neighborhood councils that can increasingly take over direct democratic control of municipal governments.

The success of such a left-libertarian municipalist movement will depend on its ability, over time, to democratize one community after another and establish confederal regional relationships between these local communities. We will need such a geographical, political, and economic base if we are ever to challenge seriously the nation-state and multi-national corporations. We will need to create such a *dual power* in order to wrest important and immediate concessions from the existing system and ultimately to supplant it. In the absence of such a truly participatory politics, I see no other realistic alternative for creating a genuinely ecological society.

Permaculture

Bill Mollison

To many of us who experienced the ferment of the late 1960s, there seemed to be no positive direction forward, although almost everybody could define those aspects of the global society that they rejected, including military adventurism, the bomb, ruthless land exploitation, the arrogance of polluters, and a general insensitivity to human and environmental needs.

From 1972-74, I spent some time (latterly with David Holmgren) in developing an interdisciplinary earth science—permaculture—with a potential for positivistic, integrated, and global outreach. It was January 1981 before the concept of permaculture seemed to have matured sufficiently to be taught as an applied design system, when the first 26 students graduated from an intensive 140-hour lecture series. Today, we can count thousands of people who have attended permaculture design courses, workshops, lectures, and seminars. Graduates now form a loose global network, and are effectively acting in many countries. The permaculture movement has no central structure, but rather a strong sense of shared work. Everybody is free to act as an individual, to form a small group, or to work within any other organization. We cooperate with many other groups with diverse beliefs and practices; our system includes good practices from many disciplines and systems, and offers them as an integrated whole.

By 1984, it had become clear that many of the systems we had proposed a decade earlier did, in fact, constitute a sustainable Earth care system. Almost all that we had proposed was tested and tried, and where the skills and capital existed, people could make a living from products derived from stable landscapes, although this is not a primary aim of permaculture, which seeks first to stabilise and care for land, then to serve household regional and local needs, and only thereafter to produce a surplus for sale or exchange.

In 1984, we held our first international permaculture conference, and awarded about 50 applied diplomas to those who had served two years of applied work since their design course. Those of us who belong to the permaculture family have cause to be proud, but not complacent. Work has scarcely begun, but we have a great team of people which increases in numbers daily. To empower the powerless and create "a million villages" to replace nation-states is the only safe future for the preservation of the biosphere. Let interdependence and personal responsibility be our aims.

Permaculture Design Philosophy

The Prime Directive of Permaculture
The only ethical decision is to take responsibility for our own existence and that of our children.

Make it now.

Most thinking people would agree that we have arrived at final and irrevocable decisions that will abolish or sustain life on this Earth. We can either ignore the madness of uncontrolled industrial growth and defence spending that is in small bites, or large catastrophes, eroding life forms every day, or take the path to life and survival.

Information and humanity, science and understanding, are in transition. Long ago, we began by wondering about what is most distant; astronomy and astrology were our ancient preoccupations. We progressed, millennia by millennia, to enumerating the wonders of Earth, first by naming things, then by categorizing them, and more recently by deciding how they function and what work they do within and without themselves. This analysis has resulted in the development of different sciences, disciplines, and technologies; a welter of names and the sundering of parts; a proliferation of specialists; and a consequent inability to foresee results or to design integrated systems.

The present great shift in emphasis is on how the parts interact, how they work together with each other, how dissonance or harmony in life systems and society is achieved. Life *is* cooperative rather than competitive, and life forms of very different qualities may interact beneficially with one another and with their physical environment. As Lewis Thomas said in *The Lives of a Cell*, even "the bacteria...live by collaboration, accommodation, exchange, and barter."

Principle of Cooperation

Cooperation, not competition, is the very basis of existing life systems and of future survival.

There are many opportunities to *create* systems that work from the elements and technologies that exist. Perhaps we should do nothing else for the next century but apply our knowledge. We already know how to build, maintain, and inhabit sustainable systems. Every essential problem is solved, but in the everyday life of people this is hardly apparent. The wage-slave, peasant, landlord, and industrialist alike are deprived of the leisure and life spirit that is possible in a cooperative society which applies its knowledge. Both warders and prisoners are equally captive in the society in which we live.

If we question why we are here and what life is, then we lead ourselves into both science and mysticism which are coming closer together as science itself approaches its conceptual limits. As for life, it is the most open of open systems, able to take from the energy resources in time and to re-express itself not only as a lifetime but as a descent and an evolution.

In *Gaia: A New Look at Life on Earth*, J.E. Lovelock has perhaps best expressed a philosophy, or insight, which links science and tribal beliefs: he sees the Earth, and the universe, as a thought process, or as a self-regulating, self-constructed and reactive system, creating and preserving the conditions that make life possible, and actively adjusting to regulate disturbances. Humanity, however, in its present mindlessness, may be the one disturbance that the Earth cannot tolerate.

The Gaia hypothesis is for those who like to walk or simply stand and stare, to wonder about the Earth and the life it bears, and to speculate about the consequences of our own presence here. It is an alternative to that pessimistic view which sees nature as a primitive force to be subdued and conquered. It is also an alternative to that equally depressing picture of our planet as a demented spaceship, forever travelling, driverless and purposeless, around an inner circle of the sun.— J. E. Lovelock, *Gaia: A New Look at Life on Earth*

For every scientific statement articulated on energy, the Aboriginal tribespeople of Australia have an equivalent statement on life. Life, they say, is a totality neither created or destroyed. It can be imagined as an egg from which all tribes (life forms) issue and to which all return. The ideal way in which to spend one's time is in the perfection of the expression of life, to lead the most evolved life possible, and to assist in and celebrate the existence of life forms other than humans, for all come from the same egg.

A young woman once came to me after a lecture in which I had considered the various concepts of after-life...Her view was, "This is heaven, right here. This is it. *Give it all you've got.*"

The totality of this outlook leads to a meaningful daily existence, in which one sees each quantum of life eternally trying to perfect an expression towards a future, and possibly transcendental, perfection. It is all the more horrific, therefore, that tribal peoples, whose aim has been to develop a conceptual and spiritual existence, have encountered a crude, scientific, and material culture which lacks a stated life aim and relies on pseudo-economic and technological systems for its existence.

The experience of the natural world and its laws has almost been abandoned for closed, artificial, and meaningless lives, perhaps best typified by the dreams of those who would live in space satellites and abandon a dying Earth.

I believe that unless we adopt sophisticated, aboriginal belief systems and learn respect for all life, we will lose our own opportunity to achieve maturity, balance, and harmony in our lives. This is the essential issue facing the present generation.

A young woman once came to me after a lecture in which I wondered at the various concepts of after-life; the plethora of "heavens"offered by various groups. Her view was, "This is heaven, right here. This is it. *Give it all you've got."*

I couldn't better that advice. The heaven, or hell, we live in is of our own making. An after-life, if such exists, can be no different for each of us.

Ethics

In earlier days, several of us researched community ethics, as adopted by older religious and cooperative groups, seeking for universal principles to guide our own actions. Although some of these guidelines contained as many as 18 principles, most of these can be included in the three below (and even the second and third arise from the first):

The Ethical Basis of Permaculture

1. CARE OF THE Earth: Provision for all life systems to continue and multiply.

2. CARE OF PEOPLE: Provision for people to access those resources necessary to their existence.

3. SETTING LIMITS TO POPULATION AND CONSUMPTION: By governing our own needs, we can set resources aside to further the above principles.

This ethic is a very simple statement of guidance, and serves well to illuminate everyday endeavors. It can be coupled to a determination to make our own way: to be neither employers nor employees, landlords nor tenants, but to be self-reliant as individuals and to cooperate as groups.

For the sake of the Earth itself, I evolved a philosophy close to Taoism from my experiences with natural systems. As stated in *Permaculture Two*, it is a philosophy of working with rather than against nature; of protracted and thoughtful observation rather than protracted and thoughtless action; of looking at systems and people in all their functions, rather than asking only one yield of them; and of allowing systems to demonstrate their own evolutions. A basic question that can be asked in two ways is:

"What can I get from this land, or person?"or

"What does this person, or land, have to give if I cooperate with them?"

Of these two approaches, the former leads to war and waste, the latter to peace and plenty.

Most conflicts, I find, lie in how such questions are asked, and not in the answers to any question. Or, to put it another way, we are clearly looking for the right questions rather than for answers. We should be alert to rephrase or refuse the "wrong"question.

It has become evident that unity in people comes from a common adherence to a set of ethical principles, each of us perhaps going our own way, at our own pace, and within the limits of our resources, yet all leading to the same goals, which in our own case is that of a living, complex, and sustainable Earth. Those who agree on such ethics, philosophies, and goals form a global nation.

How do a people evolve an ethic, and why should we bother to do so?

Humans are thinking beings, with long memories, oral and written records, and the ability to investigate the distant past by applying a variety of techniques from dendrochronology to archaeology, pollen analysis to the geological sciences. It is therefore evident that behaviors in the natural world which we thought appropriate at one time later proven to be damaging to our own society in the long-term (e.g., the effects of biocidal pest controls on soils and water).

Thus, we are led by information, reflection, and careful investigation to moderate, abandon, or forbid certain behaviors and substances that in the long-term threaten our own survival; *we act to survive*. Conservative and cautious rules of behavior are evolved. This is a rational and sensible process, responsible for many taboos in tribal societies.

From a great many case histories we can list some rules of use, for example, the RULE OF NECESSITOUS USE—that we leave any natural system alone until we are, of strict necessity, forced to use it. We may then follow up with RULES OF CONSERVATIVE USE—having found it necessary to use a natural resource, we may insist on every attempt to:

- reduce waste, hence pollution;
- thoroughly replace lost minerals;

- do a careful energy accounting; and
- make an assessment of the long-term, negative, biosocial effects on society, and act to buffer or eliminate these.

In practice, we evolve over time to various forms of *accounting for our actions*. Such accounts are fiscal, social, environmental, aesthetic, or energetic in nature, and all are appropriate to our own survival.

Consideration of these rules of necessitous and conservative use may lead us, step by step, to the basic realization of our inter-connectedness with nature; that we depend on good health in all systems for our survival. Thus, we widen the self-interested idea of human survival (on the basis of past famine and environmental disaster) to include the idea of "the survival of natural systems," and can see, for example, that when we lose plant and animal species due to our actions, we lose many survival opportunities. Our fates are intertwined. This process, or something like it, is common to every group of people who evolve a general Earth-care ethic.

Having developed an Earth-care ethic by assessing our best course for survival, we then turn to our relationships with others. Here, we observe a general rule of nature: that cooperative species and associations of self-supporting species (like mycorrhiza on tree roots) make healthy communities. Such lessons lead us to a sensible resolve to cooperate and take support roles in society, to foster an interdependence which values the individual's contributions rather than forms of opposition or competition.

Although initially we can see how helping our family and friends assists us in our own survival, we may evolve the mature ethic that sees all humankind as family, and all life as allied associations. Thus, we expand *people care* to *species care*, for all life has common origins. All are "our family."

We see how enlightened self-interest leads us to evolve ethics of sustainable and sensible behavior. These, then, are the ethics expressed in permaculture. Having evolved *ethics*, we can then devise *ways to apply them* to our lives, economies, gardens, land, and nature.

Permaculture in Landscape and Society

As the basis of permaculture is beneficial design, it can be added to all other ethical training and skills, and has the potential of taking a place in all human endeavors. In the broad landscape, however, permaculture concentrates on already-settled areas and agricultural lands. Almost all of these need drastic rehabilitation and rethinking. One certain result of using our skills to integrate food supply and settlement, to catch water from our roof areas, and to place nearby a zone of fuel forest which receives wastes and supplies energy, will be to free most of the area of the globe for the rehabilitation of natural systems. These need never be looked upon as "of use to people," except in the very broad sense of global health.

The real difference between a cultivated (designed) ecosystem, and a natural system is that the great majority of species (and biomass) in the *cultivated* ecology is intended for the use of humans or their livestock. We are only a small part of the total primeval or natural species assembly, and only a small part of its yields are directly available to us. But in our own gardens, almost every plant is selected to provide or support some direct yield for people. Household design relates principally to the needs of people; it is thus human-centred (anthropocentric).

This is a valid aim for *settlement design*, but we also need a nature-centred ethic for wilderness conservation. We cannot, however, do much for nature if we do not govern our greed, and if we do not supply our needs from our existing settlements. If we can achieve this aim, we can withdraw from much of the agricultural landscape, and allow natural systems to flourish.

Recycling of nutrients and energy in nature is a function of many species. In our gardens, it is our own responsibility to return wastes (via compost or mulch) to the soil and plants. We actively create soil in our gardens, whereas in nature many other species carry out that function. Around our homes we can catch water for garden use, but we rely on natural forested landscapes to provide the condenser leaves and clouds to keep rivers running with clean water, to maintain the global atmosphere, and to lock up our gaseous pollutants. Thus, even anthropocentric people would be well-advised to pay close attention to, and to assist in, the conservation of existing forests and the rehabilitation of degraded lands. Our own survival demands that we preserve all existing species, and allow them a place to live.

We have abused the land and laid waste to systems we need never have disturbed had we attended to our home gardens and settlements. If we need to state a set of ethics on natural systems, then let it be thus:

- opposition to further disturbances of any remaining natural for-

ests, where most species are still in balance;
- vigorous rehabilitation of degraded and damaged natural systems to stable states;
- establishment of plant systems for our own use on the *least* amount of land we can use for our existence; and
- establishment of plant and animal refuges for rare or threatened species.

Permaculture as a design system deals primarily with the third statement above, but all people who act responsibly in fact subscribe to the first and second statements. That said, I believe we should use all the species we need or can find to use in our own settlement designs, *providing they are not locally rampant and invasive.*

Whether we approve of it or not, the world about us continually changes. Some would want to keep everything the same, but history, paleontology, and commonsense tell us that all has changed, is changing, will change. In a world where we are losing forests, species, and whole ecosystems, there are three concurrent and parallel responses to the environment:

1. CARE FOR SURVIVING NATURAL ASSEMBLIES, to leave the wilderness to heal itself.

2. REHABILITATE DEGRADED OR ERODED LAND using complex pioneer species and long-term plant assemblies (trees, shrubs, ground covers).

3. CREATE OUR OWN COMPLEX LIVING ENVIRONMENT with as many species as we can save, or have need for, from wherever on Earth they come.

We are fast approaching the point where we need refuges for *all* global life forms, as well as regional, national, or state parks for indigenous forms of plants and animals. While we see our local flora and fauna as "native," we may also logically see all life as "native to Earth." While we try to preserve systems that are still local and diverse, we should also build new or recombinant ecologies from global resources, especially in order to stabilize degraded lands.

In your own garden, there are likely to be plants, animals, and soil organisms from every major land mass and many islands. Jet travel has merely accelerated a process already well-established by continental drift, bird migration, wind transport, and the rafting of debris by water. Everything will, in time, either become extinct, spread more widely, or evolve to new forms. Each of these processes is happening at once, but the rate of extinction and exchange is accelerating. Rather than new species, adapted hybrids are arising—for example, as palms, sea grasses, snails, and micro-organisms from many continents meet, mix, and produce new accommodations to their "new" environments.

Even the smallest garden can reserve a few square metres of insect, lizard, frog, or buterfly habitat, while larger gardens and farms can fence off forest and wetland areas of critical value to local species.

The very chemistry of the air, soil, and water is in flux. Metals, chemicals, isotopes, gases, and plastics are loose on Earth that have never before been present, or never present in such form and quantity before we made it so.

It is my belief that we have two responsibilities:

- to get our house and garden, our place of living, in order, so that it supports us;
- to limit our population on Earth, or we ourselves become the final plague.

Both these duties are intimately connected, as stable regions create stable populations. If we do not get our cities, homes, and gardens in order, so that they feed and shelter us, we must lay waste to all other natural systems. Thus, truly responsible conservationists have gardens which support their food needs, and are working to reduce their own energy needs to a modest consumption, or to that which can be supplied by local wind, water, forest, or solar power resources. We can work on providing biomass for our essential energy needs on a household and regional scale.

It is hypocrisy to pretend to save forests, yet to buy daily newspapers and packaged food; to preserve native plants, yet rely on agrochemical production for food; and to adopt a diet which calls for broad-scale food production.

Philosopher-gardeners, or farmer-poets, are distinguished by their sense of wonder and real feeling for the environment. When religions cease to obliterate trees in order to build temples or human artifacts, and instead generalize love and respect for all living systems as a witness to the potential of creation, they too will join the many of us now deeply appreciating the complexity and self-sustaining properties of natural systems, from whole universes to simple molecules. Gardener, scientist, philosopher, poet, and adherent of religions, all can join together in admiration of, and reverence for, this Earth. We create our own life conditions, now and for the future.

In permaculture, this means that all of us have some part in identifying, supporting, recommending, investing in, or creating wilderness habitats and species refuges. The practical way to proceed (outside the home garden) is to form or subscribe to institutes or organizations whose aims under their legal charter are to carry out conservation activities. While the costs are low, in total the effects are profound. Even the smallest garden can reserve a few square metres of insect, lizard, frog, or butterfly habitat, while larger gardens and farms can fence off forest and wetland areas of critical value to local species. Such areas should be *only* for the conservation of local species.

Permaculture as a design system contains nothing new. It arranges what was always there in a different way, so that it works to conserve energy or to generate more energy than it consumes. What is novel, and often overlooked, is that *any* system of total common sense design for human communities is revolutionary!

References

King, F. H., *Farmers of Forty Centuries: Permanent Agriculture in China, Korea, and Japan*, Rodale Press, 1911.
Lovelock, J. E., *Gaia: A New Look at Life on Earth*, Oxford University Press, 1979.
Odum, Eugene, *Fundamentals of Ecology*, W.B. Saunders, 1971.
Thomas, Lewis, *The Lives of a Cell*, Viking Press, 1974.
Watt, Kenneth, *Principles of Environmental Science*, McGraw-Hill, 1973.

3

Inventing
the Sustainable City

Introduction

Doug Aberley

Once a person has evolved an ecological world view that guides and sustains a commitment to social change, then it stands to reason that an arena for this action must be chosen. In the recent past, it has been expected that we limit the work of our lives within the confines of a profession or cultural role—planner, parent, engineer, laborer, artisan. It's time to look at alternatives to this reductionist specialization.

To survive, humans must have shelter. To *flourish*, humans need community—a physical stage upon which all the drama of our kind can be played. These simple imperatives have led to the use of hide, mud, stone, and wood to create homesteads, villages, towns, provincial cities, metropolitan cities, conurbations, edge cities, and world cities. The city is by far the most favored scale of human gathering, due to the fundamental human preference for contact with other humans and the opportunities intrinsically associated with coalesced groups of producers and consumers. In a very real sense, the greatest expression of human agency is the silhouette of the physical shell of a city against the sky.

As cities have become larger, responsibility for their continuous expansion and maintenance has been appropriated by professional élites. Supposedly, only planners, architects, engineers, and their institutional and corporate masters are able to manage the complexities of the settlements we inhabit. The result? We are told that to be efficient and safe, cities must be totally accessible to automobiles, must have strictly separated land uses, must be constructed to a single industrial standard, and must be able to grow in size and/or complexity forever. But, in fact, traffic doesn't flow, disease and accidents are epidemic, class and ethnic barriers are fossilized, and security has become the fastest growing urban industry. We need to transform radically the shape and governance of human settlement.

Up until the 1980s social change activists incorporated cities into their work in two ways. The tradition of leaving existing cities in order to build new and more humane settlements was maintained, in particular by Paolo Soleri. On a second front, activists attempted to fix only narrow aspects of city life—poverty, housing, transportation. With notable exceptions, such as Saul Alinsky and Jane Jacobs, it was not until the concept of the green city, or eco-city, that a more wholistic vision of urban transformation came into wider being. As pioneered by Richard Register and others, the idea of the eco-city is the logical extension of an ecological world view that seeks an avenue of actualization. We will not necessarily abandon existing cities, but with vision and persistence, we can transform them into self-reliant and socially just configurations.

Each contributor to this section considers a different aspect of the challenge of urban transformation. Richard Register places the idea of eco-cities in firm intellectual and practical context. Mark Roseland next describes how urban governments across the planet are acting to implement parts of the eco-city ideal. Janice Perlman explains how even the largest human agglomerations, mega-cities, are being creatively transformed to respect human need and ecological necessity. Christopher Canfield then introduces us to Cerro Gordo, a prototype eco-village in Oregon whose evolution has been carefully nurtured for over twenty years. And, finally, Melanie Taylor tells how *new urbanism*—the adaptation of vernacular settlement morphology to new urban development—is being promoted by a new generation of architects and planners. Taken together, these authors provide an excellent introduction to ways in which an ecological world view can be applied, bringing a whole new meaning to the term "home ownership."

◆

Eco-Cities: Rebuilding Civilization, Restoring Nature

Richard Register

As we build, so shall we live. As we build our cities, so shall we determine what is possible and impossible, culturally and in relation to living in balance with nature.

Few people seem to understand the importance of this proposition. Environmentalists call for efficient recycling—without calling for a city structure that makes it possible. Then they drive around town with ten pounds of paper in a 2,000 pound car. Some architects call for healthy buildings—without placing the building into a city layout that could make the building function in its town in a healthy way. Then people go on consuming gasoline and paving paradise between "healthy buildings." Some gardeners and naturalists promote planting trees, grass and shrubs in the suburbs—without recognizing the larger infrastructure and natural systems the suburbs are part of. Then, in drier climates, the watering of the trees, grass, and shrubs depletes the rivers, causing salt intrusion into estuaries, impoverishing water and marsh environments for fish, waterfowl, and humans who need or enjoy them, creating excess siltation which requires more dredging for shipping, and so on.

Everywhere the environmentalist, conscientious architect, and caring citizen come up against apparent contradictions. But if we look at the structure of cities, towns, and villages, and realize that they can be built upon ecological principles, the contradictions are explained and we can proceed to build in a healthy manner. That insight, though—that the structure of the built habitat is at the foundation of environmental and social success or failure—is almost totally missing from the current debate. It is the foundation for all that I will present. I call it the ecological city insight, or, most simply, the eco-city insight.

If this insight is missing, it doesn't matter who is doing the planning—

the professional with a contract, the concerned citizen with a democratic process, the developer with a pile of investment money, the elected official with a mandate for improving the environment of his or her town, country, or planet. The eco-city insight should be the starting point for all efforts to improve the future. Without it we will be lost in contradictions, fooling ourselves that we are making progress when we are actually taking one step forward and two backward.

With the eco-city insight we will have a real opportunity to pursue a creative human presence on Earth while letting nature thrive in all her diversity, beauty, and glory. First things first! I call it "the missing insight" simply because in all my wanderings from Australia to South America, North America to Europe, I practically never hear it mentioned, and certainly not mentioned in the pivotal position it should occupy in our deliberations on how to improve the world.

Organizing for Ecological Rebuilding

I put together organizations that are attempting to reshape cities. I am a community activist, a citizen trying to make a better world, as all citizens should. My father is an architect, and I grew up thinking of myself as an artist. I was a sculptor at 21 when I met Paolo Soleri and was taken by his ideas of building ecologically healthy cities in a single structure; to me, his "arcologies" were something like large sculptures for people to live in. Ecological architecture still strikes me as building something that is a cross between three-dimensional playground equipment for adults, a stage for us all to strut and fret upon, and a "machine" or "organism" (pick your favored analogy) for the work of culture and economy.

Seventeen years ago, with six or seven friends, some of whom worked for Soleri at Arcosanti, his experimental ecological town in Arizona, I founded Urban Ecology in Berkeley, California, as a non-profit organization to "rebuild cities in balance with nature." Between then and now the organization has participated with others in the community to build a "Slow Street," bring back part of a creek culverted and covered eighty years earlier, plant and harvest fruit trees on streets, design and build solar greenhouses, pass energy ordinances, establish a bus line, promote bicycle and pedestrian alternatives to automobiles, delay and maybe stop construction of a local freeway, and hold conferences on these and other related subjects. We convened the First International Eco-city

Conference in 1990, and a spin-off group, Urban Ecology Australia, held the Second International Eco-city Conference in Adelaide in April, 1992. Those folks, led by architect Chérie Hoyle, have gone on to produce a "community-driven design process" that aspires to build housing, shops, offices, community centers, rooftop gardens, and many other elements of a full-blown ecologically-tuned community. Their Halifax project for 800-1000 residents has been approved by Adelaide's City Council, and they were given option to one block of a community re-development area immediately adjacent to downtown Adelaide.

In order to have an independent and focused organization to build demonstration projects—ecological architecture in the right locations for evolving the ecologically healthy city—I started another non-profit organization called Eco-city Builders. That group is currently planning what we call "Restoration Development Projects" that involve two sites in the same town at the same time. At one site we restore nature or agriculture, and at the other, the "development site," we develop more of whatever we remove at the first "restoration site." But we put the new development in exactly the right place for the future healthy development of the town. In these projects we are consciously moving away from automobile dependence while withdrawing from sprawl, placing development near transit and helping create full community, with lots of "mixed uses" close together.

City Theory

When I speak of "eco-cities" I am referring to the structure of our built community, our constructed habitat. Eco-city principles apply to villages, towns and cities. At all scales there are common ecological principles, and many common issues. At different scales and in different locations, there are also many very different conditions that require very different interpretation of those universal eco-city principles. From this mix of universal principles and vastly differing local circumstances comes the wonderful, infinite variety of possible interpretations and applications of eco-city thinking. The panorama of the eco-city future is extraordinarily rich and vital, and for me, delightful to contemplate.

There is a good deal of theory (by Lewis Mumford, Jane Jacobs, Ian McHarg and others) that defines the city as a created physical entity— tool, device, apparatus, machine, organism, artifact, etc.—different terms with shifting nuances of meaning. According to this theory, the city embodies and makes possible a variety of values and spiritual perspectives and results. To a large extent, the city serves human cultural communion and expression, particularly by serving economic, creative, and exploration purposes. Some point out the almost metaphysical function of the city as something we humans create to help us invent our creative selves, both personally and collectively. Paolo Soleri and others have taken that literally to mean that cities are participating in evolution— transforming our species genetically while evolving consciousness and conscience on the planet Earth and in its very flesh-and-blood biosphere.

The city is an invention for maximizing exchange and minimizing travel.

On the more functional level, David Engwicht, Australian author of *Reclaiming Our Cities and Towns: Better Living With Less Traffic* says "the city is an invention for maximizing exchange and minimizing travel." By that he means exchange of all sorts: goods, money, ideas, emotions, genetic material, etc.. Over the years, I have used the slogan, "access by proximity, not transportation,"meaning that we should build diversity into our cities so we can just walk around the corner to get to whatever we need, rather than being forced to get into a car and drive for it. Access is what transportation is supposed to deliver, but we can get access far more efficiently by simply building it into our communities. David Engwicht was washing windows to make a living until about four years ago, when he got involved in a fight against freeway expansion in his neighborhood. As he dug deeper into the issues and realized that transportation was attacking the very fibre of community, he began to learn more and more about ecologically healthy cities. He has proven to be a very imaginative theorist on the subject, and now travels widely giving lectures.

As I was mulling over his statement that cities maximize exchange and minimize travel, I realized he was describing what access is all about. Then I realized that all living creatures, when viewed from the perspective of their tissues, organs, and organ systems, are inventions for maximizing exchange and minimizing travel: their sap or blood, nutrients, waste materials, enzymes, white corpuscles, etc., all have elegantly efficient and short-as-possible distances to travel relative to their function. And so, from the organism to the city, we are dealing with similar principles, the principles of whole complex systems and how they function.

Engwicht points out that at first glance cities look chaotic, as do bioregions, but on closer examination, the patterns begin to make sense. If we study ecological systems, we begin to deepen our knowledge about the ways cities can function well, and why they are failing in so many ways today.

In the simplest view, cities are collections of buildings, streets, vehicles, supply lines such as water mains, electric lines, and sewer pipes, with gardens and vestiges of nature in or nearby. In the broadest view, cities are home to almost half of humanity and are physically the largest of our creations. To fail to mention them while pursuing ecological solutions is something like missing the log in your eye while dealing with someone else's speck. You would think that all the attention on energy in the 1970s would have made it very clear that the city form is the chief culprit in energy squandering. It is well known that in developed nations, close to a third of the energy is used for transportation and close to a third for heating and cooling buildings, and much of the rest is consumed in processes that build the transportation systems, vehicles, and the scattered buildings. It is obvious that a city built for pedestrians, which could actually be negotiated almost entirely by foot and bicycle, would save enormous quantities of energy. It is a little more subtle to notice that buildings that share walls between each other use far less heating and cooling energy than those that stand alone which, enveloped by the atmosphere, lose the energy after essentially only one use. But obvious though it is that city and town structure is the primary energy-demand determinant once you have looked at the situation carefully, you have to ask the right questions to get that answer from planners and politicians—who will then need to be willing to entertain major changes.

And the biggest, simplest lesson we can glean from the present condition of this, the largest thing we humans make, is that cities should be built for people, not machines, and certainly not for cars. Pedestrians are almost an after-thought in the complex process of planning cities. We should take the leap and design first and rigorously for pedestrians. Even transit should be thought of as supportive of the pedestrian environment, not an end in itself. It is not good enough at this point in history to plan for the energy conservation of streetcars as compared with automobiles. We should be thinking of pedestrians and bicyclists not because they use less energy than a car but because they use no fuel energy at all—other than breakfast, lunch, and dinner. *That's* the transportation system of the future, the transportation system that is the city itself, the eco-city, eco-town, eco-village.

Ultimately, our built habitats, our constructed communities, should not just leave nature undamaged, but should actually contribute to the diversity of healthy environment. At present, cities expend resources, deplete soils, and contribute to the extinction of species; they should instead recycle materials almost 100 percent, actually build soils with human, kitchen, and garden "wastes," and provide such a benefit to nature that, over the ages, they would preserve biodiversity and help foster more species, not fewer.

Proposal

For years I have asked myself why governments don't make plans for the benefit of life on Earth. The straightforward answer is that governments don't represent people who think that broadly; they represent many other more limited and self-centered interests. It could be added that they, like most people, are also not equipped with "the missing insight."

That means that it is up to those of us who do want an ecologically healthy future to create such a plan if we hope ever to see such a pleasant reality, or if we want to give our children or grandchildren such an opportunity. What would such a scheme look like? We need a new vision of cities and of architecture, and a program with which to build such cities and buildings.

What would the ecological city look like? Structurally it would look more like the European or colonial city than their North American or Australian counterpart: relatively dense, with great diversity of land uses close together. These European and colonial cities were built largely for the pedestrian—a big head start, though this design guideline was reduced in importance after the railroad locomotive was invented and was virtually forgotten after cheap energy and cars came along.

The ecological city would support appropriate, sustainable technologies: it would glint with sunshine reflecting off solar collectors and greenhouses, it would shimmer with the motion of wind electric generators and wind water pumps twirling overhead or on nearby hills or plains.

The ecological city would be green with rooftop gardens and its pedestrian streets would be alive with fruit trees, song birds, flower boxes, bees, butterflies. Creeks, shorelines, ridgelines, and other sensitive or rich biological zones would be recovered, along with agricultural land right up to the city limits. And since the infrastructure would be literally highly miniaturized relative to the megastructure of today's sprawled vascular system of asphalt, water, sewage, gas, electric, and phone lines, much less of society's investment would be in building and getting around what's built. There should be, then, far more freedom to engage in the arts, contemplation, recreation, and deeper forms of human contribution than the economic maintenance that seems to dominate social, political, and economic imagination today.

We should try to visualize much more thoroughly what the ecologically healthy city might look like. Again, if not us, who will do it?

In looking back over two years of conferences on ecological building, I realize that even among those most deeply involved in these issues, the vision is not very clear—shaping up, but not very clear yet. In most cases, the best examples of movement towards eco-cities are individual buildings with ecologically sensitive features, redesigned "street calming"projects, and policies in cities like Toronto that have made an official effort to bring workers closer to work while promoting transit and bicycle alternatives to cars, sprawl, freeways, and oil. It strikes me that cities like Toronto don't *look* much different from other less advanced cities, and they perform a little better, though not radically better, according to any such measures as: energy conservation, recycling, reclamation of natural lands, transit use, lower miles traveled per capita, leisure and cultural opportunities available and so on. They don't perform so much better that we can say we are on our way to solving Earth's human/life crisis.

To be fair, we who work on such efforts haven't had much time yet and we are still vastly overwhelmed by the negative forces that have been building momentum for several hundred years. So we can be forgiven for the meagreness of our progress to date. However, we should not let down our guard, and we should try to visualize much more thoroughly what the ecologically healthy city might look like. Again, if not us, who will do it?

As much as I like European cities and hold them up as partial models for the future, after traveling to Australia and Brazil and considering the U.S. Southwest where I grew up, I began to realize that a certain stuffy uncomfortable feeling I experienced in some European cities suggested that the eco-city of the future should have an air of wildness that is missing among the manicured garden parks, the highly managed forests and the "working" agricultural landscapes of Europe. People control nature in Europe, in some places disastrously and in others with lovely results, but results that nonetheless show the human influence in every detail, every stone wall, every goat-nibbled grassland, every fifty- or sixty-times replanted forest.

The indigenous people allowed nature to manage them more than vice versa and even built their religions and cosmologies around that agreement. The present "American Dream" has nearly exterminated that world view, about proportionally with its genocide of the Native Americans who held it. Yet this happened relatively recently in history and the wildness echoes through the country's mythological bones and asserts itself everywhere another rusty barbed wire fence snaps, curls and opens to the wide open spaces.

In such places there is a greater sense that nature surrounds culture, that nature is in control. In fact, people in North America seem totally out of control, even of themselves. There is a wildness in their dreams, no doubt often twisted, that results in buildings one hundred storeys tall and cars designed to go well over a hundred miles per hour across the plains and deserts, when the reality is that people are stuck in freeway traffic jams inching along at a stop-and-go pace averaging 15 to 25 miles per hour. Much of the wilderness and wildness of North America, and probably Australia and other less developed countries as well, is illusion and foolishness, no doubt. But something of it strikes me as valuable to keep alive in our future cities. Somehow, we have to give nature large zones of freedom, as we design our built environments to give ourselves our own kinds of cultural freedoms. We should leave—or recover from over-developed, frequently sprawling development—very large areas for nature to do with pretty much as she would like with absolutely minimal human interference. This means we should make a very serious commitment to restoring such natural features as creeks and shorelines and to re-establishing wildlife corridors for continuous habitats of plants and animals in their seed dispersal, ranging, and migrations. Cities should shrink back to finite limits. Some should coalesce around nucleii of activity in the suburbs. The whole process might look something like galaxies of stars condensing into bright sparks of light out of a vast, relatively uniform cloud of gases. The establishment of greenbelts represents the moment that hangs in time before the pattern is reversed, and then we can begin withdrawing from car-dependent sprawl and restoring nature in a big way.

There are two approaches to eco-city transformation. We can build new towns—Soleri is attempting to build Arcosanti, Arizona as a laboratory for these eco-city ideas, for example, and there are a number of "eco-villages" in various stages of planning and construction. Or we can attempt to transform our existing cities. The new-town approach has the advantage of not requiring the clearing away of existing infrastructure and all the bad habits that go along with it, but has the disadvantage of starting in a location that lacks proximity to existing, strong economic forces. Existing cities also occupy the most natural locations for cities—that's why they were established there in the first place. The approach that attempts to transform the existing city has the reverse advantages and disadvantages. Choose whatever suits you best, but *do something* because this rebuilding stands at the foundation of any successful future we might have!

◆

Ecological Planning
for Sustainable Communities

Mark Roseland

S eemingly mundane local decisions may have a more profound impact on the future of the global environment than all the handshaking and speech-making by heads of state. For example, a major issue at the "Earth Summit"—the United Nations Conference on Environment and Development (UNCED), held in Brazil in June 1992—was the debate in many nations over whether and how to reduce carbon dioxide emissions (a major contributor to atmospheric change and possible global warming). Yet while international bodies and national governments struggle to formulate such policies, it is at the community level where most of these policies will be implemented.

Many people use the term "sustainable development" to mean simply either environmental protection or sustained economic growth (presumably to pay for, among other things, environmental protection). The very concept of "environmental protection"is based on the separation of humanity from nature. As a society we point to a few things we think of as nature—some trees here, a pond there—draw a circle around them, then try to "protect"what's within the circle. Meanwhile, we ignore the fact that human activity *outside* that circle—housing, economic development, transportation, and so on—has a far greater impact on the environment than do our "environmental" policies.

Sustainable development must therefore be more than merely "protecting" the environment: it must be development that improves the human condition while *reducing the need for environmental protection.*

In order for the developed countries to contribute to global sustainability, the most important adaptation is a drastic reduction of our *present* levels of materials and energy consumption. This will require a more globally conscious kind of local development than we are accustomed to.

Thinking Globally, Acting Locally

Nearly half of the world's people will live in urban areas by the turn of the century[8]. Most North American (i.e., U.S. and Canadian) cities were built on technologies that place a high priority on economic goals and assumed abundant, cheap energy will always be available. In the process a wide range of environmental aspects have been neglected. On the assumption of cheap energy, many communities grew quickly and inefficiently; cheap energy made it possible to increase greatly the spatial area from which cities could draw their raw materials, and cities became dependent on lengthy distribution systems. Cheap energy affected the construction of our buildings, our addiction to the automobile, the increased separation of our workplaces from our homes, and the design and livability of our cities[2,3].

Urban sprawl is the legacy of abundant fossil fuel and our perceived right to unrestricted use of the private car whatever the social costs and externalities. Per capita gasoline consumption in U.S. and many Canadian cities is now more than four times that of European cities, and over 10 times greater than such Asian cities as Hong Kong, Tokyo, and Singapore. The biggest factor accounting for these differences in energy use appears to be not the size of cars or the price of gasoline, but the efficiency and compactness of land use patterns[4].

By creating a society in which an automobile is a virtual requirement of participation, we have marginalized the old, the young, the poor, and the disabled.

Other local and regional consequences of sprawl, such as congestion, urban air pollution, jobs-housing location "imbalance," and longer commuting times are now recognized. Yet, until recently, few researchers acknowledged that the land use pattern of North American cities also has serious *global* ecological ramifications. According to recent research at the International Institute of Applied Systems Analysis, if North American cities were to model future development on cities like Amsterdam, future carbon dioxide emissions here would be only half as much as current gloomy projections now indicate[1]. Similar arguments could be made in terms of water, waste, and energy.

The postwar pattern of Western urban development is not only ecologically unconscionable but economically inefficient and socially inequitable. The physical infrastructure costs relating to pipes, utilities, poles, roads, and so on are considerably more expensive than need be, especially given that much of the costs are borne by local taxpayers. The social infrastructure costs are high as well—by creating a society in which an automobile is a virtual requirement of participation, we have marginalized the old, the young, the poor, and the disabled.

In contrast, ecological planning implies that the use of energy and materials be in balance with such "natural capital" processes as photosynthesis and waste assimilation. This in turn implies the need for increased community and regional self-reliance to reduce dependency on imports. The benefits would be reduced energy budgets, reduced material consumption, and a smaller, more compact urban pattern interspersed with productive areas which can be used to collect energy, grow crops, and recycle wastes.

Cities with low "automobile dependence" are more centralized; have more intense land use (more people and jobs per unit area); are more oriented to non-auto modes (more public transit, foot traffic, and bicycle usage); place more restraints on high-speed traffic; and offer better public transit[4]. This suggests a new approach to transportation and land use planning in North America.

This new approach is illustrated by a recent San Jose, California study which compared development pressures with or without a "greenbelt." Without it, 13,000 exurban homes would be developed which, compared to an equivalent number of units downtown and along the transit corridor, would require at least an additional 200,000 miles of auto commuting plus an additional three million gallons of water *every day*, as well as 40 percent more energy for heating and cooling[9].

While communities may gain or lose population in response to local initiatives which create jobs or give good value for housing, most population fluctuation is due to factors beyond community control (such as rural-urban migration). However, from an ecological planning perspective, *the amount of growth is less important than the pattern of growth* in determining the level of environmental impact and the efficiency of resource use.

Thinking Long-Term, Acting Now

Local environmentalists, citizen activists, and, increasingly, municipal officials, are beginning to recognize that the way our urban areas are developed will largely determine our success or failure in overcoming environmental challenges and achieving sustainable development.

Until recently, most local governments have been hesitant to act in the face of overwhelming evidence of global environmental decline. While resources at the local government level have been scarce, they have been even more inhibited by a narrow and ineffectual conception of the domain of local government concern. The result has been a lack of mobilization to address global problems that are largely rooted in local, day-to-day activity. As the following examples attest, this situation is beginning to change dramatically. Local communities are developing thousands of concrete changes in economic, political and social behavior which are providing models for national level policies and programs.

The implications of ecological planning for North American cities are illustrated by several recent municipal and local government initiatives regarding issues such as transportation and traffic management, land use planning and housing, energy conservation and efficiency, waste reduction and recycling, improving community livability, and sustainable administration67.

Transportation planning and traffic management

Both local and global air quality problems demonstrate that transportation planning and traffic management initiatives are critical for sustainable urban development. These initiatives are usually motivated by goals to, for example, reduce the number of automobile trips; increase opportunities for non-auto transportation including bicycles, walking, rail, buses, and alternative vehicles; and reduce the use of gasoline and diesel fuel in conventional buses, autos and trucks. Examples include *trip reduction by-laws* (at least 37 California cities and towns), *road pricing* (Singapore, Hong Kong, and Oslo), *traffic calming measures* (many cities in Holland and Germany), *free or inexpensive transit* within the downtown core (Portland, Oregon), and programs to shift the emphasis from bicycle recreation to *bicycle transportation* (Palo Alto and Davis, California; Bordeaux, France).

Land use planning and housing

Land use planning and housing initiatives are also critical for sustainable urban development. They are usually motivated by the recognition that transportation planning and traffic management initiatives will eventually be thwarted or simply overwhelmed by growth unless accompanied by long-term efforts to reduce the need for travel. Examples include *proximity planning*, which seeks to make "access by proximity rather than access by transportation" a central focus of urban planning (Vancouver, B.C.); *residential intensification* in existing buildings or on previously developed, serviced land (Kingston, St. Catherines, and Metro Toronto); and *community land trusts* created to remove land from the speculative market and hold it for the benefit of a community and of individuals within the community (e.g., Philadelphia, Atlanta, and Providence).

Energy conservation and efficiency

Reducing resource consumption requires initiatives in energy conservation and efficiency, both within local government and throughout the municipality. Examples include *energy efficiency targets* designed to increase energy efficiency in all sectors of the city (Portland, Oregon), *municipal energy conservation campaigns* (Osage, Iowa), and *energy conser-*

vation retrofit ordinances which require all existing commercial and/or residential buildings to be brought up to an energy conservation standard at the time of sale (San Francisco).

Waste reduction and recycling

Reducing resource consumption also requires initiatives in waste reduction and recycling. Examples include *packaging restrictions* to encourage a recyclable and compostable waste stream (Minneapolis, Minnesota), *polystyrene plastic foam bans and restrictions* to prevent one-time use of polystyrene plastic foam by restaurants and retail food vendors (Portland, Oregon and Berkeley, California), *constructed wetlands* to treat sewage (Arcata, California), *solar aquatics waste treatment facilities* for treating sewage and septage at the neighborhood scale by mimicking natural marshes via a greenhouse (Providence, Rhode Island), and water offset requirements which require developers of new projects to replace old toilets in existing buildings with low-flow models in order to free up enough water to service the new projects (the California cities of Santa Barbara, San Luis Obispo, and Santa Monica).

Improving community livability

Initiatives to improve community livability demonstrate that efforts to fulfill human needs, improve social equity, and provide for social self-determination can and must be pursued in concert with initiatives to maintain ecological integrity. Examples include *public-community partnerships* between government and the nonprofit sector (e.g., linkage programs) to help meet community needs (Boston and San Francisco), *integrated environmental and social policy initiatives* such as a prison greenhouse aquaculture/hydroponics program that provides food for the prison and the community while training inmates for future employment (Bridgewater, Massachusetts), *gender equity* initiatives such as all-female police stations (Sao Paulo, Brazil), and *healthy community* projects (Rouyn-Noranda, Quebec; Seattle, Washington).

Sustainable Administration

The road to sustainable development is paved with failed efforts to incorporate the environment into everyday social and economic decision-making. Local governments have even passed the same environmental legislation twice in ten years—a sure sign that the intended measures were not implemented the first time[6]. Conventional wisdom considers the environment as an administrative problem, to be solved by better management—understood as cutting the environment into bite-size pieces. This approach seems increasingly unable to deal effectively, sensitively, and comprehensively with environmental complexities. Rather than the environment being an administrative problem, it would appear that administration is itself an environmental problem. The alternative to conventional urban administration is an emerging form of what has been called "environmental administration." It can be characterized as non-compartmentalized, open, decentralized, anti-technocratic, and flexible[5].

Examples of some current fledgling attempts to develop sustainable forms of administration include *environmental commitments and legislation* to, for example, reduce the threat of atmospheric change (Toronto and Vancouver), *investment and purchasing or procurement policies* which favor environmentally sound business practices or which encourage the creation of markets for recycled materials (New York City and Toronto), *eco-counselors* to review the environmental impact of all municipal practices and to recommend environmentally sound practices to various government departments (cities in at least 10 European countries), *community round tables* (many Canadian cities, e.g., Peterborough, Ontario), and *networking and cooperative research* as provided through organizations such as the International Council for Local Environmental Initiatives.

Making it Happen

Taken together, the initiatives described here begin to delineate a strategy for encouraging a globally conscious culture of sustainability in our cities. They also indicate some practical suggestions on how to design effective sustainable community development policies. Any sustainable development policy framework should recognize that:

- *Sustainable development requires sustainable communities*: Despite the concentration of population in urban areas, most city and local governments do not have the regulatory and financial authority required to effectively contribute to sustainable urban development. Other levels of government must provide resources and support for the financing, management and policy-making authority necessary for local governments to achieve sustainable development in their communities.
- *Sustainability can mean "less" as well as "more"*: So long as sustainable

development is conceived merely as "environmental protection" it will be understood as an "added" cost to be "traded" against. Once sustainable development is conceived as *doing development differently*, such trade-offs become less critical: the new focus is instead on finding ways to *stop* much of what we are already doing and use the resources thus freed for socially and ecologically sustainable activities.

- *Social equity is not only desirable but essential* : Inequities undermine sustainable development, making it essential to consider the distributive effects of actions intended to advance sustainable development. Growth management ordinances in many western U. S. cities, for example, originally enacted to safeguard the environment and protect the quality of community life, have caused local housing supplies to tighten, driving up prices and causing serious affordability problems for low- and moderate-income households. As these households leapfrog across preserved open space to less expensive communities in the region, additional commuting, traffic congestion, and air pollution threaten the very quality of life at which the control measures were aimed in the first place[7].

- *Public participation is itself a sustainable development strategy*: To a considerable extent, the environmental crisis is a creativity crisis. By soliciting the bare minimum of public "input," rather than actively seeking community participation from agenda-setting through to implementation, local and national decision-makers have failed to tap the well of human ingenuity. They have failed to recognize that it is *only* from this well that the myriad challenges necessary to redevelop our communities for sustainability can be successfully met. Effective and acceptable local solutions require local decisions, which in turn require the extensive knowledge and participation of the people most affected by those decisions, in their workplaces and in their communities.

Sustainable development requires that we develop our communities to be sustainable in global ecological terms. This strategy can be effective not only in preventing a host of environmental and related social disasters, but also in creating healthy, sustainable communities which will be more pleasant and satisfying for their residents than the communities we live in today.

Sustainable communities will emphasize the efficient use of urban space, reduce consumption of material and energy resources, and encourage long-term social and ecological health. They will be cleaner, healthier, and less expensive; they will have greater accessibility and cohesion; and they will be more self-reliant in energy, food and economic security than our communities now are. Sustainable communities will not, therefore, merely "sustain" the quality of urban life they will *improve* it.

References

1. Alcamo, J. M., "Compact City Design as a Strategy to Cut Dangerous Air Pollution," presented to the First International Eco-city Conference held in Berkeley, CA, March 29-April 1, 1990.
2. Environment Council of Alberta, *Environment by Design: The Urban Place in Alberta*, ECA88PA/CS-S3. Edmonton Council of Alberta, 1988.
3. Morris, D., *Self-Reliant Cities: Energy and the Transformation of Urban America*, Sierra Club Books, 1982.
4. Newman, P. W. G. and J. R. Kenworthy, *Cities and Automobile Dependence*, Gower Technical, 1989.
5. Paehlke, R. and D. Torgerson, eds., *Managing Leviathan: Environmental Politics and the Administrative State*, Broad View Press, 1990.
6. Roseland, M., *Toward Sustainable Communities: A Resource Book for Municipal and Local Governments*, National Round Table on the Environment and the Economy, 1992.
7. van Vliet, W., "Human Settlements in the U. S.: Questions of Even and Sustainable Development," University of Toronto Center for Urban and Community Studies; draft prepared for the Colloquium on Human Settlements and Sustainable Development, June 21-23, 1990.
8. World Commission on Environment and Development, *Our Common Future*. Oxford University Press, 1987.
9. Yesney, M., "The Sustainable City: A Revolution in Urban Evolution," *Western City*, LXVI: 3, March 1990: 444.

Editor's Note: This article is based on Mark Roseland's book Toward Sustainable Communities: A Resource Book for Municipal and Local Governments (Ottawa: National Round Table on the Environment and Economy, 1992) which is available free of charge from the National Round Table on the Environment and the Economy, 1 Nicholas Street—Suite 520, Ottawa, Canada, K1N 7B7, Tel: 613-992-7189; Fax: 613-992-7385.

♦

Mega-Cities: Innovations for Sustainable Cities of the 21st Century

Janice E. Perlman

Cities have always been the centers of culture, and the crucibles for the advancement of civilization. Throughout time they have acted as magnets for people, ideas, and entrepreneurial activity. They have also been consistently beset by seemingly insurmountable problems, and have therefore had to be at the cutting edge of innovations to cope with these crises.

As cities reach sizes unprecedented in human history, they will need their innovation capacity more than ever, and will need to share these innovations with each other so as to replicate each others' successes and avoid each others' mistakes.

In brief, the basic argument can be summarized in ten points:

1. In the year 2000, the majority of the world's population will live in cities—23 of which will be mega-cities with over ten million people each.

2. These mega-cities—whether rich or poor, capitalist or socialist—are experiencing critical environmental degradation pushing to the limit their ability to sustain human life, and seriously affecting their surroundings.

3. While all urbanites are affected, the urban poor are the most vulnerable, since they often live in the shantytowns on floodplains, steep hillsides, or adjacent to dangerous industries, and are least able to protect themselves.

4. Given the scale and complexity of these cities, conventional approaches adapted from 19th century technological and managerial systems are not adequate to meet the burgeoning needs of the existing population—not to mention the future growth.

5. There is thus an urgent need to find creative ways to better utilize

human, natural, and financial resources in these cities in the service of the urban poor and their ecosystems.

6. But where can we find these? Since intelligence was not distributed by status, experts are not always the best source for non-conventional solutions. The most promising innovative approaches tend to come from those local communities, governments, or entrepreneurs closest to coping with the problems on a daily basis.

7. There is enough energy and creativity in the cities today to address the problems, but too few mechanisms to channel these forces into the policy-making process, or to multiply the effects of approaches that work.

8. The seeds of tomorrow's solutions can be found in today's experiences, but need to be carefully sought out within each sector, neighborhood, and policy area. We know too much about failures and needs, too little about successes.

9. Practical innovative solutions that deal with decentralized urban management to take advantage of local participation; increasing the productivity of the informal economy (particularly for women); and circular rather than linear systems for water, garbage, sewerage, energy and food, will have significant implications not only for the cities and their hinterlands, but also for sustainable development world-wide.

10. The challenge is how to find these innovations, distill their essence, and replicate and transfer them so as to maximize their impact (i.e. identify and multiply "best practice").

The underlying question is: given the deeply vested interest in the status quo, how can we find the political will and motivation for significant urban transformation?

The Mega-Cities Project

The Mega-Cities Project was initiated to meet these challenges. It is a collaborative effort among government, business and community leaders in the search for successful approaches to urban poverty and the environment. It aims to shorten the time lag between innovative ideas and their implementation and diffusion. The project is designed not only to identify, distill, and disseminate positive approaches, but to strengthen the leaders and groups who are evolving them and find sources of support to multiply their efforts.

The project follows a dual strategy, functioning simultaneously at the practical and theoretical levels. On the one hand, it shares "best practice"

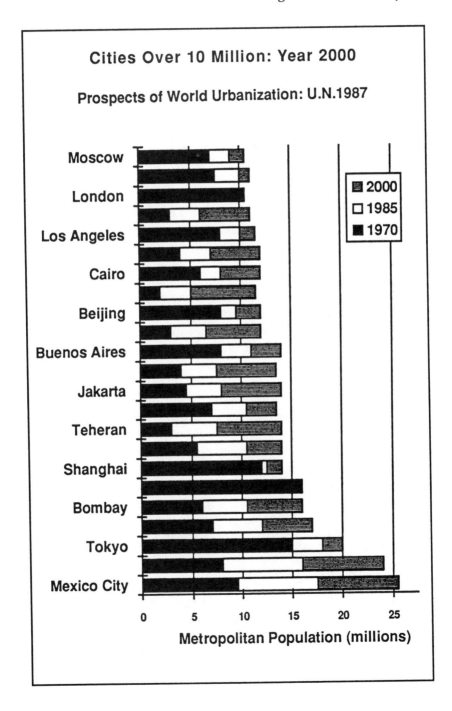

Cities Over 10 Million: Year 2000

Prospects of World Urbanization: U.N.1987

Metropolitan Population (millions)

among cities and puts the lessons of experience in the hands of decision-makers and the public; and, on the other hand, it seeks to gain a deeper understanding of the process of innovation and the consequences for deliberate social change in cities.

Initiated in August, 1987, the Mega-Cities Project is now functioning in 16 cities around the world: Bangkok, Bombay, Buenos Aires, Calcutta, Delhi, Jakarta, Lagos, London, Los Angeles, Manila, Mexico City, New York, Rio de Janeiro, Sao Paulo, and Tokyo. The structure of the project is based on a local coordinator in each city, backed up by a multi-sectoral steering committee, representing the most creative leaders from the public, private and voluntary sectors, media and academia.

The participating cities have achieved what many thought was impossible. Each city started out by saying they had no successes, only failures, problems and needs; but after following the project methodology, every one of them was able to identify between 20 and 200 successful innovations. Awareness of their own achievements made them considerably more receptive to learning from those of the other cities. The use of the network of cities as a laboratory for experimentation, as well as a reference group for achievement, is creating a catalytic effect on urban problem solving.

In terms of this exchange, the coordinators have now met together seven times—most recently in Jakarta where they made 14 specific bi-lateral agreements to transfer innovations. As part of our overall strategy for the dissemination of urban innovations, the novel experiences in each city will be part of a series of Urban Innovations Expositions and the best of these will be documented by in-depth case studies and videos, and will receive Urban Innovation Awards.

Innovative Aproaches to Poverty and the Environment

So what are some of the innovations they've identified? They range in scope from the neighborhood to the metropolitan area, and they can be initiated by the public, private, or grassroots sectors. All of them, however, meet our basic criteria of being socially just, ecologically sustainable, politically participatory, and economically viable. For the purposes of this article, we have selected some examples of innovations in the areas of air pollution; litter and solid waste disposal; water supply and sanitation; regenerating the natural environment; and appropriate technology:

A. Air Pollution

1. *The Alerta II Program in Sao Paulo.* Sao Paulo has launched a long range strategic plan to reduce pollution by promoting the use of alternative fuels, stressing the need to curb industrial emissions and installing devices in automobiles to lower carbon monoxide levels. While these strategies are going into effect, the city has initiated the "Alerta II" program to help keep air quality at safe breathing levels. Digital pollution interceptors at road intersections feed information on pollution levels by cable to a central computing system. The pollution level combined with meteorological forecasts indicate when emergency levels are reached. During an emergency, no privately owned cars may enter the central business district. Trucks and buses with poor combustion are fined as well, to encourage proper engine maintenance.

2. *Curitiba Bus Tubes.* The surface metro system in Curitiba, Brazil uses dedicated, high-speed bus lanes and cylindrical loading tubes that allow passengers to pay in advance and board quickly. This increases the speed and efficiency of bus service in the city and lessens the reliance on automobiles.

B. Garbage—Recycling for Income Generation

Zabbaleen. Greater Cairo generates around 6000 tons of solid waste per day. "The Zabbaleen Environmental and Development Program" was initiated in 1981 to improve the living conditions of the Zabbaleen community where over 50 percent of Cairo's garbage collectors live in deplorable environmental and sanitary conditions. Projects were aimed at improving labor conditions, consolidating waste management, and disseminating the Zabbaleen's collection services to other neighborhoods in Cairo.

The program's components were launched over a five year period and included the following: the installation of piped water, electricity, and sewage networks; the extension of waste collection routes to include previously neglected areas; an internal clean-up project with a composting plant to remove the accumulated waste found in the Zabbaleen settlement; and projects to increase business opportunities for the community's residents, especially targeting those women who are the principal bread winners in their families.

C. Litter

Magic Eyes: Bangkok's Unique Anti-Litter Campaign. The Magic Eyes campaign is directed toward children aged 10-16, on the theory that lifetime habits are formed early in life and that children can effectively educate their parents on acceptable forms of behavior. The campaign relies heavily upon green posters which say "magic eyes are watching you" and features cartoon faces with smiles for trash cans and glares for litterbugs. The program is promoted through classroom teaching materials, "Clean School Contests," television commercials, and litter bins on the streets showing the Magic Eyes logo. In addition, special fundraising products such as bumper stickers, posters, badges, and T-shirts help to advertise the campaign.

The combined efforts of this organization and the media resulted in a campaign so successful that the name is now recognized by 89.3 percent of the Bangkok population, and has reduced litter on the streets of Bangkok by 90 percent. The campaign and related projects are financed through subscriptions from major private corporations, and are now expanding to address other environmental issues such as water and air pollution.

D. Water Supply and Sanitation

Committee of Resource Organizations (CORO). Bombay is a city where the provision of basic amenities such as lavatories and potable water drains has not kept pace with the increasing influx of lower income groups into the metropolitan area. In Bombay's slums, toilet facilities are available at the community level, but are extremely meager and have contributed to environmental degradation. The inadequate number of latrines have made most of them unserviceable and unhygienic.

Innovative approaches have emerged recently through the Community of Resource Organizations (CORO). The unique feature of CORO is that it combines the provision of toilets with provisions for reading facilities and employment generation. By providing books to low-income communities, CORO hopes to increase the literacy levels among slum dwellers and create an awareness about the importance of hygiene and cleanliness. CORO has proposed to install libraries at toilet complexes, so people can borrow literacy kits and other reading materials to promote environmental education.

E. Regenerating the Natural Environment

Paid Self-Help Reforestation Project in Rio de Janeiro. Since the start of the 1980s, the governments of the State and Municipality of Rio de Janeiro have undertaken projects to upgrade conditions in the favelas. In 1986 the Program for the Preservation and Reforestation of Low-Income Areas was set up to reduce erosion and sediment loads deposited on neighborhood roads during the rainy season. The reforestation project has benefitted roughly 25 neighborhoods, as 240 hectares have been reforested through the planting of 300,000 seedlings.

Members of the local community were contracted to work in the project, thereby garnering local support. The results of the project were consistently positive, with workers benefiting from a local source of income and acquiring technical knowledge of the environment. A measurable difference in local conditions was also noted with lower temperatures, improved soil quality, and less erosion.

F. Appropriate Technology

El Molino: Integrated Community Development in Mexico City. Mexico City has been growing at a rate of 4.4 percent per year and is expected to reach 25 to 27 million inhabitants by the end of the century. With this population explosion, Mexico City's sewage system has been unable to provide for roughly three million of its residents.

In response to these conditions, an Integrated System for the Recycling of Organic Wastes (SIRDO, its Spanish acronym) was initiated to treat organic solid waste and/or black and gray domestic waters through filters and solar heated fermentation chambers. The SIRDO collects sewage from households via tubing or manual hauling, allowing waste to decompose in a tank and creating an organic fertilizer. The SIRDO aims to be economically sustainable, thus changing people's views that waste has no productive value. It also attempts to show the value of recycling and the need to find alternative solutions to conventional waste management. Financing of the SIRDO is meant to be innovative, with communities acquiring bank credit and paying back the loans through the profits made from the SIRDO.

G. Food

PAIS Plan. During the last fifteen years, poverty has increased considerably in Argentina, particularly in the Greater Buenos Aires area. In 1989 an overwhelming wave of hyperinflation struck the nation causing food to be priced exorbitantly high. Following numerous assaults on supermarkets, the provincial government started the Programa Alimentario Integral y Solidario (PAIS) to improve the allocation of food to the poorest sectors in Buenos Aires, by supporting local micro-enterprises and Multifamily Kitchens (MK).

The plan's main feature integrates 5-20 families into a Multifamily Kitchen, which jointly purchases food at wholesalers' shops and/or large supermarkets. The plan also provides basic inputs—flour, seeds, home machinery—to encourage self-provision and subsidies to start micro-enterprises. The major impact of the project has been the successful distribution of food to nearly 470,000 members of the urban poor and to organize many into their own productive micro-enterprises.

Conclusion

The bottom line is a concern for the well-being of the urban citizens of the 21st century and for the precarious ecological balance between city and countryside. If we are to turn around the paralyzing sense of hopelessness and despair about these large urban agglomerations and create sustainable human settlements, what is required is not simply a set of interesting ideas that happen to work in one context, but the cumulative effect of these ideas in enabling us to rethink the cities of the future.

When discussing the need for a new vision of a "socially just and ecologically sustainable city of the future," we do not mean the diffusion of one "model solution" to urban problems, but each of the cities building from its own unique strengths and finding its own path. Each successful innovation is seen as an incremental advance over the previous configuration, which is bound to generate its own contradictions and new problems, as well as the next generation of solutions.

The examples illustrated in this paper are a few of the many non-governmental projects being initiated in the mega-cities to confront environmental problems. While local initiatives cannot solve the ecological crises which impact on cities, they can empower communities and foster incremental improvements in the quality of life at the local level. For grassroots programs to have influence on environmental policy decisions in the future, a major effort at program replication will have to be started. Moreover, local government programs will have to incorporate community-based schemes into the overall policy process.

What is lacking are not ideas or technical solutions, but the political will to support and replicate these local initiatives. Government leaders and policy analysts must devise new partnerships among public, private, and voluntary sectors to grapple with the growing problems found in mega-cities. Only by rethinking the way cities work will it be possible to re-allocate human, natural, and financial resources to create a sustainable city—one that is harmoniously balanced between the built environment, the natural environment, and the human beings that inhabit both.

◆

Cerro Gordo: Eco-Village Building and Eco-City Networking

Christopher Canfield

Clearly, our civilization isn't sustainable when we consume fossil sunlight at a million times the rate it was accumulated, and when our per capita production of "renewables" like fish, grain, fibre and wood has been decreasing for decades. Our civilization isn't sustainable because we've lost touch with how things are done on this planet. We've come to define wealth with ever increasing consumption, and so we're burning our house to keep warm.

Most "development" has been based upon extractive economics and a predatory or even a parasitic approach, which has been increasingly destructive to our real source of wealth: the biosphere. This four-billion-year-old miracle has brought the sun's energy to life here on Earth. In defiance of entropy, the biosphere has kept growing and evolving, becoming more and more complex. Out of life has come more life and richer life. This is real development. The evolving, developing biosphere has been the source of all of our wealth from the air we breathe to our clever little brains. If we want to figure out how to do sustainable development, sustainable cities, and a sustainable civilization, we need to look to the larger community of the biosphere, of which the human community is only a small and dependent part. Development will be sustainable only to the extent that it works with the natural life-enhancing cycles of the biosphere.

Cerro Gordo Prototype Symbiotic Community

Cerro Gordo is a prototype symbiotic community now being built for up to 2,500 people on 1,200 acres on the north shore of Dorena Lake, near Eugene, Oregon. Our purpose is to explore ways to add the human community, with as little disturbance as possible, to the existing natural community, thereby developing a more complex symbiosis. We don't pretend to have all the answers, but we do have a living laboratory with a planned population sufficient to support all of the basic everyday activities and services.

We've adopted the strategy of building a new town because we believe fundamentally different land use patterns are needed. We spent over two years searching for the right site. Cerro Gordo includes an entire south-facing valley, surrounded on three sides by government forest and on the south by Dorena Lake. About half of the property has relatively unproductive soils, so it's a good place for people: Oregon has the most rigorous state-wide land use requirements in the country, with the basic goals of preserving prime farm and forest lands.

Before we purchased the property, we conducted extensive ecological studies to determine the site's carrying capacity and intrinsic suitabilities for various land uses. Twenty-five different factors were mapped and combined in the manner advanced by Ian McHarg in *Design With Nature*. Different combinations of factors represented the perspectives of the builder, the economist, and the ecologist. A hydrological study determined carrying capacity and tolerance to impervious cover acre-by-acre. These composites guided the initial planning efforts, but later we decided to be even more protective by mapping large wildlife corridors and all of the prime forest lands, prohibiting any construction in these areas. A comprehensive wildlife management plan and a perpetual-yield forestry program are the basis of our plan to preserve the natural ecosystem at Cerro Gordo. Over 1,000 acres of natural forest and meadow are permanently protected through the Cerro Gordo Community Trust.

From the beginning, Cerro Gordo has always been an intensively participatory process. The goal is to create a genuine community, so we're working together as an extended community of future residents and supporters, starting with formulating the vision and choosing a site and continuing with planning, financing, building, and economic and community development. The participatory planning process has been invaluable as a way to clarify community values and goals and put them in a dialogue with the opportunities and constraints of the natural ecosystem. This has been a tremendous educational experience for the community members, as they get to know one another, the site, and the implications of their personal dreams for living in harmony with nature.

As people got to know one another, their motivations changed from getting away from the city to moving toward the village.

In an initial questionnaire, two-thirds of the households said they wanted to live in detached homes on acreage homesites. Most of our members come from urban and suburban settings, so their initial images are often motivated by getting away from the pressures of urban life. Less than two years later, however, after taking part in the extensive community planning process, the group reversed itself and over two-thirds said they wanted to live in attached homes in or near the village center. Part of this change was simply educational, as community members got to know the site and saw how scattering hundreds of homes across the Cerro Gordo valley would suburbanize the natural environment we want to preserve. But along with the learning process a more fundamental change occurred: the participants began to function as a community. As people got to know one another, their motivations changed from getting away from the city to moving toward the village; and along with choosing prospective neighbors, a new image of living with nature emerged. Instead of a scattering of homes across the landscape, they'll be clustered into a village, preserving over 90 percent of the site in its natural state.

As the heart of our community, we have long carried the image of the traditional pedestrian village with its shops and services, livelihood and community life. The image of the medieval European village spoke to our yearnings for genuine human community. But most of these villages were walled towns, with the landscape paved over with buildings, streets, and plazas. The wall contained the village and preserved the surrounding fields and forests, but the homes had little contact with the natural environment. Cerro Gordo will have its mixed use village center including most of the commercial and community buildings and some residences in townhouses and apartments above shops, but most of the homes will be clustered elsewhere so each home can have both village and nature. On one side of each home will be located some portion of the thousand-acre natural commons, permanently protected by the Cerro Gordo Trust. On the other side will be the village courtyard created by the neighboring homes, often including a cluster common building. Indeed, this clustering concept evolved out of the first cluster planning group which met weekly for most of 1975, and developed a plan much like the Danish *bofoellesskaber* as described by Kathryn McCamant and Charles Durrett in *Cohousing*.

The housing clusters and neighborhoods will be located within a quarter-mile radius of the village center, joined by paths to facilitate walking and bicycling and to eliminate the private automobile within the townsite. This has always been a fundamental tenet of the Cerro Gordo Plan: a community for people, not cars. How this will work is easy to envision when Cerro Gordo grows to its maximum population of 2,500, with employment and all the everyday activities located within the village. The challenge is building a no-car community one house at a time. The current reality is that our first dozen homes are dependent upon services in Cottage Grove, a town of 7,000 six miles west of us. Furthermore, county planning regulations usually require all homes to have access via two-lane roads on 60-foot rights-of-way.

After some extensive planning and negotiating, we've come up with a system that meets practical and code requirements with one-lane, one-way loops through each cluster for emergency vehicles and large deliveries, and cluster parking areas that can be moved to sites adjacent to the county road when we have a sufficient population to provide services on site. At that point many residents may eliminate the expense of a car of their own by forming a motor pool maintained by the Cerro Gordo Community Cooperative, our nonprofit residents' association. And most of the one-lane access loops will be incorporated into the bicycle and delivery path system, or built as greenways with turf growing in concrete blocks.

The Oregon state-wide planning laws provide the best protections in the country, but they have also created horrendous delays for Cerro Gordo. When we started studying the property in 1973, Lane County planners warned us we wouldn't be able to proceed until the county completed and obtained state approval for its county comprehensive plan and zoning, which would take "a year or two." Each year after that the prognosis was the same: another "year or two." Eleven years later, on its third try, the county finally obtained approval for its rural comprehensive plan from the Oregon Land Conservation & Development Commission in 1984. The saga continued when the approval was appealed to the courts, and it wasn't until 1989 that Cerro Gordo's approvals became final. Sixteen years of planning delays created serious financial and organizational problems, but Cerro Gordo survived, though several well-financed commercial developments failed, and now we're building the ecological village we've always envisioned.

In the middle of clearcut country, the Forestry Co-op is demonstrating how we can have both the forest and the trees.

So far a dozen homes have been built with a variety of passive solar and energy conservation features. The first small manufacturing business has moved on site: Equinox Industries, producers of quality bicycle trailers which is an appropriate product for the no-car community of Cerro Gordo. It provides jobs for residents who can commute to work by strolling down a forest path. The Cerro Gordo Forestry Cooperative is now in its sixth year of its perpetual-yield forestry program, producing enough lumber each year for 25 homes while permanently protecting a diverse forest ecosystem. In the middle of clearcut country, the Forestry Coop is demonstrating how we can have both the forest and the trees—a "real world," dollars-and-cents demonstration of the axiom of symbiotic community: the ecosystem is the larger economy.

Eco-city Networking

Currently we're planning construction of the Cerro Gordo Lodge and conference center, which will include a mini-village of clustered shops and offices and an outdoor amphitheatre. This new mini-village will be the focus of our increasing networking, publishing, and educational programs on Cerro Gordo and the growing global Eco-city Network. In 1990 Cerro Gordo was pleased to co-sponsor the *First International*

Eco-city Conference organized by Urban Ecology in Berkeley, California. 150 speakers addressed the broad spectrum of how we can rebuild our civilization in balance with nature; and all 80 sessions are summarized in the 128-page book we copublished with Urban Ecology, *Eco-city Conference 1990*. Cerro Gordo is taking a key role in the growing Eco-city Network organized by the conference, and we look forward to net-workng with the Los Angeles Eco-Cities Council organized by the First Los Angeles Ecological Cities Conference. In April, 1992, the international eco-city discussion continued in Australia with Eco-city 2.

For more information about Cerro Gordo and the global Eco-city Network, write to the Cerro Gordo Town Forum, Dorena Lake, Box 569, Cottage Grove, Oregon, 97424, U.S.A.. Phone: 503-942-7720; Econet: "cerrogordo." The newly up-dated Cerro Gordo Community Plan *will be available soon for US$5;* Eco-City Conference 1990 *is available for $7; and the* Cerro Gordo Town Forum, Journal of Symbiotic Community *is available for $15 per year.*

◆

The New Suburban Village

Melanie Taylor

O ver the last fifteen years a movement to reform American urban-ism and to offer alternatives to suburban sprawl—known as the New Urbanism—has emerged, spread across the U.S., and been picked up in other countries. According to its leading practitioners, "The principles underlying the New Urbanism are straightforward: the built environment must be diverse in use and population, scaled for the pedestrian, and capable of accommodating the automobile and mass transit. It must have a well-defined public realm supported by an architecture reflecting the ecology and culture of the region."

Practitioners of the New Urbanism have been planning villages since the late 1970s. The first and most well-known of these communities is the Traditional New Development (TND) of Seaside, Florida, planned by Duany and Plater-Zyberk of Miami and begun in 1982. Located on the Gulf of Mexico between Panama City and Pensacola, Seaside occupies approximately 80 acres of coastland and has about 200 homes as well as civic and commercial buildings.

The general dissatisfaction with existing urban patterns motivated a group of architects and developers to draw on the lessons of Seaside to devise a general system that could be applied to other towns and developments. An illustrated chart called Traditional Neighborhood Development Ordinance lays out very simple guidelines for site and building design. These include the close proximity of houses and work places, well-defined public spaces, a variety of streets, and strategically placed civic buildings. The ordinance categorizes these features according to the needs of different types of buildings—for example, what percentage of public land shall be used for governmental versus retail or general use, how streets are to be arranged in residential areas, and so on.

The aim of the TND is to foster independence from automobiles by keeping neighborhood needs within walking distance. Moreover, by organizing neighborhoods in ways proven to be effective in older American towns, desirable social objectives automatically fall into place. As the ordinance states, "By walking instead of driving, citizens come to know each other and the bonds of an authentic community are established." The desired end, then, is to promote the quality of life we have come to associate with generations past, using a variety of means to that end.

Some TND communities result from renovating old ones. In 1962, Mashpee Commons on Cape Cod was a parking lot at the end of a typically bland strip mall. As part of Mashpee's 1979 redevelopment plan to create a town reminiscent of the old Nantucket, the shopping center and parking lot have been turned into an authentic main street with shops on either side. The developers specified water-saving toilets, night-time irrigation, and lower-maintenance landscaping. There are provisions for housing for the elderly and plans to create and sustain a percentage of affordable homes by limiting windfall profits.

Peter Calthorpe Designs developed Pedestrian Pockets which he defines as "a balanced, mixed use area within a quarter mile walking radius of a light rail station." Peter's goal is "to create an environment in which the convenience of the car and the opportunity to walk would be blended." Calthorpe's early pedestrian pockets were designed to be implanted in California suburbs such as Sacramento, San Jose, San Diego, Long Beach, and Orange County where light rail lines are being built. Other practitioners of the New Urbanism include Elizabeth Moule who has developed "The Bill of Community Rights," Wendy Morris who is transforming public planning policy in Victoria near Melbourne, Australia, J. Carson Looney who designed Harbortown, Stefanos Polyzoides with plans for downtown Los Angeles, Ray Gindroz who is working on affordable downtown housing, and Jonathan Barnett who is devising a sophisticated method for infilling and reshaping downtown Cleveland. Prince Charles has visited American TNDs and consulted with Duany and Plater-Zyberk in connection with his own project which will be designed by Leon Krier, Europe's pre-eminent urbanist.

The New Urbanism generates various social, economic, and environmental benefits. Although ecological planning and sustainable communities may not be the explicit focus of all New Urbanist planners, the results of their approach are heartening for environmentalists. Intensive land use and responsible traffic planning are integral to the planning process. Villages are completely designed and scaled to support pedestrians, reduce automobile traffic, utilize water-saving indigenous landscaping, green spaces, and preserve wetland, wildlife and dunes. Comparison of specific New Urbanist plans with conventional developments has discovered a 55 percent reduction in infrastructure and a 40 percent reduction in the tonnes per annum of carbon dioxide released into the atmosphere from emissions, etc..

The loosely affiliated but highly committed practitioners of the New Urbanism convened the first session of the Congress for the New Urbanism (CNU) in Alexandria, Virginia during October 1993. Modeled on CIAM, an organization which influenced the course of urbanism during the modernist era, the CNU members include planners, architects, historians, landscape architects, traffic and civil engineers, developers, marketing experts, lawyers, environmentalists, municipal administrators, and sociologists. The stated purpose of the meeting was to formulate principles for building and rebuilding the city and its environs, to set standards of practice, to exchange information and to share experiences. As a measure of the New Urbanism's reach, the CNU calculates that a few specialist firms have designed more than 100,000 acres according to new principles. As the CNU notes, even established firms who were once "most responsible for suburban sprawl now offer this type of urbanism as an option." Sessions of the CNU will be coordinated by its leading practitioners: Andres Duany, Elizabeth Plater-Zyberk, Elizabeth Moule, Stefan Polyzoides, and Daniel Solomon. As the CNU's current commitment is to the elaboration of urbanistic principles and to the establishment of standards for those who are actively engaged in the creation of the New Urbanism, participation in the first four sessions of the congress is by invitation. It remains to be seen how the CNU will evolve, but it anticipates eventually taking on a more educational or grassroots role.

Editor's Note: For more information about Traditional Neighborhood Development or to obtain a copy of the Ordinance, write to Duany & Plater-Zyberk Architects, 1023 SW 25th Avenue, Miami, FL, U.S.A. 33135. For information regarding the Fall 1994 session of the Congress of New Urbanism, titled Nature, Infrastructure, and the Region, contact Peter Calthorpe at Suite 400, 246 First Street, San Francisco, CA, U.S.A. 94105, or phone 415-777-0181.

References

Bentley, Ian, et al., *Responsive Environments: A Manual for Designers*, Architectural Press, 1985.

Duany, Andres and Elizabeth Plater-Zyberk, *Towns and Town-making Principles*, Rissoli, 1991.

Katz, Peter, *The New Urbanism: Toward an Architecture of Community*, McGraw-Hill, 1993.

LeJeune, Jean Francois, ed., *The New City, Vol. 2*, University of Miami, n.d.

4

Growing the Places Where We Live: Ecoregional Stewardship in Action

Introduction

Doug Aberley

Somewhere in all of us is the need to know and understand the place that is our home. This is part of being a human animal, a fundamental genetic trait of our kind. We are a quick learning species, with great ability to adapt and evolve. Yet in the so-called modern world this capability has been subverted. We cruise to shopping malls in our cars, and have encyclopedic knowledge of the freeway routes by which they are connected. We are able to feed ourselves from packages, turn on taps from which water flows, flush toilets which dispose of our waste, and get rid of our trash by bundling it in plastic bags. Our territorial allegiance is to a city, a state or province, a nation-state, and a variety of sports teams. Our senses of orientation are kept very, very busy, but do we really know *where are we?* Is that deepest need in humans, to belong to a place and culture, satisfied?

For several decades, growing numbers of people in North America have been tuning their time and senses away from preoccupation with mass brand-name identification, searching for ways to return to an orientation to place. This has been a rocky and rewarding path, beginning in the 1960s, and passing through a number of retrospectively predictable stages. At first it was communes, isolated adventures in encapsulated and possibly even self-indulgent exploration. Next it was absorption into the ancient cultures of place, striving with all our hearts to be " rural," or "aboriginal," or "ethnic." And now, thirty years on, has come something else: an understanding that the integration of old and new ways into hybrid bioregional cultures might be the most direct path leading to fundamental social change.

Our senses of orientation are kept very, very busy, but do we really know _where we are_?

This section of the book has been included so that you can experience just a taste of how one area of the planet, the north coast of North America, is being reinhabited. The four essays each convey an aspect of the sense of place. David McCloskey uses powerful lyric prose which almost sings the bioregion of Cascadia into being. Suzy Hamilton's description of her remarkable West Kootenay region is more conversational, like a discussion around a kitchen table where most of the business of change in her rural community is instigated. Tony Pearse introductes what has become a legend of persistent and creative defiance: the Nisga'a, a First Nation society still rooted in its ancestral place, is using sophisticated computer technology to confound absolutely the institutional and corporate forces for which the technology was made. Susan Snetsinger writes of cross- boundary ecological planning, a process which is animating the perception of a Cascadian territory defined not by international borders, but by life itself.

These four examples could be joined by literally countless others, from the same region and from hundreds of regions across the planet. In all our bioregions we are rebuilders of cities and towns, blockaders of unwise development, celebrants of new and old ritual, inventors (rediscoverers?) of tools and technologies. Ecological planning is not an abstract convolution; it is a thousand variations on the same theme—process, place-related, wholistic. It is the way we live our lives.

♦

Cascadia

David McCloskey

Sometimes I feel as if I'm living in a far, forgotten country—deep green, misty, beautiful, a world all its own. You won't find this land on many maps, though, for it's a dream image of a real place. Only now is this once-and-future country coming into its own. And I remember its name, and feel at home, whenever I hear the rivers chanting: *Cascadia, Cascadia, Cascadia....*

I live in this great green land on the northeast Pacific Rim called "Cascadia." Cascadia is named not only for the mountains but also for the white waters lunging down the entire north Pacific slope, joining earth and sea and sky in endless life-giving cycles. Cascadia is a land of falling waters.

In the north Pacific, where the mountains meet the sea, there is a relentlessly dramatic landscape, one of the freshest, most diverse regions on Earth. It begins in the sea, mother of all the winds and waters and even the land itself. First, there is the Pacific Ocean, whose eternal rhythms, storm-tossed depths and upwelling zones create rich habitats over the continental shelf. But there is another whole world hidden beneath its surface: deep-sea volcanoes, red-hot spreading rift-zones, unique sulfurous life-forms and earth-plates slip-sliding past one another, then crashing together, slamming up mountains which rise straight out of the sea.

We then encounter that intense inter-tidal edge, the glare of light and wind on water, where hard rock meets the salt sea. It's a pounding, wave-cut coast line whose rhythms of headland, cove, cape, beach, bay, and estuary, of basalt, sandstone, granite, sand, and mud, play out along the northern raincoast for miles and millennia. The open coast is fringed by a thousand serrated islands, and backed by sheltered inland seas. I live here, along with millions of others in the very heart of the region. Explorers were once sent out to chart the "sea in the forest," but found

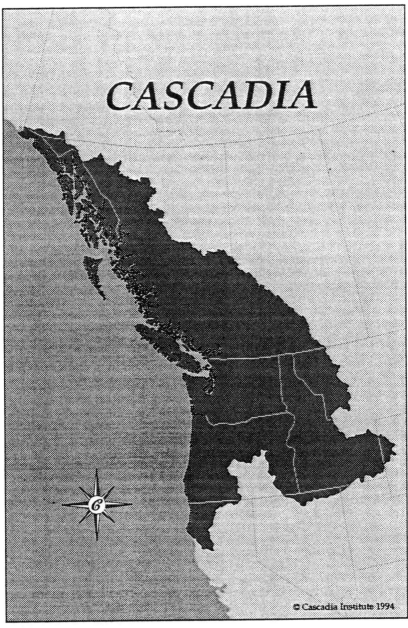

instead another forest hidden within the sea. Like them, I am trying to
discover the essential character of this place, to learn to read again the

original map of the world.

It's a world of "mountains and rivers without end." Where rivers are knives and glaciers plows. A world in which water in all its forms animates everything, inscribing a living memory into the landscape.

All along the coast, and for a thousand miles inland, we are surrounded by a great, unending cascade of mountain ranges poured from the sea, tumbling over one another, then hardening, strung out like knots on great ropes running north and south in the western Cordillera. From the summit of Glacier Peak in the heart of the North Cascades, we see a storm of stone, earth-waves blasting in from the Pacific, whitecaps frozen in the moonlight. Peaks such as these are cloud-catchers, standing tall, bringing down the rain and snow, holding the sky in a frozen embrace, mantled in glaciers and ancient, hidden, still-waiting icefields. Here is the home of the mountain king.

Lakes in the sky feed countless waterfalls plunging over the lips of hanging valleys down, down into a great green and white pulsating Cascadian plaid. From the blue mountains floating above flow sweet green valleys below, as deep as steep, carpeted in dense evergreen forests, lush vegetation, and supernatural wildlife.

The green valleys and high ranges of the western slopes are succeeded on the leeside to the east by another world—high, hot and cold, windy, wide, and lonesome, arid volcanic inter-mountain plateaus spliced by great rivers like the Columbia, Snake, Fraser, Thompson, and Stikine. Here is a vast sub-region with its own way of life. The *altiplano* is fringed by more forests, and then melts into the huge looming granite and limestone peaks riding, riding the far ridgeline of the North American continent.

It's a laminated landscape running from west to east, composed of successive layers of ocean, coast, inland valley and sound, *altiplano*, and, finally, the mountain ranges of the great divide. This is a distinctive world in many ways, a region that deserves to be recognized in its own right as a very special place.

II

If you look to the southwest on the third or fourth night of a new moon, you may see the face of Cascadia shining in the sky. For Cascadia is shaped like the top half of a quarter-crescent moon rising.

Cascadia is a curved land running from coast to crest—from the Pacific Ocean to the Rocky Mountains and the Continental Divide. Over twice as long as it is wide, this flying arc of landscapes stretches a thousand miles on its bottom and curves two thousand miles to the northwest from northern California to southeast Alaska on its western side. It runs along the Pacific coastline from Cape Mendocino in the south (where the San Andreas faultline goes out to sea, and northwest coastal native cultures begin), up to Icy Bay and the Kluane-St. Elias Icefield Ranges in the north in that odd corner where British Columbia, southeast Alaska, and the Yukon come together (where NW coastal native territory ends to the north). On its southern boundary, Cascadia runs from Mount Shasta in northern California through Oregon and Idaho above the Great Basin over to the Tetons and Yellowstone. From Yellowstone its eastern boundary follows the Continental Divide north up through Glacier National Park to the great Columbia Icefields above Banff and Jasper National Parks, thence up through the Stikine, finally curving west over to Glacier and Icy bays. Hence, Cascadia stretches from 40 to 60 degrees north latitude, and from 110 to 140 degrees west longitude.

Cascadia is one of the four great regions of western North America— its Pacific slope, northwest of the great interior valley of California, the closed Great Basin, and the high red rocks of the Colorado Plateau. Cascadia lies west of the High Plains, and south of the Arctic—a land of its own on the far northwest corner of North America.

Once known as the "Old Oregon" country (among other names), Cascadia today includes the states of Oregon, Washington, Idaho, north-western California, Montana west of the divide, two-thirds of British Columbia, and southeast Alaska, taken together as a whole. Containing over 750,000 square miles, Cascadia once enjoyed the densest native populations north of Mexico because the land was so rich, offering an incredible diversity of niches to occupy. On a continent of abundant fauna, Cascadia was once super-abundant, with wildlife bursting from every pore. Today, however, it is home to over 12 million people who have changed its character considerably.

III

She's a great green bird falling to be free, a spiral edge along the sea. But Cascadia is also center as well as edge. This is a meeting place, for instance, between land and sea, north and south, east and west, between ancient and modern cultures, Canadian and American societies. More-over, it is one of the oldest inhabited places in the western hemisphere, for it served as the major migration corridor for repeated waves of ancient peoples populating the Americas. And yet, in terms of more recent history, it is one of the last, best places to be colonized by western settlement.

Her true character is revealed as a meeting ground of different polarities, a crossing-over-and-back place of many dimensions. For instance, the inland sea where I live is located as the "inside-of-the-outside" (in relation to the coast), while at the same time it is the "outside-of-the-inside" (in relation to the plateau). My home ground functions, therefore, as a crossing-over-place which joins the high desert plateau and mountains on the east side to the ocean on the west side. Similar patterns are played out over and over again throughout the region, because such tremendous diversities are packed into such tight spaces. Indeed, located in the heart of the mid-latitudes from forty to sixty degrees, Cascadia offers us a geography of the middle ground.

In this flying arc of landscapes, you can feel tremendous forces working, a tension or torque of powers in the sky above and the earth below, a curve of binding energy revealed in the shape of Cascadia herself.

Forty to sixty degrees latitude on the north Pacific slope represents a special region in other important ways. In terms of climate, Cascadia is located half way between the equator and the North Pole, in between the sub-tropic and sub-arctic zones. The double proximity to these zones (south and north) on the one hand, and the sea and high mountain desert (west and east) on the other, generates Cascadia's distinctive climate of maritime and (moderately) continental regimes. It is a climate repeatedly modified by the mountainous terrain into an alternating series of windward and leeward sides that echo from coast to crest.

Cascadia is a fertile meeting ground of winds and waters, located in between the contrasting pressure cells of the Aleutian low and the Pacific high. These swirling gyres spin out the powerful mid-latitude jet streams which spray storm fronts one after another in great wave-trains across the face of our region. The migrating border between the two weather cells as they move up and down the coast from the deserts of Baja to the taiga of Alaska is called "spring and fall." Thus, Cascadia is winter wet and summer dry; the first seasonal pulse is twice as long as the other one. We enjoy the longest, deepest, most beautiful springtime in the world here.

Forty to sixty degrees north latitude is also where the sub-arctic boundary intersects the north Pacific (or Kuroshio) ocean current which bends down to warm northern California. In terms of salinity and water temperature, as well as rainfall, the north Pacific boundary is very important. For instance, south of this area, evaporation exceeds precipitation, while north of 40 degrees, precipitation exceeds evaporation. This region contains the preferred water temperature zone of the five great Pacific salmon families. Each family has its own niche in the vast house of Cascadia: for instance, King (or Chinook) salmon run the mainstems of the great rivers like the Columbia, Fraser, Skeena, Stikine, and Klamath, while Sockeye love the high lakes, and the Chum and Coho radiate out into the small feeder and coastal streams.

Cascadia once enjoyed the greatest salmon runs the world has ever known. "You could walk across the river on their backs," the old timers said. Indeed, salmon is the totem species of our region. When the ice receded, it was totem salmon who first reinhabited the barren landscape, bringing life back by swimming up the streams. Carrying the riches of the sea as a gift to the land, it was salmon who called eagle and bear and raven and all others back into this world. And it was this first "giveaway" from the "salmon people under the sea" that served as the prime model for all Cascadian tribal potlatch cultures.

Forty to sixty degrees is also the home of the ancient forests which, even in their degraded condition, remain the greatest temperate zone coniferous forests in the world. Here were vast primeval belts of enormous Sitka spruce, western red cedar (the sacred tree), western and mountain hemlocks, Douglas fir, silver, grand and red firs, Englemann spruce, white spruce, black spruce, ponderosa pine, white pine, limber pine, aspen and mountain larch. This once was a land of giants, home of the tallest trees in the world, with the greatest biomass per acre, exceeding even that of the tropics.

Once, the forests fed the sea, while the sea fed the forests, but that time is no more. Salmon are a kind of current pulsing between the forests and the sea, as Tom Jay says, silver shuttles in the great loom. Today, only remnants of the once-great forests and salmon runs remain, members of a dwindling tribe, leaving an entire ecosystem hovering on the limits of viability. In the present age, the great loom is almost broken and needs, above all, to be restored. I live for the day when the rivers will be set free, and the forests and sea join together again, feeding each other in endless life-giving cycles.

Like the summit of the mountain, Cascadia is a center at the edge of the world.

IV

"Mountains are fountains of the waters," John Muir said. Nowhere is this more true than in our region, for Cascadia "waters" much of the North American continent. Here many beautiful and powerful rivers rise: the great Columbia, Fraser, Skeena, Snake, and Stikine systems, the Willamette of Oregon, Alsek-Tatshenshini of the Yukon and B.C., the Kootenay and Thompsons of British Columbia, the Pend Oreille of Montana and Idaho, Klamath of southern Oregon and northern California, Skagit of western Washington, Lillooet of southern B.C., Clearwater and Salmon of central Idaho and ten thousand other rivers and white-water streams. The great "river of the west"—the Columbia—is the largest river on the Pacific coasts of both North and South America. Cascadia is truly a country of "mountains and rivers without end."

But in addition to her own westward flowing waters, Cascadia sends sweet green rivers down the other side of the Continental Divide. She is the prime source or major contributor to many of the great river systems of the continent, such as the Sacramento and the Humboldt on her southern slopes, the Missouri-Yellowstone, Saskatchewan and Athabasca on her eastern slopes, and the Peace-Liard-Mackenzie, Copper and Yukon on her northern slopes.

Perhaps a third or more of North America is fed by waters from Cascadian slopes pouring down the continental divide into the Pacific, Arctic and Atlantic oceans. Although Cascadia covers less than ten percent of the total area of the continent, it contributes 20 to 25 percent of the total surface runoff: twenty of the forty largest (by volume) rivers on the continent are fed by Cascadian waters, including the Mackenzie (third largest), Columbia (fifth), Yukon (sixth), Fraser (seventh), Missouri (ninth), Copper (thirteenth), Skeena (fourteenth), Snake (fifteenth), Stikine (sixteenth), Willamette (twenty-fourth), and Alsek (twenty-fifth). Cascadia truly is the fountain of North American waters.

Today, Cascadia's own rivers, forests, salmon, and human communities are in deep crisis. Long-standing threats to the waters have reached critical levels with the prospect of a unified North American market for natural resources. But there must be no "inter-basin transfers" of water. To buy or sell rivers like other commodities on the market, and ship waters anywhere to the highest bidder, is an ecological travesty.

Above all, the ecological integrity of Cascadia as a bioregion must be maintained. Ecology and community, not greed, must lay the foundation for any larger sustainable society.

The fountains of the waters must be protected and restored.

The West Kootenays: Something Special

Suzy Hamilton

There has always been something special about the Kootenays. As tangible as the salmon and the gold, as intangible as the protective embrace of the mountains, the lure is as strong and as potentially destructive as it ever has been.

Like the miners in the 1890s who displaced the Sinixt people and burned most mountainsides to bedrock, today's urban refugees bring with them dreams of riches. The wealth they seek is more than money. It includes a safer place for their kids, cleaner air and water, and a saner integration of work and play. Still, their numbers threaten to destroy the very life they seek. Predictions are that, by the year 2000, 50,000 people will live between the small communities of Balfour and Slocan, where 18,000 now dwell.

Yet it appears the West Kootenay region, in particular, will be able to deal with the inevitable onslaught of growth in a manner unlike its Okanagan counterparts where development runs rampant. In part this is due to the self-sufficient goals designed by the people who live here. They are making use of the groundwork laid for them by visionaries of the past and the remarkable natural, but isolated, setting that calls to be protected.

The West Kootenay is framed by the wheat fields and marshlands of Creston on the east, the arid ranchland of Grand Forks on the west, the

Laska wilderness mappers McKenzie and Batycki.
Photo: Suzy Hamilton

lush timber and farmland of the Slocan Valley to the north and the
industrial sectors of Trail and Castlegar south to the U.S. border. In
between are countless watersheds of the Columbia River system and a
diminishing wilderness that provided the Lakes people, known to themselves as Sinixt, a way of life for thousands of years.

No one can be proud of the way the Sinixt, the "court system" of the
Salish, were forced off the land 100 years ago and classified "extinct" by
Ottawa in 1956. The rush of white settlers in the Kootenays around the
1890s brought religion, smallpox, and a lust for gold and silver. By this
time, Canada and the United States had drawn the border at the 49th
parallel. Many Sinixt, who travelled freely up and down the Columbia
River from Revelstoke to eastern Washington, were forced to join the
Colville Confederated Tribes in Washington State in 1872.

By the early 1900s, their numbers were reduced from 100,000 to 2,500
people. Smallpox, disease, displacement, and murders had taken their
toll. Once the native people were reduced and absorbed by other bands,
the real rush began. Fifteen hundred Doukhobors, themselves displaced
for their pacifist beliefs from Czarist Russia in the early 1900s, were given
Sinixt lands by the government to homestead. Nelson, Trail, Rossland
and Kaslo thrived and developed from the wealth provided by silver,

lead, and gold.

Victorian architecture—the rage in Spokane and San Francisco—celebrated the wealth and gave a sense of permanence. Three-storey granite, marble, and brick buildings with towers, gables, dormers, bay windows, and balconies dominated downtown Nelson. Those were the days of the sternwheelers, affectionately known as White Swans, which moved ore and people up and down the Columbia River, and the Arrow and Kootenay lakes.

But as the ore ran out, the railways and roads replaced the sternwheelers. "Residents began to look upon the Kootenays as home, rather than a stopover to riches," writes historian Barry Bondar. "There was a longing for a sense of community." This longing continues to be the glue that keeps the fabric of the West Kootenay intact.

By the 1980s, timber extraction had replaced mining. The magnificent buildings in Nelson had been covered with cheap facades, the provincial government had closed the David Thompson University as well as the plywood plant and sawmill in Nelson. Industries such as Eddy Match, the Boeing plant, the pole yard, and the jam factory were gone. But the spirit of the land remained.

The region's complexion had changed somewhat with the arrival of young Americans seeking refuge from the Vietnam War, the back-to-the-landers from all lands, the artistic and educated populace who remained from the days of the university and the Kootenay School of Art. Land was cheap and under attack by the logging companies.

It was clear that the forests of the Valhalla Range, which formed the magnificent scenic backdrop for New Denver and Silverton residents, would be lost to logging. In 1975, a group of residents led by Wayne McCrory, his sister Colleen McCrory, and Grant Copeland, formed the Valhalla Society to lobby the government for a 60,000-hectare park in the area. It took eight years of intense involvement to win the park, but the victory gave the directors the experience in political crisis intervention that would help them provincially, nationally, and internationally in the years to come.

Since 1975, the society has helped create the Valhalla Wilderness provincial park, South Moresby National Park Reserve on Haida Gwaii, and the Khutzeymateen Grizzly Sanctuary north of Prince Rupert. In 1987, exhausted by thirteen years' work, the directors realized there was no hope for remaining B.C. wilderness if efforts continued on a park-by-park basis. The society published the first *British Columbia's Endangered Wilderness Map* which played a part in generating a promise from the B.C. government to increase protected areas from 5.2 percent to 12 percent of the land base.

Colleen McCrory has won many awards for her work and a $60,000 prize from the Goldman Foundation in San Francisco. The first thing she did with her money was pay debts and "buy a car that runs." Her "Brazil of the North" campaign has drawn world-wide attention to logging practices in B.C. and Alberta. In 1990-91 she travelled across Canada to document the extent of increased logging in Canada's vast boreal forests, forming national networks along the way.

Her brother Wayne, a bear biologist, and his partner Erica Mallam have relentlessly pursued the protection of bear habitat not only in the Kootenays, but throughout B.C.. The Khutzeymateen will be the first area preserved for grizzly bears in Canada. Now they are working on four other areas: Princess Royal Island near Kitimat, home of the white Kermode black bear; the White Grizzly Wilderness in the Kootenays; the Kitlope, largest intact temperate rainforest; and the Stikine National Park.

"This work demands more than we ever thought when we started," said Colleen, born and raised in a mining family in New Denver. "You always have to put out energy and be pro-active. More is always asked than we are prepared to give. But even though the whole Slocan Valley is clearcut, we have some jewels to hold up as examples."

"The corporations are entrenched, developing every piece of Earth. Even if we put the brakes on, we're going to go through difficult times. Working together is really important. The key is the value of the other people. We see more and more young people starting to become aware. There are good people working everywhere, and this movement is happening around the world. I might never see it succeed, but I'd rather be part of a society working on it than doing nothing at all."

Down the road live Susan and Herb Hammond in Winlaw. Herb is a professional forester (RPF) who made a name for his wholistic forestry concepts ten years ago when he challenged the government's management of Tree Farm License No. 1 on Nisga'a lands north of Terrace. He termed the wasteland, "a sea of rotting stumps," and earned a reprimand from the RPF's for speaking out. He and Susan have built an extensive forestry library and consulting business at their office in Winlaw. Herb's recent book, *Seeing the Forest for the Trees*, provides a detailed framework for those who would see the forest as more than a tree farm. Realizing that some of their goals did not fit within their consulting business, the Hammonds formed the Silva Forest Foundation in January 1993. By the fall, the foundation presented two workshops, one five-day and one three-day, in wholistic forest use planning and timber management. Foresters, tree-planters, and citizen activists filled the courses. Herb taught landscape ecology, modified landscapes, protected ecosystem networks, wholistic management and economics. "Knowledge is empowerment," said Susan.

Working with the Forest Stewardship Council, the foundation is setting bioregional standards to certify wood products. Like the organically grown label on foods, the designation will label sustainably produced wood.

"We're starting really small to work the bugs out," said Susan. "This will allow us to work out the chain of custody from the ground up. It's a huge project. The idea is to change all forest practices."

Huge projects do not faze these two. They keep chipping away at the massive industrialization of the forest. "You may not attain your goals in your lifetime," said Susan. "You may not get your rewards, but you have to keep trying. Sometimes it appears you haven't gotten anywhere, but in fact...they haven't logged the watersheds yet. Most people want an instant fix, then they can get back to their personal lives. But once you *know*, can you really go back to sleep? You must act, or be a tortured person. I couldn't do anything different now."

The Valhalla Society and the Silva Forest Foundation have provided the networks and inspired other groups to use available information to educate themselves and others. The Southern Columbia Mountain Mapping project took a year and a half to complete by a dozen volunteers from the Nelson area. It was born of the frustration felt by many residents when logging plans were announced for Lasca Creek in 1992. The area is the largest intact ecosystem in the Southern Columbia Range.

"A visual map is the best way to show people how threatened old growth is in southern B.C.," said ecologist Evan McKenzie. "You use it as a tool for advocacy, as a way for people to understand their own backyards."

Much to their surprise, the B.C. Forest Service was willing to share the information needed to color the 1:50,000 scale maps. "I have never been told by the forest service I can't see something," said Candace Batycki, who now coordinates the B.C. Biodiversity campaign for the Greater

Ecosystem Alliance. "Have the government work for your community. Say to them, 'You have all this technology, now produce this for us.'"

All you need is colored pencils, someone who can read maps and the maps. "Don't color the rock and ice," warned Candace. "Start with the hot spots and what's at risk. Keep it simple. Start with existing logged areas, clearcuts, and old growth. People just flock to the maps when we put them up. There's no rosy picture; the map is telling it like it is."

"The next logical step is taking some control over what happens. Increasing public awareness empowers people. It's really the best planning tool we've got."

Nelson, which acts as a magnet for people who want to create an alternative economy to the logging industry, is unique among towns for several reasons. The city generates and sells its own electricity from a powerhouse on the Kootenay River built in 1906. The revenues, about $1.6 million annually, pay for the parks and fire department and the civic center.

"Have the government work for your community. Say to them, 'You have all this technology, now produce this for us.'"

Facing the prospect of becoming a ghost town in the mid-80's, the city elected a mayor and council who took a giant risk. They hired Slocan Valley architectural visionary Bob Inwood to strip the magnificent buildings of their facades and restore the original architecture of Nelson. Inwood, a man who realized that personal environments affect both the productivity and the well-being of an individual, designed a downtown "to make people feel good."

And it worked. The city went for broke, and instead of paving streets, restored the Capitol Theatre. Old buildings were sandblasted and colorful new awnings were mounted to shelter the sidewalks. People love the downtown and stroll under the globe street lights any night of the year. A tourist with a couple of cameras around the neck, heritage brochure in hand, is a common sight.

Inwood has completed projects in Rossland, Revelstoke, Golden, and Trail, but Nelson is the big success story. "Nelson has also seen a high quality interpretation of the renovations and has marketed itself accordingly. I truly believe this the beginning of a new era for Nelson and a prosperous one," Inwood said.

But there was a hole in Nelson. Working artists longed for the return of an art school like the Kootenay School of Art (KSA) which opened in 1958 and folded with the David Thompson University in 1983. The residents who managed to save the David Thompson Library were not ready to admit defeat.

After hundreds of hours of meetings, the Kootenay School of the Arts was reborn in 1991. By fall of 1992, the school had hired a dozen instructors—all working writers and artists—and filled 190 seats. In 1993, the B.C. government granted the KSA autonomy and $100,000 to fund the first year, while the city provided classroom space.

Potter David Lawson, who coordinates the programs, believes the real value of the school is that it teaches people to do things with indigenous materials. "We have all these raw materials and nobody is teaching the design and draft skills that will use them in a value-added way," said Lawson.

And as the circle is completed, the Sinixt have returned to the Slocan Valley. The home-coming began four years ago when residents joined the Sinixt to stop a highway from unearthing part of their burial grounds in Vallican. After a 30-day battle, they lost the fight, but won a powerful alliance with the people who had lived here for thousands of years.

Since then, Sinixt Marilyn James—who is definitely not extinct—has been given the mandate by her elders to rebury the remains of her people whose bones have been taken by archaeologists and artifact hunters. She has returned 43 remains so far. At times she is cynical about "her dance with the devil."

"In lots of ways it's been positive, but it's also been a pain in the ass. People are afraid. There is still heavy racist bigotry," said James.

It's no wonder. As Vallican resident Marilyn Burgoon pointed out, "Returning the remains releases more than bodies. It releases history. The bones represent the truth of democracy. That's what these people are up against."

But she feels the return of the Sinixt who now live near the burial site is a gift to the Slocan Valley. The struggle with land use issues continues. "If you don't have a Native person standing beside you, you don't have the same struggle," she said. "The key is they are the key."

While there is no doubt that divisive issues such as forest management, zoning, wilderness preservation, and native land claims will escalate as the land base shrinks, people in the West Kootenay have a head start on the role they will play in the outcome. After all, there's something special about the Kootenays.

◆

Tradition plus High-Tech: A First Nations Example

Tony Pearse

E arly in 1993 a team of Nisga'a land negotiators from northern British Columbia walked into a information exchange session with government officials in Victoria carrying only a black box the size of a shoeshine kit and a notebook computer. The box was a high-tech, interactive computer display device by which the operator could query a Geographic Information System (GIS) database and project the graphic results on a wall screen for immediate viewing. In a two-hour presentation, the Nisga'a team proceeded to dazzle their counterparts with a series of computer-generated slides that portrayed a variety of land and resource issues throughout different parts of their traditional territory. When the time for the government's presentation finally arrived, a rather beleagured individual abashedly made his way to the wall and taped up a single, hand-drafted map for discussion. The contradiction was powerful, and its significance was not lost on the participants of the meeting. Probably for the first time in Canada, a local government, and in this case an aboriginal one, had challenged centralized government agencies in the "information game," and had come out on top. To get here, however, had been a long road for the Nisga'a.

Background

The struggle for the recognition of aboriginal rights in Canada is one of the most prominent ongoing issues characterizing the national geopolitical landscape. Because it involves questions of power and ownership of land, British Columbia is now on the verge of a radical reconfiguration of its internal jurisdictional makeup. At long last, the great legal uncertainty of the province's claim of authority over aboriginal lands and resources has forced the start of negotiations regarding a sharing of land and resources with the First Nations whose traditional territories now comprise B.C.. The likely result of this process, probably a good decade from now, will be the transfer of control of substantial portions of the province's land and natural resources to some 26 decentralized and semi-autonomous aboriginal jurisdictions. One of the many silver linings in this situation, however, is that it has also cast an effective backdrop against which new opportunities for redesigning outmoded land use policies and practices can be exploited.

The Nisga'a team proceeded to dazzle their counterparts with a series of computer-generated slides that portrayed a variety of land and resource issues throughout different parts of their traditional territory.

This impending change is an historical irony, a colonial artifact remaining from the refusal of the province's various governments to make treaties with aboriginal groups when acquiring land for settlers. From the 1700s onward, most of Canada, quietly or otherwise, took dominion law (and sensible military precaution) to heart, and proceeded with treaty-making as immigrants filtered westward. Colonial administrators on the west coast for the most part simply surveyed and alienated lands to settlers without regard for the indigenous societies and economies long in place. History and mounting public pressure gradually caught up to the B.C. government, with the result that comprehensive land negotiations with the Nisga'a Tribal Council, the first of the province's First Nations lined up at the starting gate, commenced in 1991. A newly formed Treaty Commission, comprised of aboriginal, federal, and provincial representatives, is beginning the process of managing the negotiations for the remaining tribal groups. No one has any clear idea of what the final internal configuration of B.C. might look like, or how long it will take to determine!

The resolution of native land claims, while cloaked in uncertainties about the roles of all governments in the future disposition of land and resources, offers unsurpassed opportunities to create a meaningful place for proper ecological planning in the development of B.C.. To this point, with the vast majority of the province's land base under the control of the Ministry of Forests and subject to its preoccupation with industrial timber extraction, an ecologically and economically sound approach to land use has been demonstrably absent. While a number of other land policy reforms are currently underway (Commission on Resources and Environment, Protected Area Strategy, Old Growth Strategy, B.C. Round-table, etc.), these, to the degree they are effective, are not likely to have as far-reaching and comprehensive effects as First Nations' land negotiations.

This potential for an improved approach to land use is not simply wishful thinking. A number of aboriginal organizations have already begun the process of inventorying resources, mapping their traditional territories, and establishing independent or co-management projects, even though they are constrained by the provincial government from exercising any real jurisdiction over what goes on in their land.

The resolution of native land claims ... offers unsurpassed opportunities to create a meaningful place for proper eco-logical planning in the development of B.C..

Among these, the Nisga'a Tribal Council (NTC), negotiating for con-trol of some 9,500 square miles of northern B.C., is one of the most advanced local governments in the province in establishing a regional resource management system. Their initiative back in the late 1970s, and their progress since then, well illustrate some of the approaches that other First Nations' and local governments are likely to find beneficial.

A prominent feature of the Nisga'a evolution in this regard has been an effective ability to translate into terms appropriate to their culture both state-of-theart technology and cutting edge science of landscape ecology, and to blend it with key features of their traditional resource management system. In approximate chronological order, the following highlights stand out as Nisga'a achievements in this field:

- 1979: Inventory, assessment and mapping of regional resource potential (1:500,000 scale);
- 1982: Overlay mapping system of land use, resource potential, land use impacts (1:250,000);
- 1984-85: Land ownership & Nisga'a geography mapping project (1:50,000), including first geographic computer database;
- 1986: Extensively documented proposal for a tree farm license based on ecological and integrated-use principles;

- 1990: Installation of full-fledged GIS and transfer of all 1:250,000 and 1:500,000 scale data;
- 1991: Installation of satellite image processor; acquisition of Landsat imagery for traditional territory; integration with GIS;
- 1992 (ongoing): Developing resource spatial data base and processing capability at 1:20,000 for the entire territory; establishing GIS resource mapping system for 24 management units comprising entire traditional territory; increasing forest management capability from landscape level to stand level.

The above projects represent a natural evolution of an initial vision by Nisga'a leaders who foresaw that graphic representation and computing ability would be essential ingredients in dealing effectively with provincial government officials and private industrial developers. The jump to each level required an enhancement in the skills of the Nisga'a personnel involved in the projects, and, of course, increasing dollars to finance the acquisition of hardware, software, and data.

In understanding how the Nisga'a got to this point, however, it is instructive first to examine their traditional system of land and resource use which provides a rational foundation for the development of a totally modern resource management system.

The Traditional System of Resource Management

Ecological planning means, at its core, gearing human activity to the natural limits set by environmental processes and structures. Generally speaking, we ought not to consume resources beyond what can be replenished by the natural annual productivity of the ecosystem. For several thousand years human activity on the northwest coast corresponded in scale and style of land use to what we define today as an ecological approach. This is not to say that Nisga'a land use was the result of some synoptic and centralized planning system in the sense we know it today. But it was the result of a structured system of land tenure and resource management that had evolved functionally over time to allow a sustained and flourishing collective economic livelihood. And it did this without impoverishing the capacity of local biological systems to renew themselves.

Ironically, while contemporary centralized states like B.C. produce a lot of rhetoric about ecological planning, the actions they sanction enable resource-based capitalist development to take place with very little planning input, and with even less enforcement of what standards there are.

What are the key features of the northwest coastal cultures that typify an ecological approach to land use? At the risk of over-simplification, the following are central:

First, the fundamental spatial unit of management was a watershed-based territory, anywhere from a few square miles to several hundred square miles in size, owned collectively by a Nisga'a House (matrilineal family unit), with a chief who allocated resources and made management decisions on behalf of the House membership. Each family territory was endowed with a range of resources required for survival—a fishing station along the adjoining watercourse; forest habitat for large and small game, plants, berries, and building materials; alpine habitat for marmot, goat, and caribou; and so forth. Some territories bordered on marine waters, which further contributed to the variety of resources that could be utilized.

Second, the scale of the management unit and its intensive use by a number of harvesters meant that the information feedback loop was short. A continuing inflow of resource data enabled the managing chief to make more responsive and rational decisions. Maximizing local knowledge and shortening the turn-around time from harvester to decision-maker and back to harvester is a key requirement for an ecological approach to land use.

Third, moral constraints on behavior about hunting and use of wildlife ensured that animals were harvested according to need, and that all parts of the animal were used. Wastage of biological resources was a serious spiritual offense, and offenders were seriously castigated.

Fourth, use of various plant and animal species fluctuated throughout the year according to their distribution and abundance. The harvest of a particularly low population of a particular species would be suspended until populations were perceived to be on the rebound, and harvests would focus, where possible, on substitute species. The indigenous economy thus exploited the interest, and not the capital, of the resident biological communities.

Fifth, the aural tradition ensured that critical environmental knowledge passed from generation to generation. Knowledge accumulated over generations about the flow and ebb of animal movements, their behavior, their strengths and weaknesses, and so forth, would be delivered in condensed form on a repetitive basis to the young harvester from the old. This provided for great continuity and renewal in important management information, as well as harvesting efficiency and propriety less accessible in immigrant society.

Contemporary Approaches

Today, the Nisga'a have integrated their House territories into a single unit of approximately 9,500 square miles. They face a number of tasks, both at the negotiating table on land settlement, and for designing and implementing resource management systems for that portion of their original territory which they will ultimately retain.

To accomplish these tasks, the NTC purchased computerized GIS and satellite image analysis systems in 1991, and have been busy storing and processing data ever since. The general approach is innovative and probably unique, and it is worth describing here.

The Nisga'a landscape ranges from a temperate rainforest along the coastal mountains and inland waterways on the west to an interior boreal forest ecosystem in the central and eastern parts of the territory. The predominance of forest lands has meant that government management efforts in the past have focused on the collection of forest cover data at a relatively detailed scale of 1:20,000. The data are organized into mapsheets, of which there are approximately 240 for the entire traditional territory. These have to be cleaned of shoddy digitizing work when they arrive from the Ministry of Forests, and then edge-tied together into larger management units that the Nisga'a resource planners have defined. There are 24 of these units for the territory, the largest of which consists of approximately 43 forest cover sheets. With several thousand forest polygons on each mapsheet, each with data table attached of some three dozen parameters, one can easily see that immense computational runs are required for processing these.

Nisga'a mappers started initially with one PC workstation, but within a year were operating six similar machines on a 24-hour basis to get the mapping base completed.

Once the management units were completed, forest use zones interpreted from air photo and satellite imagery were digitized into the system. This step zoned each unit into riparian zones, alpine, steeply complex terrain, environmentally sensitive areas, and poor to good operable timber zones. The data were again processed to yield thematic maps illustrating a "netted-down" land base that was available for intensive forest use. Because the GIS is an interactive database system, it is easy to portray graphically and to calculate the net timber values in each operable forest cover polygon as well as the aggregate values for each management unit.

The exercise of calculating spatially referenced net-downs like this is a radical departure from the conventional non-spatial approach used by the B.C. Ministry of Forests to calculate an operable land base for timber harvesting. In a direct case-study comparison between the two methods of calculation, the Nisga'a approach produced a result which showed approximately 15 percent of the net area, and 12 percent of the net volume available for sustainable use as compared to the estimates of the Ministry.

The Nisga'a have more work to do on readying this package for applied forest land management. The next phase is to apply the principles of conservation biology and landscape ecology to developing a final "overlay" of protected landscape networks. Themes to be added include wildlife habitat, water, tourism/recreation potential, and domestic wildlife harvesting. Once all this is digitized into the system, a complete operability map can be generated suitable for field application in designing land use activities.

A couple of other features of this system demonstrate the flexibility, power, and utility of the Nisga'a GIS. First, the ongoing availability of satellite imagery, which tracks the same path every 18 days or so, means that monitoring of land use practices such as timber harvesting can be continually updated. This new data can be digitally spliced into the existing image, processed to enhance features such as cut-over lands, and then transferred into the GIS for incorporation into the main mapping system. The ability to annually update logged areas, for example, and to match them to forest cover information, provides the ability to calculate aggregate removals of timber in terms of both area and volume. For First Nations, the past removal of timber resources and destruction of wildlife habitat, etc., can now be quantitatively determined as an issue in negotiations with the provincial government.

Second, the system can also generate the anticipated costs of rehabilitating the landscape to ensure adequate forest regrowth and site restoration.

Finally, with customized programming on a system such as this, any First Nation can readily generate a map of the distribution of resource values for the purposes of land selection, and quickly evaluate any similar proposal from government. As one Nisga'a technician said to me recently, "We've come a long way!"

♦

Crossing Borders: Landscape Scale Planning in the Greater North Cascades Trans-boundary Ecosystem

Susan Snetsinger

The North Cascades is one of the largest intact areas remaining in the United States—a land where grizzly bears still roam in high alpine meadows and wolves howl along ridge-tops. With over 2.2 million acres of the North Cascades established in wilderness, national park, or other protected area status, it may superficially appear as though this land is secure, and we can afford to rest easy. But those of us who watch the landscape more closely, noticing the signs of changes over time, see evidence of a decline in the long-term health of this ecosystem. We see the ecological integrity of the "protected" areas erode, as fragmentation, cumulative impacts, and edge effects of clearcut borders take their toll. As wildlife species follow their migratory routes, passing through one land ownership after another, the inadequacy of management within our politically defined but ecologically meaningless boundaries becomes clear. We realize there are much larger goals to be accomplished before the security of this ecosystem can be assured over the long-term.

For the last four years, the Greater Ecosystem Alliance (GEA) has been fighting for increased protection of the North Cascades ecosystem and all its native components. GEA is a bioregional conservation group based in Bellingham, Washington, dedicated to the protection of wildness and diversity in the transboundary region of British Columbia and the northwestern U.S.. GEA's approach is to blend hard-core science with

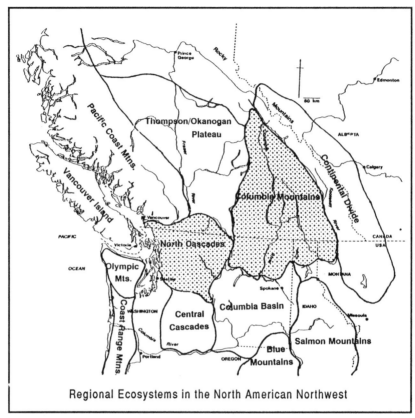

Regional Ecosystems in the North American Northwest

hard-nosed advocacy. While developing scientifically based conservation plans for the long-term, GEA works through other channels, such
as education, litigation, and legislation, to guard against loss of future
options in the short term.

Through its Regional Biodiverstiy Initiative (RBI), GEA i s compiling,
integrating, and analyzing data on patterns of biodiversity in the U.S.-
British Columbia transboundary region, from the Pacific Ocean east to
the continental divide. Two distinct regions, the Greater North Cascades
and Greater Columbia Mountains ecosystems, are encompassed in this
vast area. Within these greater ecosystems lies some of the wildest and
richest country remaining in the Pacific Northwest. All known native
species still reside here, though the persistence of some, such as the
grizzly and lynx, is increasingly precarious. Through the passage of
salmon from western ocean shores to the Columbia Mountains, and

other such wide-ranging phenomena, we know that ultimately all parts of this land are interconnected and dependent upon each other. Yet in order to allow us to plan and strategize, we must break the landscape up into units of reasonable size, with boundaries which have real meaning in the natural world.

The North Cascades ecosystem logically makes such a unit. Defined by its complex geology and characteristic plant and animal communities, the North Cascades stretch from the southern terminus of B.C.'s Coastal Mountains in the north, to Snoqualmie Pass—the transition to the Central Cascades, in the south. From tidewater to mountain top, through ancient Douglas fir forests, and montane forests of Pacific silver fir and mountain hemlock, the North Cascades rise precipitously to form one of the most rugged and dramatic ranges in all of North America. From the rock and ice of the Pacific Crest, the vegetation gives way in the east to Engelmann spruce and sub-alpine fir forests, then park-like stands of ponderosa pine at lower elevation, and finally shrub-steppe communities in the arid Okanogan River basin. One of the most remarkable aspects of this ecosystem is the juxtaposition of such wild country with one of the fastest growing urban environments in the U.S.. Thus, it is particularly imperative that ecologically sound land use plans be developed for this region now, before future options for maintaining viable populations and critical habitats are lost.

Breaking with traditions of the past, this park and reserve would be based first on the needs of the *ecosystem*.

The Greater Ecosystem Alliance's work under the Regional Biodiversity Initiative provides that planning. Using computer GIS (Geographic Information Systems) technology, GEA has compiled and integrated an extensive store of information on biodiversity in the North Cascades. With these data, GEA is conducting a full landscape analysis through which it will develop a long term conservation proposal for the North Cascades. This proposal follows the guidelines of the Wildlands Project reserve design model developed by Reed Noss. Those areas most critical to the conservation of biodiversity in the region are identified and evaluated through a set of criteria based upon the principles of conservation biology. Level of human impact (as indicated through road den-

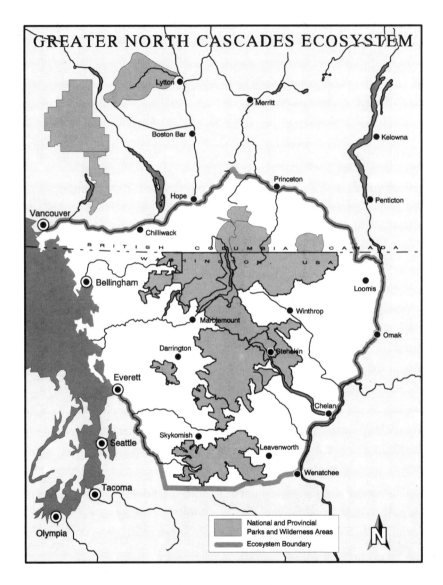

GREATER NORTH CASCADES ECOSYSTEM

National and Provincial
Parks and Wilderness Areas

Ecosystem Boundary

sities, past and present timber harvest, etc.), connectivity, distribution
and habitat of threatened and endangered species, diversity, vulnerabil-
ity, and many other factors are addressed in the analysis, and used to
identify core protected areas, buffer zones, and linkages. The proposal
also includes management recommendations on appropriate activities

within as well as outside proposed reserve areas.

The results of this analysis will provide the basis for drawing up the boundaries for a proposed Cascades International Park and Ecological Reserve. A coalition of 15 B.C. and U.S. organizations, the Cascades International Alliance (CIA), has been working to turn the long-standing vision of an international park into a political reality. Breaking with traditions of the past, this park and reserve would be based first on the needs of the *ecosystem*, and include a large enough area to support viable populations of all native species, natural disturbance regimes, and other ecosystem processes over the long term. A Cascades International Park and Ecological Reserve would be a significant step in the move towards ecosystem management in the North Cascades, especially in terms of cooperation across the international border. Although there has been a recent flurry of activity by both the U.S. and B.C. governments to come up with ecologically sound land management plans for the region, failure to look at what's happening on the other side of the 49th parallel has greatly compromised the potential of these studies. Nature does not recognize political boundaries, and until this fact is fully realized and incorporated into planning and management programs, we are likely to see the integrity of our transboundary ecosystems slowly continue to decline.

Ecosystem Planning at Another Scale

In addition to GEA and the CIA's transboundary work in the North Cascades, another planning process, being conducted by the Washington State Department of Natural Resources (DNR), is also helping to foster international cooperation. On the east side of the Cascades, high elevation plateaus, containing vast tracts of lodge-pole pine forest and key lynx habitat, spread from the Loomis State Forest northward into British Columbia. The DNR, which administers the Loomis, has recently embarked on a two-year planning process to develop a long term management plan for the Forest. This process is based on landscape scale concerns and includes biologists from a number of different agencies. The Loomis planning process is also significant in the degree to which it incorporates public participation. Interested parties and the public are encouraged to become involved through subject-specific "working groups," which help to frame the issues of concern and, in turn, the final plan. This process is a positive turning point in the move towards ecosystem management in the Cascades, and may well serve as a role model for community involvement in public land management planning projects in the future.

Nature does not recognize political boundaries.

Many public land management agencies, however, are still failing to address biodiversity issues at large enough scales and long enough time frames. And even if agencies do choose to pursue management along such lines, the data necessary to plan across administrative boundaries are often not available. Thus the compilation of data and mapping—of vegetation patterns, seral stage, watershed condition, logging activity, roads, and other important variables—that is being conducted by the Greater Ecosystem Alliance and other local groups is extremely important. Although the timely, sophisticated, and detailed mapping that is necessary to make ecologically informed decisions is, and should remain, the burden of land management agencies, a simple compilation of basic data on a regional level may be used as a tool by environmental groups to help bring such mapping and data needs to the forefront of public land agency agendas. In addition, such maps are important for providing a vision of the current and potential state of the landscape. Too often, conservation groups become locked in defensive battles, where progress is measured in terms of what *wasn't* lost, rather than what was *gained*. It is imperative that conservationists begin to take a pro-active approach by developing their own yardsticks to measure our progress towards truly ecologically sustainable systems. Places like the North Cascades, which are still relatively intact, provide us with a great opportunity to test ourselves—to test our ability and our political and social will to manage the land in the way that the science of conservation biology tells us we should. For the sake of this and all other wild landscapes and their native inhabitants—humans included—let's hope it is a test we can pass.

5

Ecological Planning
for Wild Life

Introduction

Doug Aberley

Y ou have sampled a range of ecological world views. You have perceived the importance of transforming human settlements and placing them firmly within the context of interlocking bioregions. The next big question becomes, "How do you actualize this understanding?" This is where a lot of us bog down. We travel part of the way on the path to social change, but then somehow get side-tracked. Some of us become excellent at critiquing the status quo, but don't actually do anything about it. Those who *do* resist the status quo often get sucked dry by endless confrontation, tricked into fighting symptoms and not the disease itself. Some of us work only at changing ourselves, isolated from any larger community of purpose. And, most often, we make an allegiance with a particular social change strategy, spending precious energy defending our version against that of competing movements. There are many pitfalls.

Ecological planning offers processes by which ideas from a spectrum of ecological world views can be brought together in dynamic synthesis, and then effectively put into practice. This is relatively new ground. The goal becomes not to dictate a cookie-cutter solution for all situations and locales, but to propose flexible and inclusionary processes of social change that can be adapted and applied in any bioregion. Two such techniques will be introduced. This chapter details the why and how of creating matrices of representative landscapes that maintain the integrity of environmental systems, and which guarantee the preservation of biodiversity. The next chapter then describes a process by which land that remains available for humans can be used in a manner that is socially just and ecologically sustainable. Because of the importance of placing these two ecological planning processes in proper context, they are introduced in some detail.

The idea of progress in Western civilization has been based on the belief that the entire planet is open for exploitation by humans. Added to this dogma has been implicit trust that the creation of a scattering of parks and reserves was sufficient to maintain vestiges of natural ecosystems, primarily as museum exhibits to be visited and marvelled at. The result of this approach has been the systematic decimation of virtually every bioregion on the planet, with even the small areas dedicated for preservation inundated by visitors. The demand that more and larger parks be created simply has not kept pace with the human need to visit wild space, nor the need of non-human life and environmental processes to safely maintain themselves.

There is a better way. Conservation biologist, Reed F. Noss, has best presented the idea that the preservation of local and global ecological health would be best achieved through the restoration and stewardship of webs of representative landscapes. By identifying and protecting these veins of "natural" habitat, humans would be acknowledging a fundamental change in the definition of progress. We would be accepting that life depends on life, and that the first principle of human survival is to reintegrate bioregional cultures into matrices of native ecological associations. On the land base available for human use, enterprise would become focused on qualititative growth and achievement of self-reliance, not growth for the sake of profit.

Noss has developed this concept through an exemplary mix of education and experience. In a twenty-year career he has worked as an ecologist in Ohio, Florida and with the U.S. Environmental Protection Agency. He has written over 75 technical articles, holds academic posts in Idaho, Oregon, and California, and is the editor of the prestigious journal, *Conservation Biology*. Reed Noss is also the science editor of *Wild Earth* magazine, and a prime mover of The Wildlands Project, an effort to identify and guarantee protection of a wild web of all representative ecosystems in every region of North America. This is a process far beyond the fighting of rear-guard environmental battles; it is a pro-active and wholistic vision which is rightly gaining a rapidly growing community of adherents. Some may wonder where humans fit into the uncompromising regime that Noss and his cohorts involved in The Wildlands Project develop. While Noss only partially answers this question, it is nonetheless refreshing that consideration of human habitat needs is for once placed in proper perspective—as the concern of only one species among the millions who share this planet.

◆

The Wildlands Project: Land Conservation Strategy

Reed F. Noss

W e have an opportunity, unique to our generation, to halt a mass extinction. In order to accomplish this feat, conservation must be practiced on a truly grand scale. Simply put, the tide of habitat destruction must be stopped. Despite growing dangers of pollution, acid rain, toxic wastes, greenhouse effects, and ozone depletion, direct habitat alteration by humans remains the greatest of all threats to terrestrial and aquatic biodiversity, from Panama to Alaska and beyond. The effect of habitat alteration, generally speaking, is to create conditions unlike those under which many species native to an area evolved. Whereas some species thrive under the new conditions (cheatgrass, Norway rats, and cowbirds are familiar examples), other species are not so adaptable—they go extinct. Hence, the biodiversity crisis.

In order to stop the destruction of native biodiversity, major changes must be made in land allocations and management practices. Systems of interlinked wilderness areas and other large nature reserves, surrounded by multiple-use buffer zones managed in an ecologically intelligent manner, offer the best hope for protecting sensitive species and intact ecosystems. This article is about how to select and design such systems at a regional scale.

Below, I discuss the application of conservation biology to wilderness recovery and large-scale land protection strategy in general. After reviewing the ecological goals of such a strategy and discussing approaches to reserve selection design, I outline the basic components of a wilderness recovery network: core reserves, buffer zones, and connectivity. The most important considerations in designing and managing such systems are representation of all ecosystems; population viability of sensitive species, especially large carnivores because they are usually most demanding; and perpetuation of ecological and evolutionary processes. My hope is that biodiversity activists and bioregionalists will be able to use this information in the design of ambitious wilderness recovery networks in their own regions. *Wilderness recovery, I firmly believe, is the most important task of our generation.*

Application of Conservation Biology to Wilderness Recovery

Preservation of large, wild landscapes for their natural features is not a new idea, as the history of the national parks and wilderness movements in North America attests.[27, 84] The introduction of science to the process of selecting and managing parks and other landscape-sized reserves, however, is both new and promising. Science alone, of course, is not sufficient; it must be guided by a land ethic.[43]

Most national parks, wilderness areas, and other large reserves were selected on the basis of esthetic and recreational criteria, or simply because they contained little value in terms of extractable resources. The result is that high-elevation sites (rock and ice), wetlands, and other scenic but not particularly diverse lands dominate our system of protected areas; many ecosystem types are not represented, at least not in sizable areas.[17,26,63] Because biology has been absent from design decisions, park boundaries do not conform to ecological boundaries and most parks and other reserves are too small to maintain populations of wide-ranging animals over the long term or to perpetuate natural processes.[41, 31, 58]

Increasing discussion of "greater ecosystems,"[15,30] regional landscapes,[59] regional ecosystems,[39] and ecosystem management[2] heralds a new way of looking at conservation, a way informed by ecological science. The basic idea underlying these new concepts is that most parks and other reserves are, by themselves, incomplete ecosystems. If parks or other reserves can be enlarged, and if the lands surrounding these areas are managed intelligently with the needs of native species and ecosystem processes in mind, a landscape as a whole may be able to maintain its ecological integrity over time.

If, on the other hand, surrounding lands are greatly altered from their natural condition, the chances that a reserve can maintain its integrity are slim. Animals with large home ranges (and therefore low population density) and other sensitive species will decline or fluctuate to extinction. Restoration may be needed to bring the complex of reserves and surrounding lands back to health. In any case, conservation biologists recognize that any system of parks, wilderness areas, and the public and private lands that envelop them must be managed as a whole in order to meet the goal of maintaining natural processes and native biodiversity over long spans of time.

Conservation biology and landscape ecology are both young sciences and show many signs of immaturity, such as theoretical confusion. However, the experience gained from myriad empirical case studies and observations, guided sometimes but not invariably by theory, has led to some general principles about how land might be "managed" (in a humble and non-manipulative sense of this term) to maintain biodiversity and ecological and evolutionary processes. The principles of conservation biology are not laws; we can expect them to be refined continually as the science matures. To put off implementing these principles until the science is completely developed, however, would be foolhardy; the forces that degrade natural ecosystems will not wait for the advice of scientists. Instead, the most prudent course for conservation is to proceed on the basis of the best available information, rational inference, and consensus of scientific opinion about what it takes to protect and restore whole ecosystems.

Ecological Goals

A conservation strategy is more likely to succeed if it has clearly defined and scientifically justifiable goals and objectives. Goal-setting must be the first step in the conservation process, preceding biological, technical, and political questions of how best to design and manage such systems. Primary goals for ecosystem management should be comprehensive and idealistic so that conservation programs have a vision toward which to strive over the decades.[61,64] A series of increasingly specific objectives and action plans should follow these goals and be reviewed regularly to assure consistency with primary goals and objectives.[96] Four fundamental objectives are consistent with the overarching goal of maintaining the native biodiversity of a region in perpetuity:[65, 66]

1. Represent, in a system of protected areas, all native ecosystem types and seral stages across their natural range of variation.

2. Maintain viable populations of all native species in natural patterns of abundance and distribution.

3. Maintain ecological and evolutionary processes, such as disturbance regimes, hydrological processes, nutrient cycles, and biotic interactions, including predation.

4. Design and manage the system to be responsive to short-term and long-term environmental change and to maintain the evolutionary potential of lineages.

Representation

Representation is one of the most widely accepted criteria of conservation. As an example, delegates of 62 nations at the Fourth World Wilderness Conference, in 1987, unanimously approved a resolution to preserve "representative examples of all major ecosystems of the world to ensure the preservation of the full range of wilderness and biological diversity."[17] Perhaps the best way to represent all ecosystems is to maintain the full array of physical habitats and environmental gradients in reserves, from the highest to the lowest elevations, the driest to the wettest sites, and across all types of soils, substrates, and topoclimates.[37,65] To accommodate seral stage diversity within vegetation types, reserves must either be large enough to incorporate functional natural disturbance regimes or be managed to supplement or mimic natural disturbances.[76,106] Because we do not know very well how to do the latter, as well as for ethical and aesthetic reasons, emphasis must be placed on maintaining the natural condition wherever it occurs.

Representation of all ecosystems and environmental gradients is the first step toward maintaining the full spectrum of native biodiversity in a region. Representation is subtly different from the conservation criterion of representativeness,[48] where the best or typical examples of various community types are targeted for preservation. The latter concept is typological and static; it often results in the sequestration of "museum pieces" or specimens of nature.[71] Representation does not seek to preserve characteristic types of communities so much as to maintain the full spectrum of community variation along environmental gradients. It is understood that this variation is dynamic. The best example of a conservation program based on representation goals in North America is the Gap Analysis project directed by the U.S. Fish and Wildlife Service.[89.]

Viable Populations

Simply representing a species in a reserve or series of reserves does not guarantee that it will be able to persist in those areas (or anywhere) indefinitely. The representation objective must be complemented by the goal of maintaining viable populations of every species. Population viability is a central concern in conservation biology[90,93] A viable population is one that has a high probability (say, 95 or 99 percent) of persisting for a long time (say, 100 to 1000 years). Population viability analysis is complex, with estimates depending on the mathematical model used, its assumptions, and values used for key population parameters such as population density and birth and death rates. With a few interesting exceptions, viable populations are generally on the order of thousands of individuals.[99]

Fortunately, one does not have to worry about each of the thousands of species that may live in a region in order to meet the ambitious goal of maintaining viable populations of all native species. Rather, "conservation should not treat all species as equal but must focus on species and habitats threatened by human activity."[22.] Concerns about population viability should be directed toward species at most risk of extinction in the region. Vulnerable species typically include those with small populations (limited or patchy distribution or low density), large home ranges, poor dispersal abilities, low reproductive potential, as well as those subject to exploitation or persecution or dependent on habitats that are themselves rare or threatened.[65] These are the species that require our attention; many others tolerate or even thrive on human disturbance and can get along quite well without conservation assistance. For a regional wilderness recovery strategy, large and wide-ranging carnivores—bears, wolves, jaguar, puma, wolverine—are ideal primary target species.

Although answers to population viability questions are species-specific, some general principles for managing landscapes for vulnerable species are emerging. Thomas et al.,[101] in their conservation strategy for the northern spotted owl, listed five reserve design concepts "widely accepted among specialists in the fields of ecology and conservation biology." I generalize their guidelines below to multiple species, adding a sixth guideline that applies to species such as large carnivores, that are especially sensitive to human disturbance (and therefore, greatly in need of protection).

1. Species well distributed across their native range are less susceptible to extinction than species confined to small portions of their range.

2. Large blocks of habitat, containing large populations of a target species, are superior to small blocks of habitat containing small populations.

3. Blocks of habitat close together are better than blocks far apart.

4. Habitat in contiguous blocks is better than fragmented habitat.

5. Interconnected blocks of habitat are better than isolated blocks: corridors or linkages function better when habitat within them resembles that preferred by target species.

6. Blocks of habitat that are roadless or otherwise inaccessible to humans are better than roaded and accessible habitat blocks.

Maintaining Ecological and Evolutionary Processes

One general theme of ecosystem management is that process is at least as important as pattern.[71] In other words, our concern for maintaining particular species, communities, places, and other entities must be complemented by a concern for the ecological and evolutionary processes that brought those entities into being and that will allow them to persist and evolve over the eons. Fundamental processes critical to ecosystem function include cycling of nutrients and flow of energy, disturbance regimes and recovery processes (succession), hydrological cycles, weathering and erosion, decomposition, herbivory, predation, pollination, seed dispersal, and many more. Evolutionary process, such as mutation, gene flow, and differentiation of populations, must also be maintained if the biota is to adapt to changing conditions.

Allowing For Change

Maintaining ecological and evolutionary processes implies that change must be allowed to occur without, it is to be hoped, a net loss of biodiversity. A glaring deficiency of many conservation plans is their failure to recognize and to accommodate change in nature. Conservation strategy has implicitly assumed that natural communities are unchanging entities[37] and has sought to freeze in time snapshots of nature and associations of species that may have been apart for longer periods of their evolutionary histories than they have been together. The meaning of "preservation" must be revised to emphasize processes and to interpret local patterns in the context of global biodiversity over long time periods.

The meaning of "preservation" must be revised to emphasize processes and to interpret local patterns in the context of global biodiversity over long time periods.

Short-term (years to centuries) ecological change occurs as a consequence of natural disturbance and succession. Disturbance-recovery cycles are among the most important of all ecological processes and have had a profound effect on the evolution of species (for example, many plant species are adapted to or even dependent on frequent fire). Only very large reserves or natural landscapes will be able to accommodate disturbance regimes characterized by stand replacement and large patch sizes without losing diversity.[76,92] In the Greater Yellowstone Ecosystem, for example, the lodge-pole pine forests that cover much of the area are characterized by high-intensity, stand-replacing fires that recur naturally every two or three centuries; apparently, the landscape is not in equilibrium.[82,81] Yellowstone National Park by itself is too small to exist in anything close to steady state with a natural fire regime—one more reason for managing the entire 19 million acres of the Greater Yellowstone Ecosystem as a whole.

Long-term (decades to millennia) change occurs largely as a result of changing climate. The response of plants and animals to climate change over time has primarily been to migrate with shifting climate zones. Communities did not migrate as intact units, however. Rather, plants and animals migrated at rates and in routes that were highly individualistic.[18,29] The conservation strategy of maintaining all physical habitats (soil types, slope aspects, etc.) and intact environmental gradients, with corridors or other forms of connectivity linking habitats across the landscape, is perhaps the best way to accommodate change without losing biodiversity.

Approaches to Land Conservation

How might a regional land conservation program meet the objectives of representing all ecosystems, maintaining viable populations, maintaining natural processes, and allowing for change? Four approaches emphasized in recent years appear promising: (1) identify and protect populations of rare and endangered species; (2) maintain healthy populations of species that play critical roles in their ecosystems (keystone species) or that have pragmatic value as "umbrellas" (species that require large wild areas to survive, and thus if protected will bring many species along with them) or "flagships"(charismatic species that serve as popular symbols for conservation); (3) protect high-quality examples of all natural communities; and (4) identify and manage greater ecosystems or landscapes for both biodiversity conservation and sustainable human use.

These four approaches have obvious relationships to the objectives posed above. Unfortunately, they have sometimes been presented as competing rather than complementary strategies. Advocates of one approach may get very attached to it and fail to see its limitations or the merits of other approaches. In practice, the familiar strategy of protecting sites that harbor rare species or natural communities has worked quite well for plants and animals with small area requirements, but has been less successful in protecting wide-ranging animals and has been unable to capture landscape mosaics and other higher-order expressions of biodiversity.[62] Empirical evidence has demonstrated that the small reserves selected through the site-by-site approach are heavily assaulted by external influences and often fail to retain the natural qualities for which they were set aside.

On the other hand, many so-called "ecosystem" or "landscape" approaches have lacked scientific rigor and objectivity and have failed to target those elements of biodiversity that are truly most threatened. Furthermore, most attempts to use "sustainability" as a management paradigm [85] have been anthropocentric, biased toward commodity production, and seriously flawed from a biological standpoint.[67]

These four approaches to conservation must be pursued in concert if the full spectrum of biodiversity is to be protected. Again, this can only be accomplished by representing all ecosystems (from small habitat patches to large landscape mosaics), maintaining viable populations of all native species (plant and animal, big and small), maintaining ecological and evolutionary processes, and accommodating change. The most difficult challenge is to meet all these objectives while still allowing for some kinds of human use. Most conservation biologists agree that compatible human uses of the landscape must be considered and encouraged in large-scale conservation planning. Otherwise, the strategy will have little public support. However, the native ecosystem and the collective needs of non-human species must take precedence over the needs and desires of humans, for the simple reason that our species is both more adaptable and more destructive than any other. Putting the needs of one species—humans—above those of all other species combined, as exemplified by the sustainable development theme, is one of the most pernicious trends in modern conservation.

Putting the needs of one species—humans—above those of all other species combined, as exemplified by the sustainable development theme, is one of the most pernicious trends in modern conservation.

Regionalization is a central issue in The Wildlands Project (a.k.a. the North American Wilderness Recovery Project). Trying to make sense of the distribution of biodiversity and planning reserves across all of North America at once would be overwhelming. Regionalization on the basis of physiography, biogeography, land use, and other large-scale patterns helps assure that every physically and biotically distinct region is represented in a broad conservation strategy. Omernick,[74] for example, has produced a map portraying 76 ecoregions in the 48 conterminous states, and the Canadian Parks Service recognizes 39 terrestrial natural regions.[35] Ecoregions or bioregions are a convenient scale for planning and often inspire feelings of belonging and protectiveness in their more enlightened human inhabitants. Many grassroots groups around the continent have defined bioregions and developed conservation plans for them. The Wildlands Project exists essentially to coordinate and provide technical support for these regional efforts.

Regionalization of reserve networks should be a hierarchical process; that is, we should consider regions within regions in our planning efforts. We can contemplate our homeland as a nested series, with our local watershed functioning as an interdependent part of a larger river watershed (a hydrologic unit), which in turn is part of an ecoregion or bioregion (for example, the Blue Ridge Mountains), then a biogeographical province (eastern deciduous forest), a continent, and eventually, the biosphere. Putting this nested hierarchy idea into practice means local nature reserve systems should be linked together into regional systems, which in turn are connected by inter-regional corridors that ultimately span continents. These hierarchical connections will help promote the multiple functions of connectivity discussed later in this article.

Reconnaissance and Selection

How do we choose reserves in a regional land conservation strategy? The process involves field inventory, remote sensing interpretation, and biogeographical research to determine the spatial distribution of biodiversity and wild areas, followed by an evaluation of which areas are most important to protect. The next step, drawing lines on maps, is not as easy as might be expected. Each line on a reserve design map represents a decision about areas to protect and areas to leave out. Unfortunately, not every acre can be protected or restored within the near future. Decisions must be made quickly about which areas are most valuable ecologically, before they are altered irrevocably. Such decisions should not result in any area being "trashed." Ideally, all lands should be managed, at least in part, for biodiversity. But some areas deserve and require more rigorous protection than others. We call this process of picking and choosing "conservation evaluation."[102]

Conservation evaluation is legitimate because biodiversity is not distributed uniformly across the landscape. Certain areas—call them "hot spots"—are unusually high in sheer number of species or contain concentrations of rare or endemic species or unusual natural communities. Areas of high physical habitat diversity, such as topographically complex landscapes with many distinct soil types, are often hot spots. Sites in a landscape also vary in conservation value as a result of historical influences, including past human activities. Roadless areas, especially when large,[26] are of great importance because they harbor reclusive species and are often inherently sensitive to physical disturbance due to steep terrain or highly erodible soils (which made them difficult to exploit economically and explains why they are still roadless). Parking lots and corn fields, on the other hand, would score low in a conservation evaluation. Some degraded sites, however, may be priorities for restoration due to their locations relative to other landscape features, such as lying within a corridor that links hot spots across a landscape.

Core reserves and primary corridors in a regional network should enclose and link biologically critical areas (i.e., those that contribute to the goals discussed above) in a continuous system of natural habitat whenever possible. Some critical steps in selecting core reserves (the most strictly protected areas) and primary linkages in a wilderness network, are as follows:[25,61,65,66,68,26]

1. Select areas that, on the basis of field reconnaissance and interpretation of maps, aerial photographs, or satellite images, appear to be roadless, undeveloped, or otherwise in essentially natural condition. Center proposed core reserves on these undeveloped areas. A map of land ownership will show those areas which are on public lands.

2. Add roaded landscapes that are relatively undeveloped and restorable, especially when adjacent to or near roadless areas. Addition of such areas is important to increase core reserve size and to link roadless areas into larger complexes or networks.

3. Map the distribution of rare species and community types in your region, using state natural heritage program databases (which also exist for some Canadian provinces and Latin American countries). The heritage programs use a five-point scale of global and state-wide endangerment developed by the Nature Conservancy, with rank 1 signifying the most imperilled elements. Map occurrences of all species, subspecies, varieties, and communities that rank 3 (very rare and local throughout range or found locally in a restricted range) or higher at a global scale (G3 or T3, G2 or T2, and G1 and T1; the G indicates global status and the T indicates status of taxonomic sub-categories). Add species that are imperilled or critically imperilled state-wide (S2 and S1), though they may be less rare globally. Request a computer printout from the heritage program with data on each occurrence, including township/range/section and other location information. Map occurrences on mylar overlays on maps ranging from 1:100,000 to 1:250,000 scale (e.g., Forest Service 1/2 inch = 1 mile maps are 1:126,720). Local analyses should use 1:24,000 scale (the familiar 7.5 minute quadrangle maps) or larger. If you use a Geographic Information System (GIS), you can request a disk with longitude/latitude coordinates of occurrences. In some regions, mapping the distribution of rare species and communities might be the most

practical first step in the network design process.

4. Draw polygons around clusters or constellations of rare species and community types. If not encompassed in core reserves proposed in steps 1 and 2, add these polygons to the system. Some hot spots will be naturally isolated (for instance, caves, serpentine barrens, or kettlehole bogs), so linking them by corridors is unnecessary.

5. Obtain information from the U.S. Fish and Wildlife Service GIS gap analysis (if completed for your state or states) on unprotected and underprotected vegetation types and centers of species richness in your region.[89] The purpose of gap analysis is to provide information on representation of ecosystems and species in protected areas. A similar representation study is being conducted in Canada by World Wildlife Fund-Canada (A. Hackman, personal communication). Locate areas that contain vegetation types and centers of species richness (areas where the ranges of many species overlap) that are not adequately protected in existing reserves. Add these areas to your network of sites if not already encompassed through steps 1-4.

6. You have now determined the general locations of your core reserves and some of the linkages between them. Next, you need to define boundaries more precisely, add more corridors so that all sites that would be naturally linked are reconnected, and envelop the entire network in a matrix of buffer zones (Fig. 1). To do these things, you must zoom in to the landscape scale (say, 1:24,000 or larger, if feasible). Refer to detailed road maps, land ownership maps, land-use information including grazing allotments, proposed timber sales, and mineral rights, wildlife maps such as ungulate winter range and dispersal corridors, and additional data, as available.[25,66,68] This information also tells you about threats to sites which must be averted. Using this information and knowledge of the land, based on field reconnaissance and maps, adjust proposed boundaries.

7. As part of your final proposal, indicate specific actions that must be taken to secure the system. These actions include land and mineral rights acquisitions, wilderness or other reserve designations on public lands, road closures, road modifications (such as underpasses to allow migration of animals beneath highways), cancellation of grazing leases and timber sales, tree planting, dam removals, stream dechannelization, and other restoration projects.[68]

The issue of appropriate size or scope of a regional wilderness recov-

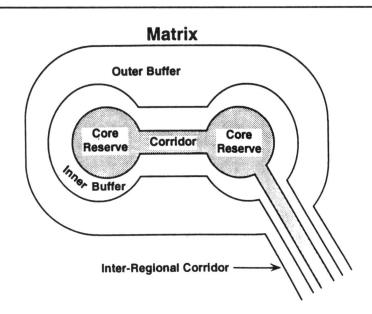

Figure 1. A regional wilderness recovery network, consisting of core reserves, connecting corridors or linkages, and buffer zones. Only two core areas are shown, but a real system may contain many reserves. Inner buffer zones would be strictly protected, while outer zones would allow a wider range of compatible human uses. In this example, an inter-regional corridor connects the system to a similar network in another bioregion. Matrix refers to the landscape surrounding the reserve network, but this is only true in the first stages of a wilderness recovery project in regions now dominated by human activity. Eventually, a wilderness recovery network would dominate a region and thus would itself constitute the matrix, with human habitations being the islands. In regions where wildland is already the matrix, the inverted model should be implemented right away.

ery network, some aspects of which will be discussed later in this article, is thorny. Each region must be assessed individually. I suggest that at least half of the land area of the 48 conterminous states should be encompassed in core reserves and inner corridor zones (essentially extensions of core reserves) within the next few decades; I also believe that this could be done without great economic hardship. Areas with more wild land remaining, such as much of Canada, Alaska, and parts of Mexico and Central America, should have higher targets. Some regions such as the Mid-western Till Plains and Northeastern Coastal

Zone, will take longer to restore to 50 percent wilderness, perhaps on the order of centuries. Nonetheless, half of a region in wilderness is a reasonable guess of what it will take to restore viable populations of large carnivores and natural disturbance regimes, assuming that most of the other 50 percent is managed intelligently as buffer zone.

Other authors, using different criteria, have arrived at similar estimates of what it might take to protect ecological integrity in a region. Odum and Odum[73] suggested that managing half of southern Florida as natural area and half as cultural land was optimal.

Earlier, Odum[72] estimated that managing 40 percent of the state of Georgia as natural, 10 percent as urban-industrial, 30 percent in food production, and 20 percent in fibre production would maximize ecological services while maintaining the current standard of living. I would offer a more ambitious long-term goal, pending human population reduction, that at least 95 percent of a region be managed as wilderness and surrounding multiple-use wildlands. The following sections provide detailed ecological criteria for designing a wilderness recovery network.

Components of a Wilderness Recovery Network

A wilderness recovery network is an interconnected system of strictly protected areas (core reserves), surrounded by lands used for human activities compatible with conservation that put biodiversity first (buffer zones), and linked together in some way that provides for functional connectivity of populations and processes across the landscape. These basic concepts are common to many conservation strategies, including the biosphere reserves of the Man and the Biosphere (MAB) Program,[103,33,6,24] and the multiple-use module idea that applies these concepts at various spatial scales.[31,71,61]

Below, I discuss core areas, buffer zones, and connectivity as they apply to wilderness recovery. I follow with a brief discussion of the "bigness" issue, that is, determining how large a reserve or reserve system must be to maintain its native biodiversity over time.

Core Areas

The backbone of a regional reserve system is formed by those protected areas managed primarily to maintain or restore their natural values. The selection of core reserves should be based on the criteria and objectives discussed above: representing all ecosystems, maintaining viable populations of all native species, maintaining ecological and evolutionary processes, and being responsive to change. Core reserves should collectively encompass the full range of communities, ecosystems, physical habitats, environmental gradients, and natural seral stages in each region. Design and management guidelines for specific core reserves require considerable site-specific research.

Buffer (Multiple-Use) Zones

A system of core reserves is necessary but not sufficient to maintain biodiverstiy. In most regions, strictly protected areas will not occupy enough land, in the short term, to meet the conservation goals suggested in this article.[11] For a largely wild region, such as much of the western United States and Canada, the multiple-use public lands that envelop reserves should be managed in a way more sensitive to natural ecosystems and processes than what is now the custom (to put it mildly). To the extent that buffer zones are managed intelligently, core reserves have a better chance of maintaining viable populations, and regional landscapes will be richer in native biodiversity than if reserves are surrounded by intensive land use.

I use the terms "multiple-use zone" and "buffer zone" interchangeably.[65] The former term, although tainted by misuse by public agencies and special interest groups, may be preferable because such zones can indeed provide for many human uses and function as much more than buffers. Multiple-use public lands adjacent to reserves should serve as at least marginal habitat for vulnerable species and should insulate reserves from intensive land uses. A reserve properly insulated from high-intensity land use by one or a series of buffer zones is, to a measurable degree, functionally enlarged as a conservation unit. In many cases, private lands will need to be acquired and added to national forests and other public lands in order to serve as effective buffers.

Physical and biotic edge effects can be serious problems for small reserves with high perimeter/area ratios,[59] buffer zones have been recommended to mitigate edge effects in these situations.[31,61] Among forest communities, deleterious edge effects are best documented for closed-canopy forest types. Forest interior species may be sensitive to a variety of edge-related environmental changes. Increased blowdown potential may extend at least two tree-heights into a stand,[28,31] Some kinds of external influences' such as invasions of weedy species, penetrate much farther—perhaps five km or more into a forest.[38] Weedy, exotic species of plants and animals are often abundant in human-disturbed environments; buffer zones may help screen these pests away from reserves. Core reserves, if designed according to the criteria discussed in this article, will generally be large enough that edge effects from their boundaries should not be a significant problem. Edge effects from internal fragmentation, such as that caused by road-building and clearcutting, will be a threat until artificially disturbed habitats are restored.

Multiple-use zones have functions other than ameliorating edge effects. If maintained in low road density, they can protect core reserves from poaching and other harmful human activities that otherwise would be intense near reserve boundaries. They may also protect developed areas from depredating large mammals (such as grizzly bears and wolves) that will hopefully thrive in core reserves. Outer zones of vegetation resistant to high-intensity fire (such as grasslands), supplemented by fire lanes on the perimeter, may protect private forests and settlements from fires originating in core reserves.

An ideal function of multiple-use zones is to provide supplementary habitat to native species inhabiting a core reserve, thus increasing population size and viability. To the extent that multiple-use zones can be restored and managed to increase habitat area for those species most vulnerable to extinction, they will enlarge the effective area of the reserve. In some cases, animals that depend on several different habitat types, perhaps on a seasonal basis, will require areas not represented in a reserve to meet a portion of their annual life-history needs. Obvious examples are elk and deer that make seasonal migrations between high-elevation summer ranges and low-elevation winter ranges.[1] Core reserves can be created or enlarged to protect the most critical migration corridors, but many other movement areas will need to be protected by buffer zones.

Population dynamics across reserve boundaries can be complex. The notion of "source" versus "sink" habitats is germane here. As discussed by Pulliam,[79] source habitats are those that can support a net population increase whereas "sink" habitats have in situ death rates higher than birth rates—they are "black holes" for wildlife. Populations are maintained by sink habitats only when subsidized by source habitats. Population density, therefore, may be a misleading indicator of habitat quality.[104] Concentration of socially subordinate individuals (for instance, female and sub-adult male bears, or juvenile songbirds) in sink habitats may lead to mistaken impressions about habitat quality in those areas. Although most of the population may exist at any given time in the sink habitat, conservation of the source habitat is absolutely essential to the survival of the whole population.[79,34]

The source-sink dichotomy (really a continuum) is relevant to the planning of buffer zones, because whenever habitat quality or population density for a species differs across a boundary, we can expect net movement of individuals across that boundary. This gradient-aligned dispersal is in addition to any movements made by animals that use resources on both sides of the boundary.

The developed landscape is often a sink, relative to reserve habitat, for native species.[38,88,12] In the absence of well protected buffer zones, surplus animals produced in a park or other reserve may disappear into the developed landscape matrix, seldom reproducing and often dying there. Areas near roads and developments are well known population sinks for Yellowstone grizzly bears, even within the National Park.[50] Across the Greater Yellowstone Ecosystem, illegal shooting and management "removals" are the major causes of mortality for the grizzly and are associated with real or perceived threats to humans or livestock, particularly sheep.[40,49] Road closures and removal of sheep allotments are probably essential to grizzly bear recovery in this region.[53]

If, on the other hand, lands surrounding core reserves are managed for the benefit of a sensitive species and contain habitat of moderate or high quality for that species, those lands may be minor sinks or no sink at all. If death rates in the buffer are approximately equal to birth rates, there will be no drain on the reserve population. Furthermore, a recent model suggests that sink habitats can actually contribute to meta-population persistence.[34] Although the highest priority is to identify and protect source habitats where annual reproduction exceeds mortality, a large fraction of a species' population may exist in sink habitats and those areas may extend the survival time of the meta-population as a whole (meta-population is a collection of local populations linked by dispersal[44]). A buffer zone of marginal habitat quality, even if technically a sink, can be managed to reduce mortality and contribute to meta-population persistence. Dispersal is a key factor in meta-population persistence (Fig. 2) and can be enhanced if buffer zones are managed to minimize road density, artificial openings, and other potential barriers.

Another advantage of buffer zones around reserves may be to allow plants and animals to shift their distributions in response to disturbances and other changes. In the long-term, or perhaps rather quickly (within the next few decades, if prevailing models of anthropogenic global warming prove true), organisms will need to shift their ranges in response to climate change.[75] Buffer zones or habitat corridors between reserves will help organisms make these distributional shifts and avoid extinction (see connectivity discussion, below).

In order to protect species sensitive to legal or illegal hunting or persecution, such as grizzly bear, jaguar, and wolf, buffer zones must have low road density (say, no more than 0.5 miles of road per square mile). Research has shown that road densities as low as 0.8 or 0.9 miles per square mile may make habitat unsuitable for large carnivores and omnivores.[10,98,55] Road access is a major threat to wildlands throughout North America.[23] Road closures are one of the most effective ways to make multipleuse lands function as buffers.

Connectivity

A fundamental principle for designing regional reserve systems is connectivity. Unless many millions of acres in size, individual core reserves will not be able to function alone as whole ecosystems, in the sense of maintaining viable populations of large animals and ecological and evolutionary processes (see the following section on bigness). In the long-term, regions themselves must be functionally interconnected to allow for long distance dispersal and migration in response to climate change. In order to maintain their ecological integrity, many or most core reserves will have to be functionally joined to other protected areas.

Habitat fragmentation, one of the greatest of all threats to biodiversity,[59,61,31,109,108] is a process where large blocks of natural habitat are broken up into smaller and isolated pieces. Connectivity is in many respects the opposite of fragmentation. A reserve system with high connectivity is one where individual reserves are functionally united into a whole that is greater than the sum of its parts.[71]

As suggested above, properly managed buffer zones in which a constellation of reserves is embedded may provide adequate habitat connectivity. Key qualities of buffer zones that provide for animal movement are low road density and minimal development, clearcutting, or other forms of habitat fragmentation. In some cases, however, distinct corridors of suitable habitat may be needed to link core reserves or reserve complexes into a functional network. These corridors may range in scale from short connectors a few dozen meters wide to regional corridors one hundred miles or more in length and many miles in width[68,69] I use the term "linkages" to emphasize the many types and functions of connectivity.

Linkages as Habitat: Some types of corridors are distinct in the natural landscape, riparian corridors being a good example. Riparian forests are highly productive and often very rich in species. As an illustration of how many animals may depend on riparian forests, in the Blue Mountains of Oregon and Washington 285 (75 percent) of the 378 species of terrestrial vertebrates either depend on or strongly prefer riparian zones over other habitats.[100] Riparian forests are immensely valuable in their own right, aside from any role they may play as conduits for wildlife movement.

Wide protected corridors are basically extensions of core reserves. The width of corridor needed to contain an adequate amount of forest interior habitat and minimize edge effects is uncertain and depends on habitat quality both within and outside the corridor.[69] For example, the edge effect of increased blowdown risk extends at least two tre-eheights into a forest.[31] If forest trees average 40 metres in height, a corridor would have to be at least 360 metres (approximately one-quarter mile) wide to maintain a modest 200 metre-wide strip of interior forest. Another consideration for determining optimal corridor width is the territory or home range size of target species expected to use the corridor. Because this issue also affects the ability of a corridor to promote dispersal, I discuss it below in the dispersal section.

Linkage for Seasonal Movements: The conservation function most commonly associated with corridors is to allow movement of animals between reserves. For wide-ranging animals, a small core reserve may not encompass a single annual home range. Some large carnivores have annual ranges of 1,000 or more km^2, and elk and mule deer may travel over 100 km in linear distance between summer and winter ranges.[65,69] Maintaining safe travel opportunities for these species is largely a matter of protecting them from human predation; wide, roadless corridors will best serve this purpose.

Vertebrates often use traditional migration routes between summer and winter range. Elk generally use forested travel lanes, when available, for migratory movements.[1] Elk migration has been disrupted by removal

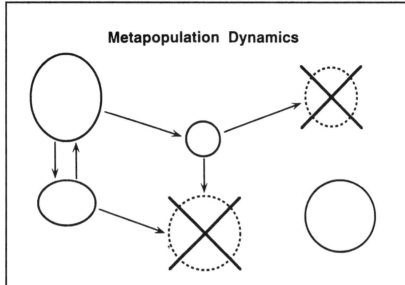

Metapopulation Dynamics

Figure 2. A hypothetical example of metapopulation dynamics. Sub-populations are connected by dispersal, which may keep local populations
from going extinct (the "rescue" effect) and thus stabilizes the metapopulation. In this example, two sub-populations (each marked by an "x")
have recently gone extinct. Dispersal from other sub-populations allows
for these areas to be recolonized. The sub-population in the lower right
is not receiving any immigrants, perhaps because developments or other
barriers lie between it and other sub-populations. Should this isolated
sub-population go extinct, it can only be recolonized by restoration of
dispersal corridors or active reintroduction by humans.[78, 56]

of security cover by logging in many regions, for example on the Targhee
National Forest near Island Park, Idaho. Travel corridors used by grizzly
bears include ridgetops, saddles and creek bottoms;[42] grizzlies avoid
crossing clearcuts and other large openings (D. Mattson, personal communication). Traditional wildlife migration routes should be incorporated into corridors between reserves. Habitat nodes or staging areas for
migratory animals also should be identified and protected.

Linkages for Dispersal: Dispersal refers to the movement of organisms
away from their place of origin, such as the movement of sub-adult
animals out of the parental home range. Many species are distributed as
metapopulations (Fig. 2). Dispersal can counteract the isolating effects
of habitat fragmentation, but only if adequate dispersal habitat remains.

For a regional meta-population of a species to persist, movement of individuals between patches must be great enough to balance extirpation from local patches.[19] Late successional species tend to be poorer dispersers and more vulnerable to extinction in fragmented landscapes than species associated with early successional stages.[20] Therefore, dispersal corridors are most important for late successional species and for species, such as large carnivores or ungulates, likely to be killed by humans or vehicles in developed or heavily roaded landscapes.

Dispersal is more often successful when habitat in a corridor or other linkage is similar to the habitat in which a species lives,[107] with some exceptions.[8] Just how similar it must be is a question yet to be answered. Thomas et al.[101] predicted, on the basis of a collective best guess, that maintaining 50 percent of the landscape matrix between proposed habitat conservation areas in forest stands averaging at least 11 inches dbh and 40 percent canopy closure would provide adequate dispersal habitat for the northern spotted owl. Other scientists might have opted for more stringent standards, for example, 75 percent of the matrix, more canopy closure, lower road density, and less edge to protect owls from shooting and great horned owl predation. In any case, maintaining matrix suitability, as in the multiple-use zoning strategy reviewed above, is another way to provide connectivity between core reserves. For those species most sensitive to human harassment, barrier effects of roads, or edge effects, the prudent strategy is to maintain wide corridors with roadless core zones and true interior habitat.[69]

Corridors that maintain resident populations of animals are more likely to function effectively as long-distance dispersal conduits for those species.[7] Minimum corridor widths, then, might be based on average home range or territory diameters of target animals.[32] Consider the grizzly bear, with an average male life-time home range of approximately 3,885 km[2] (1500 square miles) in the Greater Yellowstone Ecosystem.[53] A male life-time home range may contain, at any one time, one or two adult males, and up to a few females; thus, it would provide an adequate width for an inter-regional corridor.

If the population of grizzlies in the Greater Yellowstone Ecosystem is to be connected to other populations, which seems to be necessary to assure population viability, then wide corridors with resident grizzlies must connect Yellowstone with the Northern Continental Divide Ecosystem (about 200 miles away) and the wildlands of central Idaho.[78,56]

Considering rectangular life-time home ranges twice as long as wide, a between-population corridor for grizzly bears should be at least 44.25 km (27.5 miles) wide. A corridor based on annual or seasonal home ranges would be much narrower but also less secure; it is best to risk erring on the side of caution. Because road densities above about 0.5 miles of road per square mile of habitat may be a threat to grizzlies,[4] road closures would be required to make inter-regional corridors safe. Figure 1 portrays a wide inter-regional corridor of the type discussed here and others are shown in the state-wide network proposed for Florida (Fig. 3[60,61] and *Wild Earth* (1)).

Linkages for Long-Distance Range Shifts: A final function of connectivity

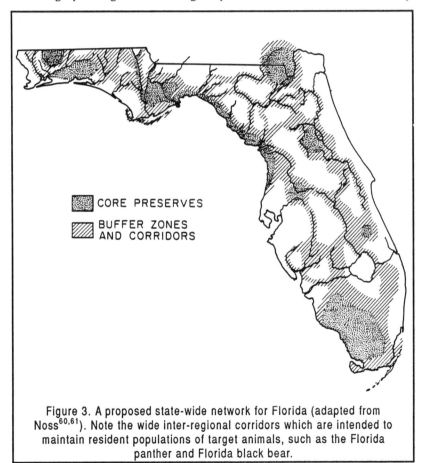

CORE PRESERVES

BUFFER ZONES
AND CORRIDORS

Figure 3. A proposed state-wide network for Florida (adapted from Noss[60,61]). Note the wide inter-regional corridors which are intended to maintain resident populations of target animals, such as the Florida panther and Florida black bear.

is to provide for long distance migration of species in response to climate change. Models of anthropogenic global warming predict dramatic shifts in vegetation in most regions. In the Greater Yellowstone Ecosystem, for example, the upper and lower tree-lines are expected to move considerable distances.[83] Human activities have imposed a new set of barriers on the landscape that, in addition to natural barriers, may interfere with long distance movements. Unfortunately, if rates of global warming in the next few decades are as fast as predicted, many species will be unable to migrate quickly enough, even along ideal corridors. In Yellowstone, as elsewhere, species with short and rapid life histories, such as introduced weeds, will probably adjust well to climate change, as will broadly distributed species such as lodgepole pine. On the other hand, whitebark pine and many alpine species, which already show limited and discontinuous distributions, are at high risk of extirpation.[83]

Mountainous regions with broad elevational spans are better suited for adaptation to climate change than flatter regions. A three degree (C) rise in temperature, as predicted with greenhouse warming, translates to a latitudinal range shift of roughly 250 km (155 miles), but an elevational range shift of only 500 metres (1,640 ft.).[46] Perhaps the best way to facilitate adaptive migration of species in response to climate change is to maintain intact environmental gradients, as discussed earlier in this article. Complete, unfragmented elevational gradients, for example, from foothill grasslands and shrub steppe up to alpine tundra, will offer the best opportunities for up-slope migration of species in response to global warming.

The Issue of Bigness

The question that has most occupied conservation biologists for the last two decades has been "How large does a reserve need to be to maintain its diversity over time?" Researchers have sought answers in various ways and have discovered many reasons why large reserves are preferable to small ones. The desirability of large reserves, all else being equal, is one of the few almost universally accepted principles of conservation biology.[94,101]

Some of the best reasons for large reserves are quite practical: per unit area, they are usually cheaper to buy and require less management effort to maintain their natural qualities than smaller reserves.[80,106,59] Due to the species-area relationship and its many potential causes,[14] larger reserves also contain more species than smaller reserves in the same biogeographic region. Island biogeographic theory suggests that large islands or nature reserves contain more species because they experience higher colonization rates and lower extinction rates than smaller areas.[47,21] But perhaps the most compelling arguments for large reserves have to do with population viability and habitat diversity in the face of environmental change.

Reserve Size and Population Viability. Estimates of minimum viable population sizes and corresponding reserve sizes are alarmingly high. Small populations are vulnerable to extinction due to a number of factors, including environmental change, demographic stochasticity, social dysfunction, and genetic deterioration.[90,93] All populations fluctuate over time; small populations are more likely to fluctuate down to zero. A recent review of empirical studies [99] concluded that an average population of 1,000 individuals must be maintained in order to assure population viability of species with average levels of fluctuation in abundance. Bird and mammal species with highly variable populations may require average populations of about 10,000 individuals for long-term persistence. In some cases, however, populations can persist for long periods at surprisingly small sizes, even less than 50 individuals (e.g., Walter[105]). It seems wise, however, to strive for large populations of vulnerable species whenever possible.

Habitat quality, social behavior, and other factors will determine how minimum population estimates translate to reserve size estimates. Schonewald-Cox[87] estimated that reserves of 10,000 to 100,000 hectares (25,000 to 250,000 acres) might maintain viable populations of small herbivorous and omnivorous mammals, but that large carnivores and ungulates require reserves on the scale of 1 to 10 million hectares (2.5 to 25 million acres). Using a minimum viable population size of 50 (which is reasonable only under very short planning horizons), it has been estimated that grizzly bear populations in Canada require an average of 49,000 km^2 (12.1 million acres), wolverines, about 42,000 km^2 (10.4 million acres), and wolves, about 20,250 km^2 (5 million acres).[36] For a minimum viable population of 1,000,[99] the figures would be 242 million acres for grizzly bears, 200 million acres for wolverines, and 100 million acres for wolves. And, of course, it is not prudent to manage down to the minimum!

Such immense areas could not be contained today within individual reserves, but only with regional and inter-regional systems of interlinked reserves, for example, the Greater Yellowstone Ecosystem linked to the Northern Continental Divide Ecosystem and on to the Canadian Rockies; the Florida network (Fig. 3) linked to a network that parallels the Appalachian Trail to Maine;[86,37] and a southern Arizona network linked to the rest of the Southwest and to Mexico. Regional and inter-regional systems of protected areas connected by wide corridors appear to be necessary to maintain viable and well-distributed populations of most large carnivores, hence the importance of these species as targets for wilderness recovery planning.

Reserves making up a habitat system for large carnivores should be predominately wilderness, but should include appropriately managed buffer zones. In order to protect these species, which are very sensitive to human predation and harassment,[98,52,54,40,16,50,51] open roads and other means of human access must be tightly restricted. Recognizing (on paper) the threats posed by open roads, the Gallatin National Forest in Montana has implemented an open road density (ORD) standard of 0.5 miles of road per square mile in critical grizzly bear and big game habitat. The 0.5 ORD standard is assumed to maintain a habitat effectiveness of at least 70 percent, an accepted minimum for population viability of grizzlies and elk.[4] Road closures to reduce the density of roads to an acceptable level (less than 0.5 miles per square mile) in each region will be among the most difficult actions politically, but most necessary ecologically.

Reserve Size and Disturbance Regimes. Maintaining habitat diversity and the full range of species associated with different seral stages requires that natural disturbance regimes be taken into account when considering reserve size. Disturbances are patchy in time and space, so that a landscape can be viewed as a "shifting mosaic" of patches in various stages of recovery from disturbance.[9] The mosaic appears to shift because new disturbances occur in some portions of the landscape at the same time as formerly disturbed areas are growing back into forest or other mature vegetation. Reserves that are small relative to the spatial scale (patch size) of disturbance may experience radical fluctuations in the proportions of different seral stages over time, which in turn threaten populations that depend on certain stages. Many nature reserves are smaller than the area likely to be disturbed by a single wildfire or windstorm, and therefore are quite vulnerable to loss of habitat diversity and associated species.

If a core reserve is to maintain a relatively stable mix of seral stages and species over time, it must be large enough that only a relatively small part of it is disturbed at any one time. Another requirement is that a source of colonists (that is, reproducing population of the same species) exists within the reserve or within a reasonable dispersal distance so that populations can be re-established on disturbed sites (see Fig. 2). Disturbance patch sizes and spatial distribution, successional dynamics, potential refugia (areas within the reserve, or nearby, that are not likely to be disturbed), and dispersal capacities of species, are the ecological factors to keep in mind when planning reserves around natural disturbance regimes.

Pickett and Thompson[76] used these criteria to define a "minimum dynamic area" as "the smallest area with a natural disturbance regime, which maintains internal recolonization sources, and hence minimizes extinction." In theory, a minimum dynamic area should be able to manage itself and maintain habitat diversity and associated native species with no human intervention. Shugart and West[92] estimated that landscapes must be some 50-100 times larger than average disturbance patches in order to maintain a relative steady-state ("quasi-equilibrium") of habitats. In a steady-state landscape, the proportions of different seral stages in the overall landscape would be relatively constant over time, even though the sites occupied by various seral stages would change. A steady state may never be reached in some ecosystem types, such as those regularly experiencing large, catastrophic fires.[5] Romme and Knight[82] concluded that Yellowstone National Park is not large enough to exist in equilibrium with its disturbance regime, and that a steady state for the Greater Yellowstone Ecosystem as a whole is unlikely.

Very large but infrequent fires are characteristic of many landscapes in the central and northern Rocky Mountains. Surveys by Ayres[3] in the Lewis and Clarke Reserve of Montana (which included what are now the Bob Marshall, Great Bear, and Scapegoat Wilderness Areas) showed that over 300,000 hectares (750,000 acres) burned in the area in one year, 1889, and up to 136,000 hectares in a single fire. About 100,000 ha burned in the Canyon Creek Fire in 1988.[45] Similarly, fires in the Coast Range of Oregon have burned as much as 200,000 hectares.[95] In the Northwest, fires become smaller and less severe, but considerably more frequent, along a transect from the Washington Cascades to northern California.[97,57]

Although most fires are mosaics, a minor portion of the affected acreage being of stand-replacement intensity, the immense scale of many natural disturbances provides a strong argument for establishing large reserves. Active fire suppression is simply not a reasonable option in these cases. Experience and research have shown that fire is a natural part of these systems and essential to their overall diversity; moreover, many fires are impossible to suppress.[13]

A core reserve, by itself, need not encompass a minimum dynamic area. The concept implies that all natural seral stages be maintained over time and that dispersal distances between similar habitats are surmountable by native species; but there is no reason to insist that a steady state of seral stages be maintained, for this may rarely occur in nature.[77] The steady-state concept is useful, however, in the sense that reserves large enough to be close to steady state will likely experience lower extinction rates than reserves where habitat conditions fluctuate wildly over time. Larger landscapes buffer the effects of disturbance on diversity of habitats and species.[91] Thus, the scale of management planning, including core reserves and surrounding multiple-use lands, should encompass something approximating a minimum dynamic area whenever possible; the complex as a whole can be managed to maintain habitat diversity.

Conclusions

This article has reviewed some considerations for designing wilderness recovery networks at a regional scale (basic recommendations are summarized in the Appendix). The spotlight has been on North America, but projects of the type described here are urgently needed worldwide. I have emphasized terrestrial ecosystems for the simple reason that this is my area of expertise. However, protection and restoration of entire regional landscapes, as promoted by The Wildlands Project, are intended to maintain aquatic and terrestrial ecosystems alike. Nevertheless, many aquatic biota will require special recovery techniques, such as dechannelization of streams and elimination of dams and water diversion structures, in order to be healthy again. Furthermore, marine ecosystems, particularly near shore, are in serious jeopardy in many regions and need comprehensive recovery strategies of their own.

I have highlighted the needs of large carnivores in this article because they are often acutely sensitive to human activity and hence are among the best indicators of wilderness condition. However, the stated goals of The Wildlands Project should make clear that not just carnivores, but all of biodiversity is the target of our efforts. Many sensitive assemblages (for example, neo-tropical migrant songbirds, anadromous fish, freshwater bivalve mollusks, and declining amphibian species) will require focused recovery work for many years to come. Importantly, ecosystem-level protection does not imply that we neglect individual species or assemblages on the brink of extinction; endangered species legislation should be strengthened and rigorously enforced to help imperilled taxa.

No substitute exists for detailed on-the-ground knowledge of the ecology and natural history of a region. General theory and insights gained from other regions are helpful, but do not transfer directly to areas with different biotas and histories. A long-term conservation plan for a region should be hypothesis-driven and adaptive; that is, we should scientifically test various approaches and techniques to see how well they work, then adjust our management to reflect new knowledge. Activists should enlist the participation of ecologists and other scientists most familiar with a region: if the latter will not themselves get actively involved in a project (some are afraid of tarnishing their cherished credibility as impartial observers), they may at least provide information and guidance. If all else fails, become an expert yourself on the ecology of your region!

The discussions above should make clear that planning on a bioregion by bioregion basis is incomplete. Because of the huge areas required to support viable populations of some animals and the necessity for all species to be able to migrate long distances with climate change, inter-regional and inter-continental planning is mandatory. The Wildlands Project will facilitate planning among regions and provide access to critical information, both scientific and tactical, to activists and planners world-wide. We now need, all of us, to put this information and strategy into action.

Acknowledgments

The ideas presented here are part of a continually evolving text, parts of which have appeared in unpublished reports prepared on contract with the National Audubon Society and The Nature Conservancy. Many individuals, but especially Rick Brown, Peter Brussard, Blair Csuti, Jim DePree, Mitch Friedman, Dennis Murphy, Jim Pissot, Mike Scott, Michael Soulé, David Wilcove, and George Wuerthner, have commented on various versions of these reports and their predecesors. I thank John Davis for his eternally helpful editorial advice and Dave Foreman for wild inspiration.

Appendix: A Recipe for Reserve System Design and Management

A regional reserve system consists of three basic ingredients: core reserves, multiple-use (buffer) zones, and corridors. Select your core reserves first, then interconnect and buffer them across the landscape. For many species, properly managed multiple-use zones will function as corridors. An archipelago of core reserves in a matrix with low road density and low-intensity human activities will function well for most native species. Multiple-use zones at a landscape scale can be corridors at a regional scale. Whenever possible, however, significant core reserves should be linked by corridors containing roadless interiors.

I. Core Reserves

A. Selecting Sites and Drawing Boundaries

1. If large reserves (e.g. national parks, large wilderness areas) already exist in the landscape, enlarge boundaries to encompass adjacent and nearby old-growth stands, roadless areas, and other ecologically important patches.

2. If no large reserves presently exist in the landscape, draw boundaries to enclose geographic clusters of the following:

    a. managed areas (wilderness areas, RNAs, designated wildlife habitat areas, etc.)

    b. old-growth stands

    c. other natural (virgin) forest

    d. other natural areas and sensitive sites

    e. roadless areas

    f. rare species occurrences (e.g., as mapped by heritage programs)

    g. under-represented vegetation types.

3. At a regional scale, be certain that the overall system of core reserves includes the following:

    a. representative examples of all major ecosystem (vegetation) types native to the region, and all seral stages within each type

    b. centers of species richness and endemism (as determined, for example, by gap analysis projects)

    c. population centers of large, wide-ranging species (especially large carnivores)

    d. populations of other rare species

    e. entire environmental gradients (all physical habitat types).

B. How Large Should a Core Reserve Be?

    1. The basic issue is context. Core reserves surrounded by adequate buffer zones and/or well inter-connected by corridors can be quite small (say, 10,000 to 100,000 acres) and still function effectively for most target species.

    2. Assuming that core reserves are isolated and surrounded by hostile habitat (tree farms, agriculture, urban areas), they may need to be one to 10 million hectares (2.5 to 25 million acres) or more in size to maintain viable populations of large mammals in the long term.

    3. For vegetation types prone to high-intensity fire, core reserves millions of acres in size are needed to maintain seral stage diversity across the landscape. Silvicultural manipulations or prescribed fires will be necessary to maintain seral stage diversity in cases where core reserves are too small.

C. How Should Core Reserves Be Managed?

    1. All else being equal, the smaller the reserve, the more management is necessary (particularly to protect the reserve from human activity and other external influences).

    2. Core reserves should be managed as roadless areas (wilderness). All roads should be permanently closed. The more roads remain open, the less viable the reserve for many sensitive species.

    3. Restoration will be the management emphasis in most cases. This is particularly true when a core reserve encompasses a cluster of relatively pristine sites in a matrix of human disturbed habitat, or where no pristine habitat remains for a certain vegetation type.

    4. Restorative management includes the following:

        a. thinning of plantations and planting of other native species, if necessary, to diversify structure and species composition.

        b. thinning of fire-suppressed (and artificially dense) stands of naturally open-structured forest types (e.g., longleaf pine or ponderosa pine) prior to reintroduction of fire;

        c. reintroduction of fire, either by allowing natural fires to burn or by prescribed fires that mimic natural fires in intensity, frequency (return interval), and seasonality;

d. road closures and (where necessary) re-vegetation;

e. soil innoculation with mycorrhizal fungae, where necessary to re-establish native vegetation;

f. control or (where possible) elimination of exotic species (including livestock);

g. reintroduction of extirpated native species (for example, large carnivores).

II. Multiple-Use Zones

A. Primary Functions of Multiple-Use Zones

1. Ameliorization of edge effects on small core reserves (insulate core reserves from intensive land use).

2. Provision of a suitable matrix for animals to move between core reserves (i.e., enhance connectivity).

3. Provision of supplemental habitat for populations of native species inhabiting reserves, and stabilize population dynamics.

4. Protection of developed areas from depredating large mammals that reach relatively high densities in core reserves.

B. Design and Management Criteria

1. Two or more zones are recommended, so that a gradation of use intensity exists from the core reserve to the developed landscape.

2. Inner zones should have low road density (no more than 0.5 mile/square mile) and low-intensity use. Uses might include:

a. non-consumptive recreation (hiking, cross-country skiing, birding);

b. primitive camping;

c. wilderness hunting and fishing;

d. low-intensity silviculture (light selective cutting);

e. limited habitat manipulation for target plant and animal species.

3. Outer zones may have higher road density (but still no more than one mile/square mile) and more intensive use. Uses might include:

a. heavier recreational use (but no off-road vehicles) and camp-grounds;

b. New Forestry silviculture (e.g., partial retention harvests), selection forestry, or other forestry experiments;

c. habitat manipulations to favor target wildlife.

III. Corridors

A. *Primary Functions of Corridors*

1. Provision of dwelling habitat, as extensions of reserves.
2. Provision for seasonal movements of wildlife (e.g., elk and mule deer migrations).
3. Provision for dispersal and genetic interchange between core reserves.
4. Allowance for latitudinal and elevational range shifts with climate change.

B. *Design and Management Criteria*

1. Connect small core reserves within clusters by corridors at a landscape scale. Connect clusters of reserves by bigger corridors at a regional scale.
2. Multiple corridors inter-connecting a network of core reserves provide functional redundancy and mitigate against disturbance.
3. Corridors aligned up-slope, coast-inland, and south-north will facilitate migration of species with climate change.
4. Known wildlife migratory routes should be incorporated into corridors.
5. When possible, corridors should be zoned to have roadless core areas in their centers, enveloped by buffer zones.
6. When possible, route corridors through parts of the landscape with lowest road density.
7. When intersecting roads, corridors should include wildlife underpasses, tunnels, bridges, viaducts, and other structures that allow wildlife to cross roads safely.
8. Width considerations:
    a. if centred on a river, a corridor should extend each slope to overlap the ridge line (ridgetop to ridgetop);
    b. if centred on a ridge, the corridor should extend downslope on either side to encompass the riparian zones;
    c. longer corridors, all else being equal, need to be wider;
    d. corridors surrounded by inhospitable habitat (i.e., unbuffered) need to be wider;
    e. corridors at a landscape scale should be at least three times wider than the longest distance penetrated by edge effects (for example, if edge effects penetrate 200 metres, the corridor should be 600 metres wide in order to include a 200 metre-wide core of interior habitat);

f. corridors at a regional scale (say, more than 10 miles long), should average at least one mile wide, with bottlenecks no thinner than 1/4 to 1/2 mile. Corridors several miles wide are needed if the objective is to maintain resident populations of large carnivores (necessary if the corridor is longer than normal dispersal distances);

g. a corridor designed with a particular species in mind will function better the more similar its habitat is to the preferred dwelling habitat of that species; corridors with resident populations of target species are optimal.

9. When designing inter-connected networks of reserves at a regional scale, the planning area should be at least the minimum area necessary to insure demographic and genetic integrity of the most space-demanding species.

10. Do not allow corridors to substitute for the protection of large, intact core reserves or to divert attention from managing the landscape as a whole in an ecologically responsible manner.

References (literature cited):

1. Adams, A. W., "Migration Papers," in *Elk of North America: Ecology and Management*, J.W. Thomas and D.E. Toweill, eds. Stackpole Books, 1982, pages 301-32.
2. Agee, J. K., and D. R. Johnson, *Ecosystem Management for Parks and Wilderness*, University of Washington Press, Seattle, 1988.
3. Ayres, H. D., "Lewis and Clarke Forest Reserve," in *21st Annual Report, Part 5*, U. S. Department of Interior, Geological Survey, 1901, pages 27-80.
4. Bader, M., "Biological Geography: Think Big for Northern Rockies Wildlife," *The Networker*, June 1991: 3-10.
5. Baker, W. L., "Landscape Ecology and Nature Reserve Design in the Boundary Waters Canoe Area," *Ecology* 70 (1989): 23-35.
6. Batisse, M., "Development and Implementation of the Biosphere Reserve Concept and its Applicability to Coastal Regions," *Environmental Conservation* 17 (1990):111-116.
7. Bennett, A. F., *Habitat Corridors: Their Role in Wildlife Management and Conservation*, Arthur Rylah Institute for Environmental Research, Dept. of Conservation and Environment, Victoria, Australia, 1990.
8. Bleich, V. C., J. D. Wehausen, and S. A. Holl, "Desert-dwelling Mountain Sheep: Conservation Implications of a Naturally Fragmented Distribution," *Conservation Biology* 4 (1990): 383-390.
9. Bormann, F. H., and G. E. Likens, *Pattern and Process in a Forested Ecosystem*, Springer-Verlag, 1979.

10. Brody, A. J., *Habitat Use by Black Bears in Relation to Forest Management in Pisgah National Forest, North Carolina,*. M.S. Thesis, University of Tennessee, 1984.
11. Brussard, P. F., "The Role of Ecology in Biological Cconservation," *Ecological Applications* 1 (1991): 6-12.
12. Buechner, M., "Conservation in Insular Parks: Simulation Models of Factors Affecting the Movement of Animals Across Park Boundaries," *Biological Conservation* 41 (1987): 57-76.
13. Christensen, N. L., J. K. Agee, P. F. Brussard, J. Hughes, et al., "Interpreting the Yellowstone Fires of 1988," *BioScience* 39 (1989): 67-685.
14. Connor, E. F., and E. D. McCoy, "The Statistics and Biology of the Species-Area Relationship," *American Naturalist* 113 (1979): 791-833.
15. Craighead, F. C., Track of the Grizzly, Sierra Club Books, 1979.
16. Craighead, J. J., K. R. Greer, R. R. Knight, and H. I. Pac, *Grizzly Bear Mortalities in the Yellowstone Ecosystem 1959-1987*, Montana Fish, Wildlife, and Parks, Inter-agency Grizzly Bear Study Team, Craighead Wildlife-Wildlands Institute, National Fish and Wildlife Foundation, 1988.
17. Davis, G. D., "Preservation of Natural Diversity: The Role of Ecosystem Representation within Wilderness," Paper presented at National Wilderness Colloquium, Tampa, Florida, January 1988.
18. Davis, M. B., "Quaternary History and the Stability of Forest Communities," D. C. West, H. H. Shugart, and D. B. Botkin, eds., *Forest Succession*, Springer-Verlag, 1981.
19. den Boer, P. J., "On the Survival of Populations in a Heterogeneous and Variable Environment," *Oecologia* 50 (1981): 39-53.
20. den Boer, P. J., "The Survival Value of Dispersal in Terrestrial Arthropods," *Biological Conservation* 54 (1990): 175-192.
21. Diamond, J. M., "The Island Dilemma: Lessons of Modern Biogeographic Studies for the Design of Natural Preserves," *Biological Conservation* 7 (1975): 129-146.
22. Diamond, J. M., "Island Biogeography and Conservation: Strategy and Limitations, *Science* 193 (1976): 1027-1029.
23. Diamondback, "Ecological Effects of Roads (or, The Road to Destruction)," J. Davis, ed. *Killing Roads: A Citizen's Primer on the Effects and Removal of Roads*, Earth First! Biodiversity Project Special Publication, 1990.
24. Dyer, M. L., and M. M. Holland, "The Biosphere-Reserve Concept: Needs for a Network Design," *BioScience* 41 (1991): 319-325.
25. Foreman, D., *How to Conduct a Wilderness Study*, Unpublished report, The Wilderness Society, Southwest Region, 1976.
26. Foreman, D., and H. Wolke, *The Big Outside*, Ned Ludd Books, 1989.

27. Fox, S. R., *John Muir and His Legacy: The American Conservation Movement*, Little, Brown and Co., 1981.
28. Franklin, J. F., and R. T. T. Forman, "Creating Landscape Patterns by Cutting: Ecological Consequences and Principles," *Landscape Ecology* 1 (1987): 5-18.
29. Graham, R. W., "Response of Mammalian Communities to Environmental Changes During the Late Quaternary," in J. Diamond and T. J. Case, eds., *Community Ecology*, Harper and Row, 1986.
30. Grumbine, R. E., "Protecting Biological Diversity Through the Greater Ecosystem Concept," *Natural Areas Journal* 10 (1990): 114-120.
31. Harris, L. D., *The Fragmented Forest: Island Biogeography Theory and the Preservation of Biotic Diversity*, University of Chicago Press, 1984.
32. Harris, R. L., "Toward a Theory of Inter-refuge Corridor Design," *Conservation Biology* 6 (1992): 293-295.
33. Hough, J., "Biosphere Reserves: Myth and Reality," *Endangered Species Update* 6 (1988): 1-4.
34. Howe, R. W., G. J. Davis, and V. Mosca, "The Demographic Significance of 'Sink' Populations," *Biological Conservation* 57 (1991): 239-255.
35. Hummel, M. ed., *Endangered Spaces: The Future for Canada's Wilderness,*. Key Porter Books, 1989.
36. Hummel, M., *Conservation Strategy for Large Carnivores in Canada*, World Wildlife Fund Canada, 1990.
37. Hunter, M. L., G. L. Jacobson, and T. Webb, "Paleoecology and the Coarse-filter Approach to Maintaining Biological Diversity," *Conservation Biology* 2 (1988): 375-385.
38. Janzen, D. H., "The Eternal External Threat," *Conservation Biology: The Science of Scarcity and Diversity*, M. E. Soulé, ed., Sinauer Associates, 1986.
39. Keystone Center, *The, Final Consensus Report of the Keystone Policy Dialogue on Biological Diversity on Federal Lands*, The Keystone Center, 1991.
40. Knight, R., B. M. Blanchard, and L. L. Everhardt, "Mortality Patterns and Population Sinks for Yellowstone Grizzly Bears, 1973-1985," *Wildlife Society Bulletin* 16 (1988): 121-125.
41. Kushlan, J. A., "Design and Management of Continental Wildlife Reserves: Lessons from the Everglades," *Biological Conservation* 15 (1979): 281-290.
42. LeFranc, M. N., M. B. Moss, K. A. Patnode, and W. C. Sugg., eds., *Grizzly Bear Compendium*, National Wildlife Federation and Interagency Grizzly Bear Committee, 1987.
43. Leopold, A., *A Sand County Almanac*, Oxford University Press, 1949.
44. Levins, R., "Extinction," *Some Mathematical Questions in Biology. Lec-*

tures on Mathematics in the Life Sciences, Vol. 2, M. Gerstenhaber, ed., American Mathematical Society, 1970.

45. Losensky, B. J., *A Comparison of the 1988 Fire Season to the Historical Role of Fire for the Bob Marshall-Great-Bear-Scapegoat Wilderness Complex*, Unpublished Report, 1990.

46. MacArthur, R. H., *Geographical Ecology: Patterns in the Distribution of Species*, Princeton University Press, 1972.

47. MacArthur, R. H., and E. O. Wilson, *The Theory of Island Biogeography,*. Princeton University Press, 1967.

48. Margules, C., and M. B. Usher, "Criteria Used in Assessing Wildlife Conservation Potential: A Review," *Biological Conservation* 24 (1981): 115-128.

49. Mattson, D. J., "Human Impacts on Bear Habitat Use", *International Conference on Bear Research and Management* 8 (1990): 33-56.

50. Mattson, D. J., and R. R. Knight, *Effects of Access on Human-caused Mortality of Yellowstone Grizzly Bears,*. USDI National Park Service Interagency Grizzly Bear Study Team Report, 1991B.

51. Mattson, D. J., and R. R. Knight, *Application of Cumulative Effects Analysis to the Yellowstone Grizzly Bear Population*, USDI National Park Service Interagency Grizzly Bear Study Team Report, 1991C.

52. Mattson, D. J., R. R. Knight, and B. M. Blanshard, "The Effects of Developments and Primary Roads on Grizzly Bear Habitat Use in Yellowstone National Park, Wyoming," *International Conference on Bear Research and Management* 7 (1987): 259-273.

53. Mattson, D. J. and M. M. Reid, "Conservation of the Yellowstone Grizzly Bear," *Conservation Biology* 5 (1991): 364-372.

54. McLellan, B. N., and D. M. Shackleton, "Grizzly Bears and Resource Extraction Industries: Effects of Roads on Behaviour, Habitat Use, and Demography," *Journal of Applied Ecology* 25 (1988): 451-460.

55. Mech, L. D., S. H. Fritts, G. L. Radde, and W. J. Paul, "Wolf Distribution and Road Density in Minnesota," *Wildlife Society Bulletin* 16 (1988): 85-87.

56. Metzgar, L. H., *Comments on USFWS, 1990, Grizzly Bear Recovery Plan, Revised Draft*, University of Montana, 1990.

57. Morrison, P. H. and F. J. Swanson, "Fire History and Pattern in a Cascade Range Landscape," *General Technical Report PNW-GTR-254*, USDA Forest Service, Pacific Northwest Forest and Range Experiment Station, 1990.

58. Newmark, W. D., "Legal and Biotic Boundaries of Western North American National Parks: A Problem of Congruence," *Biological Conservation* 33 (1985): 197-208.

59. Noss, R. F., "A Regional Landscape Approach to Maintain Diversity," *BioScience* 33 (1983): 700-706.

60. Noss, R. F., "Wilderness Recovery and Ecological Restoration: An

Example for Florida," *Earth First!* 5(8) (1985): 18-19.

61. Noss, R. F., "Protecting Natural Areas in Fragmented Landscapes," *Natural Areas Journal* 7 (1987): 2-13.

62. Noss, R.F., "From Plant Communities to Landscapes in Conservation Inventories: A look at the Nature of Conservancy (USA)," *Biological Conservation* 41 (1987): 11-37.

63. Noss, R. F., "What Can Wilderness do for Biodiversity?" *Preparing to Manage Wilderness in the 21st Century*, P. Reed, ed., General Technical Report SE-66, USDA Forest Service, Southeastern Forest Experiment Station, 1990.

64. Noss, R. F., "Indicators for Monitoring Biodiversity: A Hierarchical Approach," *Conservation Biology* 4 (1990): 355-364.

65. Noss, R. F., *Protecting Habitats and Biological Diversity. Part I: Guidelines for Regional Reserve Systems*, National Audubon Society, 1991.

66. Noss, R. F., *Landscape Conservation Priorities in the Greater Yellowstone Ecosystem, Report to The Nature Conservancy, 1991.*

67. Noss, R. F., "Sustainability and Wilderness," *Conservation Biology* 5 : (1991)120-122.

68. Noss, R. F., "Wilderness Recovery: Thinking Big in Restoration Ecology," *Environmental Professional* 13 (1991): 225-234.

69. Noss, R. F., "Wildlife Corridors," *Ecology of Greenways*, D. S. Smith and P. A. Hellmund, eds., University of Minnesota Press, 1993.

70. Noss, R. F., "Sustainable Forestry or Sustainable Forests?" *Defining Sustainable Forestry*, J. T. Olson, ed. Island Press, in press.

71. Noss, R. F., and L. D. Harris, "Nodes, Metworks, and MUMs: Preserving Diversity at All Scales," *Environmental Management* 10 (1986): 299-309.

72. Odum, E. P., "Optimum Population and Environment: A Georgia Microcosm," *Current History* 58 (1970): 355-359.

73. Odum, E. P. and H. T. Odum, "Natural Areas As Necessary Components of Man's Total Environment," *Transactions of the North American Wildlife and Natural Resources Conference* 37 (1972): 178-189.

74. Omernick, J. M., *Ecoregions of the United States*, Map, U.S. Environmental Protection Agency, 1986.

75. Peters, R. L. and J. D. S. Darling, "The Greenhouse Effect and Nature Reserves," *BioScience* 35 (1985): 707-717.

76. Pickett, S. T. A. and J. N. Thompson, Patch dynamics and the design of nature reserves, *Biological Conservation* 13 (1978): 27-37.

77. Pickett, S. T. A. and P. S. White, *The Ecology of Natural Disturbance and Patch Dynamics*, Academic Press, 1985.

78. Picton, H. D., "A Possible Link Between Yellowstone and Glacier Grizzly Bear Populations," *International Conference on Bear Research and Management* 6 (1986): 7-10.

79. Pulliam, H. R. "Sources, Sinks, and Population Regulation," *American*

Naturalist 132 (1988): 652-661.

80. Pyle, R. M., "Management of Natural Reserves," *Conservation Biology: An Evolutionary-Ecological Perspective*, M. E. Soulé and B. A. Wilcox, eds., Sinauer Association, 1980.

81. Romme, W. H. and D. G. Despain, "Historical Perspective on the Yellowstone Fires of 1988," *BioScience* 39 (1989): 695-699.

82. Romme, W. H. and D. H. Knight, "Landscape Diversity: The Concept Applied to Yellowstone Park," *BioScience* 32 (1982): 664-670.

83. Romme, W. H. and M. G. Turner, "Implications of Global Climate Change for Biogeographic Patterns in the Greater Yellowstone Ecosystem," *Conservation Biology* 5 (1991): 373-386.

84. Runte, A., *National Parks: The American Experience*, Second edition. University of Nebraska Press, 1987.

85. Salwasser, H., "Sustainability as a Conservation Paradigm," *Conservation Biology* 4 (1990): 213-216.

86. Sayen, J., "The Appalachian Mountains: Vision and Wilderness," *Earth First!* 7(5) (1987): 26-30.

87. Schonewald-Cox, C. M., "Conclusions, Guidelines to Management: A Beginning Attempt," *Genetics and Conservation: A Reference for Managing Wild Animal and Plant Populations*, C. M. Schonewald-Cox, S. M. Chambers, B. MacBryde, and W. L. Thomas, eds., Benjamin/Cummings, 1983.

88. Schonewald-Cox, C. M., and J. W. Bayless, "The Boundary Model: A Geographical Analysis of Design and Conservation of Nature Reserves," *Biological Conservation* 38 (1986): 305-322.

89. Scott, J. M., B. Csuti, K. Smith, J. E. Estes, and S. Caicco, "Gap Analysis of Species Richness and Vegetation Cover: An Integrated Biodiversity Conservation Strategy," *Balancing on the Brink of Extinction: The Endangered Species Act and Lessons for the Future*, K. Kohm, ed., Island Press, 1991.

90. Shaffer, M. L., "Minimum Population Sizes for Species Conservation," *BioScience* 31 (1981): 131-134.

91. Shugart, H. H., and S. W. Seagle, "Modeling Forest Landscapes and the Role of Disturbance in Ecosystems and Communities," *The Ecology of Natural Disturbance and Patch Dynamics*, S. T. A. Pickett and P. S. White, eds. Academic Press, 1985.

92. Shugart, H. H., and D. C. West, "Long-term Dynamics of Forest Ecosystems," *American Scientist* 69 (1981): 647-652.

93. Soulé, M. E. ed., *Viable Populations for Conservation*, Cambridge University Press, 1987.

94. Soulé, M. E., and D. Simberloff, "What Do Genetics and Ecology Tell Us About the Design of Nature Reserves?" *Biological Conservation* 35 (1986): 19-40.

95. Spies, T. A., and S. P. Cline, "Coarse Woody Debris in Forests and

Plantations of Coastal Oregon," *From the Forest to the Sea: A Story of Fallen Trees*, C. Maser, R. F. Tarrant, J. M. Trappe, and J. F. Franklin, eds., General Technical Report PNW-GTR-229, USDA Forest Service, Pacific Northwest Research Station, 1988.

96. Stankey, G. H., "The Role of Management in Wilderness and Natural-area Preservation," *Environmental Conservation* 9 (1982):149-155.

97. Swanson, F. J., J. F. Franklin, and J. R. Sedell, "Landscape Patterns, Disturbance, and Management in the Pacific Northwest, USA," *Changing Landscapes: An Ecological Perspective*, L. S. Zonneveld and R. T. T. Forman, eds., Springer-Verlag, 1990.

98. Thiel, R. P., "Relationship Between Road Density and Wolf Habitat Suitability in Wisconsin," *American Midland Naturalist* 113 (1985): 404-407.

99. Thomas, C. D., "What Do Real Population Dynamics Tell Us About Minimum Viable Population Sizes?" *Conservation Biology* 4 (1990): 324-327.

100. Thomas, J. W., ed., *Wildlife Habitats in Managed Forests: The Blue Mountains of Oregon and Washington*, USDA Forest Service Agricultural Handbook No. 553, 1979.

101. Thomas, J. W., E. D. Forsman, J. B. Lint, et al., *A Conservation Strategy for the Northern Spotted Owl*, USDA Forest Service, USDI Bureau of Land Management, USDI Fish and Wildlife Service, USDI National Park Service, 1990.

102. Usher, M. B., ed., *Wildlife Conservation Evaluation*, Chapman and Hall, 1986.

103. UNESCO, *Task Force on Criteria and Guidelines for the Choice and Establishment of Biosphere Reserves*, Man and the Biosphere Report No. 22, 1974.

104. Van Horne, B. "Density as a Misleading Indicator of Habitat Quality," *Journal of Wildlife Management* 47 (1983): 893-901.

105. Walter, H. S., "Small Viable Population: The Redtailed Hawk of Socorro Island," *Conservation Biology* 4 (1990): 441-443.

106. White, P. S., and S. P. Bratton, "After Preservation: Philosophical and Practical Problems of Change," *Biological Conservation* 18 (1980): 241-255.

107. Wiens, J. A., *The Ecology of Bird Communities, Vol. 2, Processes and Variations*, Cambridge University Press, 1989.

108. Wilcove, D. S., C. H. McLellan, and A. P. Dobson, "Habitat Fragmentation in the Temperate Zone," *Conservation Biology: The Science of Scarcity and Diversity*, M. E. Soulé, ed., Sinauer Associates, 1986.

109. Wilcox, B. A. and D. D. Murphy, "Conservation Strategy: The Effects of Fragmentation on Extinction", *American Naturalist* 125 (1985): 879-887.

6

Ecological Planning
for Human Use

Introduction

Doug Aberley

Once a web of cores and corridors is created across the landscape, human communities will need to very clearly understand the capacity of the remaining space and ecosystems to provide for their sustenance. With much of the planet's surface bounded away from exploitation in this manner, there will be much less land left for human activities such as settlement, cultivation, resource extraction, and transportation. A critical question thus becomes, "How then will communities in bioregions decide how to use the limited land, water, soil and other resources in a manner that is equitable and sustainable?"

The disciplines of community, regional and resource planning were established to deal with this question and have each operated from a belief in the same basic action model. Goals and objectives are formulated, alternatives are then examined for actualizing these goals, the consequences of each alternative is predicted and evaluated, a decision for action is made, the decision implemented and the results of the chosen action are monitored. At the core of this model reside the dual beliefs that broadly informed rationality can be applied towards the achievement of public good, and that the planning process must be subservient to the will of those who hold political or economic power. It is clearly evident that this method of guiding human action has not entirely worked. As a consequence, many citizens and planners have been attempting to describe new or adapted planning processes that center on the quest for qualitiative progress based upon the achievement of social justice and ecological sustainability.

Frederick Steiner is one such individual. Trained as a planner at the University of Pennsylvania during a turbulent and exciting time, he was taught in part by Ian McHarg, an expatriate Scot who had adapted the Geddesian regional survey technique to a contemporary graphic format. He went on to become both an academic and working planner, taking the Geddes/McHarg survey technique into real communities and regions and making significant positive modifications. The result is the descripition of a socially and ecologically balanced planning process that is as well evolved as any that professional planning has devised. It proposes a step-by-step means by which human communities can understand their social requirements for achieving a good quality of life, and then how they can relate these aspirations to biophysical opportunities and constraints. This ecological planning process is especially notable because it is described in a manner that demystifies professional practice into inventory and implementation steps that can be navigated by any diligent citizen of any bioregion.

The ecological planning processes proposed by Steiner and Noss approach the issue of sustainability from two different directions. One is based entirely on the protection of an interconnected, continent-wide system of all representative ecosystems, placing the esssential requirement to protect biological diversity before the immediate needs of human communities. The second process describes how individual human communities can identify social, economic and cultural goals for sustainability and then match these aspirations to constraints and opportunities associated with surrounding landscapes. What becomes obvious from the juxtapositioning of these two strategies is that they would benefit from a severe intertwining. This is the fundamental challenge of the bioregional movement: how will it unify action to transform human societies that are embedded in a web of representative, protected ecosystems? While the answer to this question has not been totally defined yet, it is quickly evolving from the practice of social change activists rooted in scores of bioregions. We can only hope that this experience is communicated to a broader, anxiously awaiting audience in the same courageous manner that Reed Noss, Frederick Steiner, and their contemporaries have demonstrated.

♦

The Living Landscape: An Ecological Approach to Landscape Planning

Frederick Steiner

There is a need for a common language among all those concerned .about social equity and ecological parity, a common method which can transcend disciplinary territorialism, be applicable to all levels of government, and incorporate both social and environmental concerns. For, as the poet Wendell Berry has observed, "The mentality that destroys a watershed and then panics at the threat of flood is the same mentality that gives institutionalized insult to black people then panics at the prospect of race riots." [3]

An approach is needed that can assist planners to analyze the problems of a region as they relate to each other, to the landscape, and to the national and local political economic structure. This might be called an applied human ecology. Each problem is linked to the community in one or more specific ways. Banking is related to real estate, is related to development pressure, is related to schools, is related to rising tax base, and is related to retirees organizing against increasing property taxes. This approach identifies how people are affected by these chain reactions and presents options for the future based on those impacts.

Aldo Leopold, the University of Wisconsin wildlife biologist, was perhaps the first to advocate an "ecological ethic" for planning. [17,18] He was joined by such individuals as Lewis Mumford and Benton MacKaye, [23] who were strongly influenced by the Scottish biologist and town planner, Patrick Geddes and the English garden city advocate

Ebenezer Howard. Others who have proposed and/or developed ecological approaches for planning include the Canadian forester, G. Angus
Hills;[13] the Israeli architect and town planner, Artur Glikson;[11] the American landscape architects, Philip Lewis,[19] Ian McHarg,[26] Anne Spirn,[39] and
John Lyle;[21] the American regional planner, Jon Berger (with John Sinton[2]), and the French geographer and planner, Jean Tarlet.[43]

Ecological Planning Method

What is meant by ecological planning? Planning is a process which
utilizes scientific and technical information for considering and reaching
consensus on a range of choices. Ecology is the study of the relationship
of all living things, including people, to their biological and physical
environments. *Ecological planning* may be defined as the use of biophysical and sociocultural information to suggest opportunities and constraints for consensual decision-making about the use of the landscape.

Ian McHarg has summarized a framework for ecological planning in
the following way:

All systems aspire to survival and success. This state can be
described as syntropic-fitness-health. Its antithesis is entropic-mis-
fitness-morbidity. To achieve the first state requires systems to find
the fittest environment, adapt it and themselves. Fitness of an
environment for a system is defined as that requiring the minimum
of work and adaptation. Fitness and fitting are indications of health
and the process of fitness is health giving. The quest for fitness is
entitled adaptation. Of all the instrumentalities available for man
for successful adaptation, cultural adaptation in general and planning in particular, appear to be the most direct and efficacious for
maintaining and enhancing human health and wellbeing.[27]

Arthur Johnson explained the central principle of this theory in the
following way:

The fittest environment for any organism, artifact, natural and
social ecosystem, is that environment which provides the [energy]
needed to sustain the health or well-being of the organism/arti-
fact/ecosystem. Such an approach is not limited by scale. It may
be applied to locating plants within a garden as well as to the
development of a nation.[15.]

The ecological planning method is primarily a procedure for studying
the biophysical and sociocultural systems of a place to reveal where a
specific land use may be best practiced. As Ian McHarg has summarized

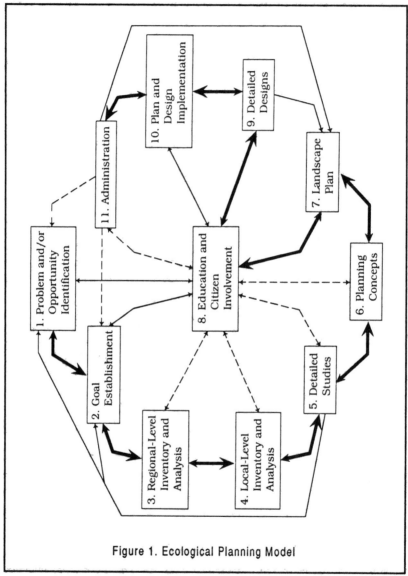

Figure 1. Ecological Planning Model

repeatedly in his writings and many public presentations:

The method defines the best areas for a potential land use at the convergence of all or most of the factors deemed propitious for the use in the absence of all or most detrimental conditions. Areas meeting this standard are deemed intrinsically suitable for the land use under consideration.

As presented in Figure 1, there are eleven interacting steps. An issue or group of related issues is identified by a community—that is, some collection of people—in step 1. These issues are problematic or present an opportunity to the people or the environment of an area. Goals are then established in step 2 to address the problem(s). Next, in steps 3 and 4, inventories and analyses of biophysical and sociocultural processes are conducted, first at a larger level, such as a drainage basin or an appropriate regional unit of government, and second at a more specific level, such as a watershed or a local government.

In step 5, detailed studies are made that link the inventory and analysis information to the problem(s) and goal(s). Suitability analyses are one such type of detailed study. Step 6 involves the development of concepts and options. A landscape plan is then derived from these concepts in step 7. Throughout the process, a systematic effort is made to educate and involve citizens. Such involvement is important in each step but especially so in step 8 when the plan is explained to the affected public. In step 9, detailed designs are made that are specific at the individual land-user or site level.

These designs and the plan are implemented in step 10. In step 11, the plan is administered. The heavier arrows in Figure 1 indicate the flow from step 1 to 11. Smaller arrows between each step suggest a feedback system whereby each step can modify the previous step and, in turn, be changed from the subsequent step. Additional arrows indicate other possible modifications through the process. For instance, detailed studies of a planning area (step 5) may lead to the identification of new problems or opportunities or the amendment of goals (steps 1 and 2). Detailed designs (step 9) may change the landscape plan, and so on. Once the process is complete and the plan is being administered and monitored (step 11), the view of the problems and opportunities facing the region and the goals to address these problems and opportunities may be altered, as is indicated by the dashed lines in Figure 1.

This process is adapted from the conventional planning process and its many variations (see, for instance Hall;[12] Roberts;[37] McDowell;[25] Moore;[30] and Stokes et al.,[42] as well as those suggested specifically for landscape planning: Lovejoy;[20] Fabos;[8] Zube;[51] Marsh ;[24] and Duchhart[6]). Unlike some of these other planning processes, design plays an important role in this method. Each step in the process contributes to and is affected by a plan and implementing measures, which may be the official controls of the planning area. The plan and implementing measures may be viewed as the results of the process, although products may be generated from each step. The approach to ecological planning developed by McHarg and his colleagues at the University of Pennsylvania differs slightly from the one presented here. The Pennsylvania, or McHarg, model places a greater emphasis on inventory, analysis, and synthesis. This one places more emphasis on the establishment of goals, implementation, administration, and public participation, yet does attempt to do so in an ecological manner.

Step 1: Identification of Planning Problems and Opportunities

Human societies face many social, economic, political, and environmental problems and opportunities. Since a landscape is the interface between social and environmental processes, landscape planning addresses those issues that concern the inter-relationship between people and nature. The planet presents many opportunities for people and there is no shortage of environmental problems.

Problems and opportunities lead to specific planning issues. For instance, suburban development is occurring on prime agricultural land, which local officials consider a problem. A number of issues arise, such as land-use conflicts between new suburban residents and farmers, and division of financial responsibility for public services for the newly developed areas. Another example might be an area with the opportunity for new development because of its scenic beauty and recreational amenities, such as an ocean beach or mountain town: how can the new growth be accommodated while protecting the natural resources that are attracting people to the place?

Step 2: Establishment of Planning Goals

In a democracy, the people of a region establish goals through the political process. Elected representatives will identify a particular issue affecting their region—a steel plant is closing, suburban sprawl is threatening agricultural land, or a new power plant is creating a housing boom. After issues have been identified, then goals are established to address the problem. Such goals should provide the basis for the planning process.

Goals articulate an idealized future situation. In the context of this method, it is assumed that once goals have been established there is a commitment by some group to address the problem or opportunity identified in step 1. Problems and opportunities can be identified at various levels. Local people can recognize a problem or opportunity and then set a goal to address it. As well, issues can be national, international, or global in scope. Problem solving, of which goal setting is a part, may occur at many levels or combinations of levels. Although goal setting is obviously dependent on the cultural-political system, the people affected by a goal should be involved in its establishment.

Goal-oriented planning has long been advocated by many community planners. Such an approach has been summarized by Herbert Gans:

The basic idea behind goal-oriented planning is simple; that planners must begin with the goals of the community—and of its people—and then develop those programs which constitute the best means for achieving the community's goals, taking care that the consequences of these programs do not result in undesirable behavioral or cost consequences.[10]

There are some good examples of goal-oriented planning, such as Oregon's mandatory land-use law.[34,7,16] However, although locally generated goals are the ideal, too often goals are established by a higher level of government. Many federal and state laws have mandated planning goals for local government, often resulting in the creation of new regions to respond to a particular federal program. These regional agencies must respond to wide-ranging issues that generate specific goals for water and air quality, resource management, energy conservation, transportation, and housing. No matter at what level of government goals are established, information must be collected to help elected representatives resolve underlying issues. Many goals, particularly those which are the focus of this essay, require an understanding of biophysical processes.

Step 3: Landscape Analysis, Regional Level

After a community has identified the problems and opportunities that it faces and has reached some consensus concerning its goals to address those issues, then the information can be collected to achieve community goals. Information about nature has often been used in an ad hoc manner in planning. Only that information needed to achieve a specific goal is collected—and too often it is disconnected information. For instance, since flooding is recognized by a community as a hazard to human safety, the responsible elected officials adopt a goal to prevent buildings in flood-prone areas. These areas are mapped and building restricted. The goal is one-dimensional.

The basic premise of ecology is that everything is connected to everything else. As a result, the ecological approach differs from more traditional methods. Whereas in conventional planning only the flood-prone areas are identified, in ecological planning, the complex matrix of factors related to flooding would be considered. Flooding is the result of the interaction of several natural phenomena—rainfall, bedrock, terrain, temperature, and vegetation, for instance. Since ecological planning rests on an understanding of relationships, broader-range information about the biophysical processes of an area must be collected and analyzed. Moreover, the sequence of collecting it is important.

Older, larger-scale components of the landscape exert a strong influence on more ephemeral elements. Regional climate and geology help determine soils and water drainage systems of an area that, in turn, affect what vegetation and animals will inhabit a place. As a result, in ecological planning one begins the inventory with the older elements and proceeds to the youngest.

When conducting such an inventory, it is useful to identify boundaries so that the various biophysical elements can be compared with each other over the same spatial area and at the same scale. Often such a planning area is defined by legislative goals, as, for instance, with the New Jersey Pinelands.

Ideally, several levels of inventories from regional to local are undertaken. A hierarchy of levels is identified so that the planning area may be understood as part of a larger system and specific places may be seen as parts of a whole. The drainage basin at the regional level and the watershed more locally are ideal units of analysis for ecological planning. A *watershed* is an area drained by a river or river system, also called a *catchment area* or, at a larger scale, a *drainage basin*. Eugene Odum suggests the watershed as "a practical ecosystem unit for management that combines natural and cultural attributes,"[33] while Peter Quinby[36] notes that watershed boundaries can be used as ecosystem boundaries. The watershed is a handy unit that contains biological, physical, social, and economic processes. Watersheds have discrete boundaries yet can vary in scale, providing flexibility for adaptation to social, economic, and political concerns. Watersheds also offer linkages between the elements of regions, making them an ideal unit of analysis since the flow of water, which provides the linkage throughout the watershed, may be easily visualized.

The use of drainage basins and watersheds for planning is not new. John Wesley Powell, who introduced the term *region* to North America, essentially suggested the use of watersheds in his 1879 plan for the American West. The use of watersheds is also consistent with past efforts of watershed conservancies and river basin commissions, such as the Delaware River Basin Commission, the Columbia River Basin Commission, and the Tennessee Valley Authority; with programs of the U.S. Soil Conservation Service (which may be renamed the Natural Resources Conservation Service), the Army Corps of Engineers, the National Parks Service, and the U. S. Forest Service; and with joint Canadian-American efforts in the Great Lakes region. But more often than not, units other than watersheds—political boundaries, most frequently—are used. Still the principle of hierarchy can apply to political boundaries, with counties or other similar levels of government forming the regional scale, and cities or towns being used as the unit for local landscape analysis.

Conventional approaches to planning have incorporated socio-economic analyses. Connecting such studies to biophysical information for planning is relatively new. Planners use a variety of types of social information, and these materials fall into three basic categories: existing data, new information from existing data, and original information. These data include quantitative information, such as the number of people living in an area counted by a census, as well as more qualitative data, such as the perceptions of people about the visual impacts of a new roadway or dam.

Planning projects and programs require different types of social information. For example, a growth management plan requires an estimate of future population, and economic and development trends. This quantitative information can be derived from existing sources. Conversely, for the placement of a new electric transmission line, planners need to collect original, qualitative information about perceptions and reactions through interviews with affected residents. Because of the variety of possible planning projects and programs, a blanket prescription cannot be given for the specific social inventories that should be conducted. The issues that have stimulated the planning process as well as the goals that have been identified to resolve those problems and opportunities will determine the types of data to be collected and analyzed.

An understanding of current and possible future population trends and characteristics will probably be essential for a community to achieve many of its goals. In Oregon, for instance, local governments are required to address specific goals concerning agriculture and housing. As a result, planners must inventory and analyze information concerning trends in farm population (such as whether it is growing or declining) and characteristics of the agricultural community (such as the average age of farmers). Planners must also analyze population trends and characteristics and forecast future possibilities to make recommendations about housing needs.

To accomplish this, planners need to understand local economies. For example, it is important to know the percentage that farming contributes to the economic base of a community, as well as the primary commodities and their markets. Through an analysis of the local agricultural economy, planners can determine how healthy it is, whether or not it is worth protecting, and if intervention is necessary to improve local farming systems. The economic base of the community helps planners analyze community needs. If the economic base is comprised of primary industries (such as farming, fishing, mining, and logging) rather than those of the tertiary sector (such as retail, wholesale, and services), then demands for housing, for instance, will be different. Where primary industries are involved, it may be necessary for houses to be relatively close to farmland, the ocean, the mountains, or forests. With tertiary industries, the linkage between home and workplace may be less spatially dependent.

Conventional planning processes have considered and incorporated population and economic studies. But the social characteristics have not been related to the landscape—a major difference between conventional approaches and ecological planning. Through an ecological approach, social processes are connected to landscape features. For instance, agriculture can be related to specific combinations of biophysical elements that vary with crops. Wheat requires different climate, water, and soil characteristics than do cranberries. Rural housing has different needs than highrise apartments. Different users of the land—cranberry farmers or highrise apartment dwellers—place different demands on the landscape as well.

Each human community must be viewed as having unique characteristics. The population growth of a major Texas city—Dallas, Texas, for

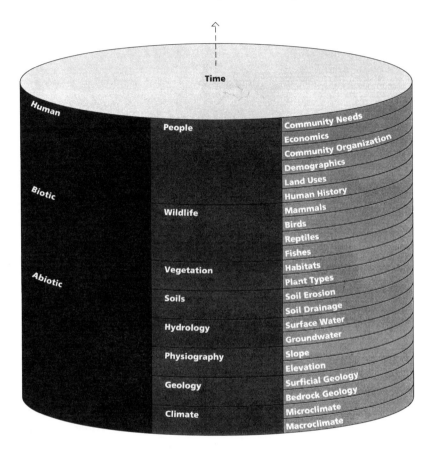

Figure 2. The layer-cake model illuminates the relationship among elements across the landscape. The elements are mapped and superimposed to reveal landscape ecological process for planning and design. The layer-cake model is based on the work of McHarg[44] as reinterpreted by Steiner[40] and drawn by Alfred C. Sanft.

instance—of 500 people per year may not be dramatic or even the source of concern. But in a rural west Texas country, the same growth may be quite significant and have consequences for several land uses, especially agriculture and housing. Although ranching may have great symbolic value in Dallas, the number of real cowboys may be few, while in a west Texas county, people actively engaged in ranching may constitute the most important economic sector. Certainly, the landscape in Dallas, and the biophysical process that created it, differs from that of west Texas. As a result, each place—whether in Texas, Oregon, or New Jersey, or Wales, North Holland, or Tuscany—must be inventoried and analyzed for its special qualities.

Step 4: Landscape Analysis, Local Level

During step 4, processes taking place in the more specific planning area are studied. The major aim of local-level analysis is to obtain insight into natural processes and human plans and activities in the immediate area. Such processes can be viewed as the elements of a system, with the landscape a visual expression of the system.

This step in the ecological planning process, like the previous one, involves the collection of information concerning the appropriate physical, biological, and social elements that constitute the planning area. Since cost and time are important factors, existing published and mapped information is the easiest and fastest to gather. If budget and time allow, however, inventory and analysis may be best accomplished by an interdisciplinary team collecting new information. In either case, this step is an interdisciplinary collection effort that involves search, accumulation, field checking, and mapping of data.

Ian McHarg and his colleagues have developed a layer-cake simulation model that provides a central group of biophysical elements for the inventory. McHarg's model has been expanded in Figure 2. Categories include geology, physiography, groundwater, surface water, soils, climate, vegetation, wildlife, and people. UNESCO, in its Man and the Biosphere Program, has developed a more exhaustive list of possible inventory elements (Table 1).

Land classification systems are valuable for analysis at this stage because they may allow the planner to aggregate specific information into general groupings. Such systems are based on inventoried data and on needs for analysis. Many government agencies in the United States and elsewhere have developed land classification systems that are helpful. The Soil Conservation Service, the U.S. Forest Service, the U.S. Fish and Wildlife Service, and the U.S. Geological Survey (USGS) are agencies that have been notably active in land classification systems. However, there is not a consistency of data sources even in North America. In urban areas, a planner may be overwhelmed with data for inventory and analysis. In remote rural areas, on the other hand, even a Soil Conserva-

Table 1. UNESCO Total Environmental Checklist: Components and Processes

Natural Environment — Components

Soil	Energy Resources
Water	Fauna
Atmosphere	Flora
Mineral Resources	Micro-organisms

Natural Environment — Processes

Biogeochemical cycles	Fluctuations in animal and plant growth
Irradiation	Changes in soil fertility, salinity,
Climatic processes	alkalinity
Photosynthesis	Host/parasite interactions, and
Animal and plant growth	epidemic processes

Human Population — Demographic Aspects

Population Structure:	Population size
• Age	Population density
• Ethnicity	Fertility and mortality rates
• Economic	Health statistics
• Educational	
• Occupational	

Human Activities and the Use of Machines

Migratory movements	Mining
Daily mobility	Industrial activities
Decision making	Commercial activities
Exercise and distribution of	Military activities
authority	Transportation
Administration	Recreation activities
Farming, fishing	Crime rates

Societal Groupings

Governmental groupings	Information media
Industrial groupings	Law-keeping media
Commercial groupings	Health services
Political groupings	Community groupings
Religious groupings	Family groupings
Educational groupings	

Products of Labor

The built-environment:	Food
• Buildings	Pharmaceutical products
• Roads	Machines
• Railways	Other commodities
• Parks	

Culture

Values	Technology
Beliefs	Literature
Attitudes	Laws
Knowledge	Economic System
Information	

Source: Boyden, 1979.

tion Service survey may not exist, or may be old and unusable. An even larger problem is that there is little or no consistency in scale or in the terminology used among agencies. A recommendation of the National Agricultural Lands Study[31] was that a statistical protocol for federal agencies concerning land resource information be developed, led by the Office of Federal Statistical Policy and Standards. One helpful system that has been developed for land classification is the USGS Land Use and Land Cover Classification System (Table 2) .

Several American agencies are developing integrated mapping programs using geographic information systems (GIS). The U.S. Environmental Protection Agency's environmental monitoring and assessment program (EMAP) is partially based on the ideas of McHarg.[28] EMAP was proposed to be a broadly conceived ecosystem inventory integrating regional and national scales, allowing for monitoring and assessment, and designed to influence decision-making. The U.S. Fish and Wildlife Service has developed a comprehensive, national biological diversity information system, using GIS technology, to organize existing data and improve spatial aspects of environmental assessment.[5] The system is called Gap Analysis and identifies gaps in the representation of biological diversity in protected areas. Gap Analysis uses vegetation types and vertebrate and butterfly species as indicators of biodiversity.[38] The U.S. Fish and Wildlife Service and other federal agencies are collaborating with states in the Gap Analysis Program. In 1993, Secretary of the Interior Bruce Babbitt recommended a National Biological Survey which would provide nation-wide ecological data. These efforts indicate massive environmental data will soon be available, ultimately in digital form, in North America and globally.

The ability of the landscape planner and resource manager to inventory biophysical processes at the regional level may be uneven, but it is far better than their capability to assess human ecosystems. An understanding of human ecology is essential in conducting a socio-cultural inventory and analysis. Since humans are living things, *human ecology* may be thought of as an expansion of ecology—how humans interact with each other and their environments. Interaction then is used as both a basic concept and an explanatory device. As Gerald Young,[46,48,49,50] who has illustrated the multidisciplinary scope of human ecology, noted:

In human ecology, the way people interact with each other and with the environment is definitive of a number of basic relation-

Table 2: U.S. Geological Survey Land-Use and Land-Cover Classification System for Use With Remote Sensor Data

Level I	Level II
1. Urban or built-up land	11 Residential 12 Commercial and services 13 Industrial 14 Transportation, communications, and services 15 Industrial and commercial complexes 16 Mixed urban or built-up land 17 Other urban or built-up land
2. Agricultural land	21 Cropland and pasture 22 Orchards, groves, vineyards, nurseries, and ornamental horticulture 23 Confined feeding operations 24 Other agricultural land
3. Rangeland	31 Herbaceous rangeland 32 Shrub and brush rangeland 33 Mixed rangeland
4. Forest land	41 Deciduous forest land 42 Evergreen forest land 43 Mixed forest land
5. Water	51 Streams and canals 52 Lakes 53 Reservoirs 54 Bays and estuaries
6. Wetlands	61 Forested wetland 62 Non-forested wetland
7. Barren land	71 Dry salt flats 72 Beaches 73 Sandy areas other than beaches 74 Bare exposed rocks 75 Strip mines, quarries, and gravel pits 76 Transitional areas 77 Mixed barren land
8. Tundra	81 Shrub and brush tundra 82 Herbaceous tundra 83 Bare ground 84 Mixed tundra
9. Perennial snow ice	91 Perennial snowfields 92 Glaciers

Source: Anderson et al., 1976.

ships. Interaction provides a measure of belonging, it affects identity versus alienation, including alienation from the environment. The system of obligation, responsibility, and liability is defined through interaction. The process has become definitive of the public interest, as opposed to private interests which prosper in the spirit of independence.[47]

Step 5: Detailed Studies

Detailed studies link the inventory and analysis information to the problem(s) and goal(s). For example, suitability analyses, as explained by McHarg,[26] can be used to determine the fitness of a specific place for a variety of land uses, based on thorough ecological inventories and on the values of land users. The basic purpose of the detailed studies is to gain an understanding about the complex relationships between human values, environmental opportunities and constraints, and the issues being addressed. To accomplish this, it is crucial to link the studies to the local situation. As a result, a variety of scales may be used to explore linkages.

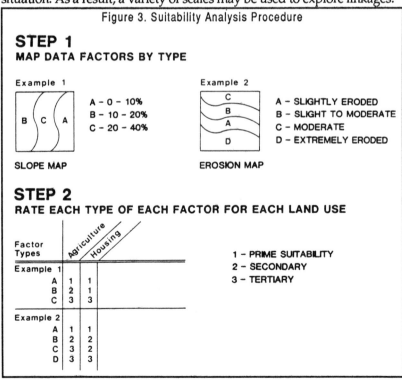

Figure 3. Suitability Analysis Procedure

STEP 1

MAP DATA FACTORS BY TYPE

Example 1

A - 0 - 10%
B - 10 - 20%
C - 20 - 40%

SLOPE MAP

Example 2

A - SLIGHTLY ERODED
B - SLIGHT TO MODERATE
C - MODERATE
D - EXTREMELY ERODED

EROSION MAP

STEP 2

RATE EACH TYPE OF EACH FACTOR FOR EACH LAND USE

Factor Types	Agriculture	Housing
Example 1		
A	1	1
B	2	1
C	3	3
Example 2		
A	1	1
B	2	2
C	3	2
D	3	3

1 - PRIME SUITABILITY
2 - SECONDARY
3 - TERTIARY

A simplified suitability analysis process is provided in Figure 3. There are several techniques that may be used to accomplish suitability analysis. Again, it was McHarg who popularized the "overlay technique."[26] This technique involves maps of inventory information superimposed on one another in order to identify areas that provide, first, opportunities for particular land uses, and second, constraints.[14] MacDougall[22] has criticized the accuracy of map overlays and made suggestions on how they may be made more accurate. Steinitz et al.[41] have provided a history of the use of hand overlays of mapped information, and Neckar[32] has written a profile of Warren Manning, who was responsible for the idea of overlaying maps to represent natural systems.

Although there has been a general tendency away from hand-drawn overlays, there are still occasions where they may be useful. For instance, they may be helpful for small study sites within a larger region or for certain scales of project planning. However, the limitations of hand-drawn overlays include, for instance, the fact that after more than three or four overlays they may become opaque. There are the accuracy

STEP 3
MAP RATINGS FOR EACH AND USE ONE SET OF MAPS FOR EACH LAND USE

Example 1   Example 2   Example 1   Example 2

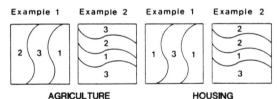

AGRICULTURE   HOUSING

STEP 4
OVERLAY SINGLE FACTOR SUITABILITY MAPS TO OBTAIN COMPOSITES. ONE MAP FOR EACH LAND USE

LOWEST NUMBERS ARE BEST SUITED FOR LAND USE

HIGHEST NUMBERS ARE LEAST SUITED FOR LAND USE

AGRICULTURE   HOUSING

questions raised by MacDougall[22] and others that are especially acute with hand-drawn maps, and there are limitations for weighting various values represented by map units.

Numerous GIS programs have been developed that overcome these limitations and replace the technique of hand-drawn overlays. Some of these programs are intended to model only positions of environmental processes or phenomena, while others are designed as comprehensive information storage, retrieval, and evaluation systems. These systems are intended to improve efficiency and economy in information handling, especially for large or complex planning projects.

Step 6: Planning Area Concepts, Options, and Choices

This step involves the development of concepts for the planning area. These concepts can be viewed as options for the future, based on the suitabilities for the use(s), that give a general conceptual model or scenario of how problems may be solved. This model should be presented in such a way that the goals can be achieved. Often more than one scenario has to be made. These concepts are based on a logical and imaginative combination of the information gathered through the inventory and analysis steps. The conceptual model shows allocations of uses and actions. The scenarios set possible directions for future management of the area and, therefore, should be viewed as a basis for discussion where choices are made by the community about its future.

Choices should be based on the goals of the planning effort. For instance, if it is the goal to protect agricultural land yet allow some low-density housing to develop, different organizations of the environment for those two land uses should be developed. Different schemes for realizing the desired preferences also need to be explored.

The Dutch have devised an interesting approach to developing planning options for their agricultural land re-allocation projects. Four land-use options are developed, each with the preferred scheme for a certain point of view. Optional land-use schemes of the area are made for nature and landscape, agriculture, recreation, and urbanization. These schemes are constructed by groups of citizens working with government scientists and planners. For instance, for the nature and landscape scheme, landscape architects and ecologists from the *Staatsbosbeheer* (Dutch Forest Service) work with citizen environmental action groups. For agriculture, local extension agents and soil scientists work with farm commodity organizations and farmer cooperatives. Similar coalitions are formed for recreation and urbanization. What John Friedmann[9] calls a dialogue process begins at the point where each of the individual schemes is constructed. The groups come together for mutual learning so that a consensus of opinion is reached through debate and discussion.

Various options for implementation also need to be explored, which must relate to the goal of the planning effort. If, for instance, the planning is being conducted for a jurisdiction trying to protect its agricultural land resources, then it is necessary not only to identify lands that should be protected but also the implementation options that might be employed to achieve the farmland protection goal.

Step 7: Landscape Plan

The preferred concepts and options are brought together in a landscape plan which gives a strategy for development at the local scale. The plan provides flexible guidelines for policy-makers, land managers, and land users about how to conserve, rehabilitate, or develop an area. Enough freedom should be left so that local officials and the land users can adjust their practices to new economic demands or social changes.

This step represents a key decision-making point in the planning process. Responsible officials, such as county commissioners or city council members, are often required by law to adopt a plan. The rules for adoption and the forms that the plans may take vary widely. Commonly in the United States, planning commissions recommend a plan for adoption to the legislative body after a series of public hearings. Such plans are officially called *comprehensive plans* in much of the United States, *general plans* in California and Arizona, and *master plans* in Colorado. In some states, such as Oregon, there are specific, detailed elements that local governments are required to include in such plans. Other states permit much flexibility to local officials for the contents of these plans. On public lands, various federal agencies—including the U.S. Forest Service, the National Park Service, and the U.S. Bureau of Land Management—have specific statutory requirements for land management plans.

The term *landscape plan* is used here to emphasize that such plans should incorporate natural and social considerations. A landscape plan is more than a land-use plan because it addresses the overlap and integration of land uses. It may involve the formal recognition of previous elements in the planning process, such as the adoption of policy goals, and should include both written statements about policies and implementation strategies, as well as a map showing the spatial organization of the landscape.

Step 8: Continued Citizen Involvement and Community Education

In step 8, the plan is explained to the affected public through education and information dissemination. Actually, such interaction occurs throughout the planning process, beginning with the identification of issues. Public involvement is especially crucial as the landscape plan is developed, because it is important to ensure that the goals established by the community will be achieved in the plan.

The success of a plan depends largely on how much people affected by the plan have been involved in its determination. There are numerous examples of both government agencies and private business suddenly announcing a plan for a project that will dramatically impact people without consulting those individuals first. The result is predictable—the people will rise in opposition to the project. The alternative is to involve people in the planning process, soliciting their ideas, and incorporating those ideas into the plan. Doing so may require a longer time to develop a plan, but local citizens will be more likely to support it than to oppose it and will often monitor its execution.

Step 9: Detailed Designs

To design is to give form and to arrange elements spatially. By making specific designs based on the landscape plan, planners can help decision makers visualize the consequences of their policies. Carrying policies through to arranging the physical environment gives meaning to the process by actually conceiving change in the spatial organization of a place. Designs represent a synthesis of all the previous planning studies. During the design step, the short-term benefits for the land users or individual citizen have to be combined with the long-term economic and ecological goals for the whole area.

Step 10: Plan and Design Implementation

Implementation is the employment of various strategies, tactics, and procedures to realize the goals and policies adopted in the landscape plan. On the local level, several different mechanisms have been developed to control the use of land and other resources. These techniques include voluntary covenants, easements, land purchase, transfer of development rights, zoning, utility extension policies, and performance standards. The preference selected should be appropriate for the region. For instance, in urban areas like King County, Washington, and Suffolk County, New York, traditional zoning has not been effective in protecting farmland. The citizens of these counties have elected to tax themselves to purchase development easements from farmers. In more rural counties like Whitman County, Washington, and Black Hawk County, Iowa, local leaders have found traditional zoning effective.

One implementation technique especially well suited for ecological planning is performance standards. Like many other planning implementation measures, *performance standards* is a general term that has been defined and applied in several different ways; basically, it means that criteria are established and must be met before a certain use will be permitted. These criteria are usually a combination of economic, environmental, and social factors. This technique lends itself to ecological planning because criteria for specific land uses can be based on suitability analysis.

Step 11: Administration

In this final step, the plan is administered. *Administration* involves monitoring and evaluating the plan on an ongoing basis. Amendments or adjustments will no doubt be necessary because of changing conditions or new information. To achieve the goals established for the process, planners should pay especial attention to the design of regulation review procedures and to the management of the decision-making process.

Administration may be accomplished by a commission comprised of citizens with or without the support of a professional staff. Citizens may also play an important role in administering local planning through participation via commissions and review boards that oversee local ordinances. To a large degree, the success of citizens' boards and commissions depends on the extent of their involvement in the development of the plans that they manage. Again, Oregon provides an excellent example of the use of citizens to administer a plan. The Land Conservation and Development Commission, comprised of seven members who are appointed by the governor and supported by a professional staff, is responsible for overseeing the implementation of the state land-use planning law. Another group of citizens, 1,000 Friends of Oregon, monitors the administration of the law. Public support of the law is evident from the defeat of several attempts to abolish mandatory state-wide land-use planning in Oregon.

Working Plans

A method is necessary as an organizational framework for landscape planners, and can be used to compare and analyze case studies. To fulfill their responsibilities to protect public health, safety, and welfare, planners should base their actions on a knowledge of what has and what has not worked in other settings and situations. A large body of case-study results can provide an empirical foundation for planners. A common method is helpful both for practicing planners and for scholars who should probe and criticize the nuances of such a method in order to expand and improve its utility.

The approach suggested here should be viewed as a working method. The pioneering forester, Gifford Pinchot, advocated a conservation approach to the planning of the national forests of the United States. His approach was both utilitarian and protectionist, and he believed "wise use and preservation of all forest resources were compatible."[45] To implement this philosophy, Pinchot in his position as chief of the U.S. Forest Service required "working plans." Such plans recognized the dynamic, living nature of forests. In the same vein, the methods used to develop plans should be viewed as a living process. However, this is not meant to imply that there should be no structure to planning methods. Rather, working planning methods should be viewed as something analogous to a jazz composition—not a fixed score but a basis for improvisation.

The method offered here has a landscape ecological—specifically human ecological—bias. As noted by the geographer Donald W. Meinig, "Environment sustains us as creatures; landscape displays us as cultures."[29] As an artifact of culture, landscapes are an appropriate focus for planners faced with land-use and environmental management issues. Ecology provides insight into landscape patterns, processes, and interactions. An understanding of ecology reveals how we interact with each other and our natural and built environments. We still know little of such relationships but our understanding is expanding all the time. As Ilya Prigogine and Isabelle Stengers have observed, "Nature speaks in a thousand voices, and we have only begun to listen."[35]

Excerpted from: Frederick Steiner, The Living Landscape: An Ecological Approach to Landscape Planning, 1991. McGrawHill, New York.

References

1. Anderson, James R., Ernest E. Hardy, John T. Roach, and Richard E. Witmer, *A Land Use and Land Cover Classification System for Use with Remote Sensor Data* (U.S. Geological Survey Professional Paper 964), USGPO, 1976, 28 pp.
2. Berger, Jonathan, and John W. Sinton, *Water, Earth, and Fire*, Johns Hopkins University Press, 1985, 228 pp.
3. Berry, Wendell, *A Continuous Harmony, Essays Cultural and Agricultural*, Harcourt Brace Jovanovich, 1972, 182 pp.
4. Boyden, Stephen, *An Integrative Ecological Approach to the Study of Human Settlements* (MAB Technical Notes 12), UNESCO, 1979, 87 pp.
5. Davis, Frank W., David M. Stoms, John E. Estes, Joseph Scepan, and J. Michael Scott, "An Information Systems Approach to the Preservation of Biological Diversity," *International Journal of Geographical Information Systems* 4(1): 55-78, 1990.
6. Duchhart, Ingrid, *Manual on Environment and Urban Development*, Ministry of Local Government and Physical Planning, Nairobi, Kenya, 1989, 86 pp.
7. Eber, Ronald, "Oregon's Agricultural Land Protection Program" in *Protecting Farmlands*, Frederick R. Steiner and John E. Theilacker (eds.), AVI Publishing Company, 1984, pp. 161-171.
8. Fabos, Julius Gy., *Planning the Total Landscape*, Westview Press, 1979, 181 pp.
9. Friedmann, John, *Retracking America*, Anchor Press/Doubleday, 1973, 289 pp.
10. Gans, Herbert J., *People and Plans*, Basic Books, 1968, 395 pp.
11. Glikson, Artur, *The Ecological Basis of Planning*, Matinus Nijhoff, 1971, 115 pp.
12. Hall, Peter, *Urban and Regional Planning*, Halsted Press/John Wiley & Sons, 1975, 312 pp.
13. Hills, G. A., *The Ecological Basis for Land-Use Planning*, (Research Report No. 46), Ontario Department of Lands and Forests, 1961, 204 pp.
14. Johnson, A. H., Jonathan Berger, and Ian L. McHarg, "A Case Study in Ecological Planning: The Woodlands, Texas" in *Planning the Uses and Management of Land*, Marvin T. Beatty, Gary W. Petersen, and Lester D. Swindale (eds.), American Society of Agronomy, Crop Science Society of America, and Soil Science Society of America, 1979, pp. 935-955.

15. Johnson, A. H., "Guest Editorial: Human Ecological Planning—Methods and Studies," *Landscape Planning* 8:107-108, 1981.
16. Knaap, Gerrit and Arthur C. Nelson, *The Regulated Landscape, Lessons on State Land-Use Planning from Oregon*, Lincoln Institute of Land Policy, 1992, 243 pp.
17. Leopold, Aldo, "The Conservation Ethic," *The Journal of Forestry*, 31(6):634-643, 1933.
18. Leopold, Aldo., *A Sand County Almanac and Sketches Here and There*, Oxford, 1949, 295 pp.
19. Lewis, Philip H., "Ecology: The Inland Water Tree," *American Institute of Architects Journal*, 51(8):59-63, 1969.
20. Lovejoy, Derek (ed.), *Land Use and Landscape Planning*, Barnes & Noble, 1973, 308 pp.
21. Lyle, John, *Design for Human Ecosystems*, Van Nostrand Reinhold, 1985, 279 pp.
22. MacDougall, E. Bruce, "The Accuracy of Map Overlays," *Landscape Planning*, 2:23-30, 1975.
23. MacKaye, Benton, "Regional Planning and Ecology," *Ecological Monographs*,10(3):349-353, 1940.
24. Marsh, William M., *Landscape Planning*, Addison-Wesley, 1983, 356 pp.
25. McDowell, Bruce D., "Approaches to Planning" in *The Practice of State and Regional Planning*, Frank S. So, Irving Hand, and Bruce D. McDowell (eds.), American Planning Association, 1986, pp. 3-22.
26. McHarg, Ian L., *Design With Nature*, Doubleday/The Natural History Press, 1969, 197 pp.
27. McHarg, Ian L., "Human Ecological Planning at Pennsylvania," *Landscape Planning* 8:109-120, 1981.
28. McHarg, Ian, John Radke, Jonathan Berger, and Kathleen Wallace, *A Protoypte Database for a National Ecological Inventory*, U.S. Environmental Agency, 1992, 113 pp.
29. Meinig, D. W., "Introduction" in *The Interpretation of Ordinary Landscapes*, D. W. Meinig (ed.)., Oxford University Press, 1979, pp. 1-7.
30. Moore, Terry, "Planning without Preliminaries," *Journal of the American Planning Association*, 54(4):525-528, 1988.
31. National Agricultural Lands Study, *Final Report*, U.S. Department of Agriculture and Council on Environmental Quality, 1981, 94 pp.
32. Neckar, Lance M., "Developing Landscape Architecture for the Twentieth Century: The Career of Warren H. Manning," *Landscape Journal* 8(2): 78-91, 1989.
33. Odum, Eugene P., *Fundamentals of Ecology*, W. B. Saunders, 1971, 574 pp.
34. Pease, James R., "Oregon's Land Conservation and Development Program" in *Planning for the Conservation and Development of Land Resources*, Frederick R. Steiner and Hubert N. van Lier (eds.), Elsevier Scientific Publishing, 1984, pp. 253-271.

35. Prigogine, Ilya and Isabelle Stengers, *Order Out Of Chaos*, Bantam Books, 1984, 349 pp.
36. Quinby, Peter A., "The Contribution of Ecological Sciences to the Development of Landscape Ecology: A Brief History," *Landscape Research*, 13(3):9-11, 1988.
37. Roberts, John C., "Principles of Land-Use Planning" in *Planning the Uses and Management of Land*, Marvin T. Beatty, Gary W. Petersen, and Lester D. Swindale (eds.), American Society of Agronomy, Crop Science Society of America, and Soil Science Society of America, 1979, pp. 47-63.
38. Scott, J. Michael, Frank Davis, Blair Csuti, Reed Noss, Bart Butterfield, Craig Groves, Hal Anderson, Steve Caicco, Frank D'Erchia, Thomas C. Edwards, Jr., Joe Ulliman, and R. Gerald Wright, "Gap Analysis: A Geographic Approach to Protection of Biological Diversity," *Wildlife Monographs*, 123:1-41, 1993.
39. Spirn, Anne Whiston, *The Granite Garden*, Basic Books, 1984, 334 pp.
40. Steiner, Frederick, *The Living Landscape*, McGrawHill, 1991, 356 pp.
41. Steinitz, Carl, Paul Parker, and Lawrie Jordan, "Hand-Drawn Overlays, Their History and Prospective Uses," *Landscape Architecture*, 66:444-455, 1976.
42. Stokes, Samuel N., A. Elizabeth Watson, Genevieve P. Keller, and J. Timothy Keller, *Saving America's Countryside*, Johns Hopkins University Press, 1989, 306 pp.
43. Tarlet, Jean, *La Planification Ecologique: Méthodes et Techniques*, Economica, 1985, 142 pp.
44. Wallace, McHarg, Roberts, and Todd, *Woodlands New Community* (4 volumes), 1971-1974, Various pages.
45. Wilkinson, Charles F., and H. Michael Anderson, "Land and Resource Planning in National Forests," *Oregon Law Review*, 64(1&2):1-373, 1985.
46. Young, Gerald L., "Human Ecology as an Interdisciplinary Concept: A Critical Inquiry," *Advances in Ecological Research*, 8:1-105, 1974.
47. Young, Gerald L., "Environmental Law: Perspectives from Human Ecology," *Environmental Law*, 6(2):289-307, 1976.
48. Young, Gerald L, *Human Ecology as an Interdisciplinary Domain: An Epistemological Bibliography*, Vance Bibliographies, 1978, 62 pp.
49. Young, Gerald L. (ed.), *Origins of Human Ecology*, Hutchinson Ross Publishing, 1983, 415 pp.
50. Young, Gerald L., "A Conceptual Framework for an Interdisciplinary Human Ecology," *Acta Oecologiae Hominis*, 1:1-136, 1989.
51. Zube, Ervin H., *Environmental Education*, Brooks/Cole, 1980, 148 pp.

7

Conclusion and Ecological Planning Reading List

Doug Aberley

This short anthology has been designed on the premise that ecological planning as a technique of applied bioregionalism could be uniquely delineated by bringing together the thoughts of a gifted group of social change activists. These contributions were then grouped around consideration of some simple questions. How is an ecological world view gained and expressed? How can human settlements and the bioregions they occupy be transformed to achieve sustainability? And, what techniques and information sources are available so that ecological planning processes are available for adaptation by reinhabitants living in a great variety of bioregions? This has been an ambitious agenda, but one adopted in the belief that an ability to nurture a sustainable future for the planet recedes with every moment that we don't challenge our ability to *act* towards change.

What conclusions do a reading of this anthology bring? From an editor's perspective, it is a mix of awe, impatience, and anxiety. These emotions are intertwined and difficult to describe, but worth the effort of exposition. The awe I feel comes from the power of the ideas that many of the authors communicate. In a great variety of styles, from poetic to journalistic to academic, these writers bring alive a great intellectual and practical purpose. They express ideas and methods that seem immediately right—no doubt connected to some remnant of tribal memory. At their best, the contributors to this volume have achieved a written "voice" that translates radical purpose with a rhythm that is powerful and enticing. Awe also comes from the perception that behind all the printed words are lives which have been wholly dedicated to the quest for positive change. In a post-modern world, there are few heroes and heroines; some of them appear in this book.

My impatience is a little harder to describe. Why don't the contributors, and many scores of their activist peers, work harder to evolve a more wholistic approach to social change? Why do we sometimes get the impression that each seer carves a separate niche, stylizes a separate vocabulary, acts on a separate stage, and guards a separate audience? It is possible to see how all the approaches to change can be combined into a greater alternative vision, but only with a degree of effort that most people have neither the time nor the interest to make. We certainly have the ability to overcome this specialization and to evolve a decentralized unity of the type that bioregionalism embodies. But my impatience stems from the desire to get on with it at a pace more in keeping with the onslaught of local and global crises that confront us.

Finally, my anxiety is rooted in the fact that, since the 1700s, there has been a tradition of resisting the idea that the world is a machine. But, at the end of the second millenium, it can be argued that the machine paradigm is *gaining*, rather than losing, strength. If the effect of all our movements has at best been limited, what impact will we have on a future world of genetic manipulation, cybernetics, instant portable communication, and corporate control of a planetary political agenda? Is it merely a dream that we can ever reform a paradigm so fundamentally and violently based on money and power as the only measures of progress?

We often hear the maxim that the work we are doing to promote social change will only be realized in the life-time of our children's children; further, that we are enlightened fools to invest so much in a result we will never see. I continue to be motivated by the first part of this thought, but I sometimes despair that our ultimate self-indulgence may be the belief that there will in fact be a recognizable future for our children to inherit. This makes me angry and even more determined that it will be much more than the illusion of a socially just and ecologically integrated human society that we achieve.

The social change that we will grow must be based on weaving many threads of knowledge and experience together. The exact strands that we choose for this weaving will be widely diverse, as will the order in which they are placed together. It will nonetheless be a process of local and regional craft made of two fundamental similarities. The new bioregion fabric we create will have a warp which designs how human life can be adapted within ecological carrying capacity, and a weft which intersects patterns of absolute social justice. In plateau and plain, in city or rural setting, the results of this patterning will be a great variety of vernacular expression, each a unique portrayal of the opportunity and limit of place. As variant as these patterns are, they will all have the same basic characteristic: they will all be flexible and strong, and able to be combined in endless patterns of wholistic association. This is as much as human society can possibly hope to achieve...futures by our own best design.

Ecological Planning Reading List

Ecological planning is not a narrow discipline with only several key texts which quickly represent its essence. It is a wholistic pursuit which requires growth of a broad range of understanding—a grounding—that can take many years to gain fully. This is not to say that one should not act to create the bioregional or reinhabitant alternative until this knowledge is perfectly achieved. It is more a signal that gaining ecological planning skills is a process that will unfold through years of reading, discussion, and practice. Ecological planning intrinsically requires familiarity with as many subjects as are needed for you to actualize a wholistic understanding of time and place, limit and opportunity, rights and responsibility.

An important purpose of this volume is to guide its readers into a process of learning about all the diverse aspects of ecological planning. To satisfy this goal I have included a reading list divided into thirty subject areas. Under each of these headings five or more key texts have been listed, each chosen for its clarity, success at summarizing subject matter, inclusion of a comprehensive background bibliography, or proven popularity. This bibliography is a tool, and as such it comes with some simple user instructions:

- The accent has been placed on contemporary titles, and books that provide access to earlier key writers through a summary or introduction to their life and thought. Please take time to read the original works which are summmarized.

- Note that there are often multiple titles listed for some authors. It is informative to see how a writer's interest changes and evolves over time.
- Although information on journal titles is listed, there are no journal articles included in the reading list. Please refer to bibliographies contributed by Reed Noss and Frederick Steiner for a sample of journal article titles currently available.
- There are no books listed which reflect local or regional treatment of each of the subject headings. Please check local bookstores for titles which relate specifically to your own territory.
- Due to space limitations the city of publication of each volume has not been included. This citation model is similarly employed by the primary reference for this reading list, *The Island Press Bibliography of Environmental Literature* (Island Press, 1993).
- *There is no substitute for experience.* As interesting as these books are, they will be pure indulgence unless leavened with walking ridgelines, driving a snow plow, growing food, arguing a point at a community meeting, or feeling the ache of *work!*

A final encouragement. Make sure that folks at your local library know that these are the books you'd like to see on its shelves. If you are a student, ask your course instructor to add them to reading lists, and to make them available in school libraries. Be persistent—without access to information that will aid the evolution of personal and community processes of social change, it can be a long and slow struggle to assemble these resources on a piecemeal basis. Good reading, good luck!

Aboriginal Peoples

Bodley, John H., *Tribal Peoples and Development Issues*, Mayfield, 1987; *Victims of Progress*, Mayfield, 1987.

Hughes, J. Donald, *Ecology in Ancient Civilzations*. University of New Mexico Press, 1975; *American Indian Ecology*, Texas Western Press, 1983.

Knudtson, Peter and David Suzuki, *Wisdom of the Elders*, Stoddart, 1992.

McNeeley, Jeffrey A. and David Pitt, eds., *Culture and Conservation: The Human Dimension in Environmental Planning*, Croom Helm, 1985.

Moody, Roger, ed., *The Indigenous Voice: Visions and Realities*, 2 Volumes, Zed Books, 1988.

Anarchism/Social Ecology

Alihen, Milla Aissa, *Social Ecology: A Critical Analysis*, Cooper Square, 1964.

Bookchin, Murray, *Post-Scarcity Anarchism*, Ramparts Press, 1971; *Toward An Ecological Society*, Black Rose Books, 1980; *The Ecology of Freedom: The Emergence and Dissolution of Hierarchy*, Cheshire Books, 1982; *Remaking Society*, Black Rose Books, 1989.

Clark, John, *The Anarchist Moment: Reflections on Culture, Nature, and Power*, Black Rose Books, 1984; ed., *Renewing the Earth: The Promise of Social Ecology*, Marshall Pickering, 1989.

Woodcock, George, *Anarchism: A History of Libertarian Ideas and Movements*, Harmondsworth, 1975.

Animals/Wildlife

DiSilvestro, Roger L., *Audubon Perspectives: Fight for Survival*, John Wiley, 1990.

Gilbert, Frederick F. and Donald G. Dodds, *The Philosophy and Practice of Wildlife Management*, Krieger, 1987.

Livingston, John A., *The Fallacy of Wildlife Conservation*, McClelland and Stewart, 1981.

Peek, James M., *A Review of Wildlife Management*, Prentice-Hall, 1986.

Singer, Peter, *In Defense of Animals*, Basil Blackwell, 1985; *Animal Liberation*, Avon Books, 1990.

Appropriate Technology

Burnham, Laurie, et al., eds., *The Renewable Energy Sourcebook*, Island Press, 1992.

Darrow, Ken and Mike Saxenian, *Appropriate Technology Sourcebook: A Guide to Books for Village and Small Scale Technology*, Volunteers In Asia, 1986.

The Real Goods Company, *Alternative Energy Sourcebook*, Ten Speed Press, 1992.

Todd, Nancy Jack and John Todd, *Tomorrow Is Our Permanent Address*, Lindisfarne/Harper and Row, 1980; *Bioshelters, Ocean Arks, City Farming: Ecology as the Basis of Design*, Sierra Club Books, 1984.

Wann, David, *Biologic: Environmental Protection By Design*, Johnson Books, 1990.

Architecture/Shelter

Alexander, Christopher, et al., *The Production of Houses*, Oxford University Press, 1985.

Crowther, Richard, *Ecologic Architecture*, Butterworth Architecture, 1992.

Fromm, Dorit, *Collaborative Communities: Cohousing, Central Living, and other*

Forms of Housing with Shared Facilities, Van Nostrand Reinhold, 1991.

Kahn, Lloyd, *Shelter*, Ten Speed Press, 1990.

McCamant, Kathryn and Charles Durrett, *Cohousing: A Contemporary Approach to Housing Ourselves*, Ten Speed Press, 1988.

Pearson, David, *The Natural House Book*, Conran Octopus, 1989.

Vale, Brenda and Robert Vale, *Green Architecture: Design for a Sustainable Future*, Thames and Hudson, 1991.

Biodiversity

Erhlich, Paul R. and Anne H. Erhlich, *Extinction: The Causes and Consequences of the Disappearance of Species*, Random House, 1981.

Grumbine, R. Edward, *Ghost Bears: Exploring the Biodiversity Crisis*, Island Press, 1992.

McNeely, Jeffrey A., *Economics and Biological Diversity*, International Union for Conservation of Nature and Natural Resources (IUCN), 1988; et al., *Conserving the World's Biological Diversity*, IUCN, 1990.

Norton, Bryan G, ed., *The Preservation of Species: The Value of Biological Diversity*, Princeton University Press, 1986; *Why Preserve Natural Variety?* Princeton University Press, 1987.

Wilson, E. O., *Biophilia*, Harvard University Press, 1984; *Biodiversity*, National Academy Press, 1988; *The Diversity of Life*, Harvard University Press, 1992.

Biogeography/Conservation Biology

Brown, J. H. and A. C. Gibson, *Biogeography*, C.V. Mosby Co., 1983.

Browne, J., *The Secular Ark: Studies in the History of Biogeography*, Yale University Press, 1983.

Fiedler, Peggy L. and Subodh Jain, *Conservation Biology: The Theory and Practice of Nature Conservation, Preservation, and Management*, Chapman and Hall, 1992.

Meilke, H. W., *Patterns of Life: Biogeography of a Changing World*, Unwin Hyman, 1989.

Primack, Richard B., *Essentials of Conservation Biology*, Sinauer, 1993.

Shafer, Craig L., *Nature Reserves: Island Theory and Conservation Practice*, Smithsonian, 1990.

Soulé, Micheal E., ed., *Conservation Biology: The Science of Scarcity and Diversity*, Sinauer, 1986.

Bioregionalism

Andruss, Van; et al., eds., *Home! A Bioregional Reader*, New Society Publishers, 1990.

Berry, Thomas, *The Dream of the Earth*, Sierra Club Books, 1988.

Plant, Christopher, and Judith Plant, *Turtle Talk: Voices For A Sustainable*

Future, New Society Publishers, 1990.

Sale, Kirkpatrick, *Dwellers In The Land: The Bioregional Vision*, New Society Publishers, 1985.

Snyder, Gary, *The Old Ways*, City Lights Books, 1977; *The Real Work: Interviews and Talks 1964-1979*, New Directions, 1980; *The Practice of the Wild*, North Point Press, 1990.

Cities

Benevolo, L., *The History of the City*, Scolar Press, 1980.

Drakakis-Smith, D., *The Third World City*, Routledge, 1990.

Gerreau, Joel, *Edge Cities, Life on the New Frontier*, Doubleday, 1991.

Gutkind, E. A., *International History of City Development*, 8 Volumes. Free Press of Glencoe/Macmillan, 1964-1972.

Jacobs, Jane, *The Death and Life of Great American Cities*, Random House, 1961; *The Economy of Cities*, Vintage Books, 1970; *Cities and The Wealth of Nations: Principles of Economic Life*, Vintage Books, 1985; *Systems of Survival*, Random House, 1992.

Mumford, Lewis, *The City in History: Its origins, its transformations, and its Prospects*, Penguin, 1961.

Sassen, Saskia, *The Global City: New York, London, Tokyo*, Princeton University Press, 1991.

Climate/Air

Gribbin, John R., *Hothouse Earth: The Greenhouse Effect and Gaia*, Grove Weidenfeld, 1990.

Lowry, William P., *Weather and Life: An Introduction to Biometeorology*, Academic Press, 1969.

Oliver, John E. and Rhodes W. Fairbridge, eds., *The Encyclopedia of Climatology*, Van Nostrand Reinhold, 1987.

Peters, Robert L. and Thomas Lovejoy, *Global Warming and Biological Diversity*, Yale University Press, 1992.

Schneider, Stephen H. and Randi Londer, *The Co-evolution of Climate and Life*, Sierra Club Books, 1984.

History of Conservation and Environmental Movements

Bramwell, Anna, *Ecology in the 20th Century: A History*, Yale University Press, 1989.

Merchant, Carolyn, *Radical Ecology: The Search For A Livable World*, Routledge, 1992.

Nash, Roderick F., *Wilderness and the American Mind*, Yale University Press, 1982; *The Rights of Nature: A History of Environmental Ethics*, University of Wisconsin Press, 1989; *American Environmentalism: Readings In Conservation History*, McGrawHill, 1990.

Sale, Kirkpatrick, *The Green Revolution: The American Environmental Move-ment 1962-1992*, Hill and Wang, 1993.
Worster, Donald, ed., *American Environmentalism: The Formative Period, 1860-1915*, John Wiley, 1973; *Nature's Economy: The Roots of Ecology*, Sierra Club Books, 1977; *The Ends of the Earth: Perspectives on Modern Environmental History*, Cambridge University Press, 1988.

Decentralism

Kohr, Leopold, *The Breakdown of Nations*, Routledge and Kegan Paul, 1957; *The Overdeveloped Nations: The Diseconomies of Scale*, Schocken Books, 1978.
Kropotkin, Peter, *Fields, Factories and Workshops Tomorrow*, Harper and Row, 1974.
Loomis, Mildred J., *Alternative Americas*, Universe Books, 1980.
Plant, Judith and Christopher Plant, eds., *Putting Power In Its Place: Create Community Control!* New Society Publishers, 1992.
Sale, Kirkpatrick, *Human Scale*, Perigee Books, 1980.
Schumacher, E. F., *Small Is Beautiful: Economics As If People Mattered*, Harper and Row, 1973.

Deep Ecology

Devall, Bill and George Sessions, *Deep Ecology: Living As If Nature Mat-tered*, Peregrine Smith, 1985.
Devall, Bill, *Simple In Means, Rich In Ends: Practicing Deep Ecology*, Pere-grine Smith, 1988; *Living Richly in an Age of Limits*, Peregrine Smith, 1993.
LaChapelle, Delores, *Earth Wisdom*, Finn Hill Arts, 1978; *Sacred Land, Sacred Sex: Rapture of the Deep*, Finn Hill Arts, 1988.
Naess, Arne, *Ecology, Community, and Lifestyle*, Cambridge University Press, 1989.
Tobias, Michael, ed., *Deep Ecology*, Avant Books, 1985.

Critique of Development/Globalization

Adams, Patricia, *Odious Debts: Loose Lending, Corruption and the Third World's Environmental Tragedy*, Earthscan, 1991; with Lawrence Solomon, *In The Name of Progress: The Underside of Foreign Aid*, Pollution Probe, 1991.
Chomsky, Noam, *Necessary Illusions: Thought Control in Democratic Socie-ties*, South End Press, 1989; *Year 501: The Conquest Continues*, South End Press, 1992.
Marchak, M. Patricia, *The Integrated Circus: The New Right and The Restruc-turing of Global Markets*, McGill-Queen's University Press, 1991.
Peet, Richard, *Global Capitalism: Theories of Societal Development*, Rout-

ledge, 1991.

Sachs, Wolfgang, ed., *The Development Dictionary: A Guide to Knowledge as Power*, Zed Books, 1992.

Shiva, Vandana, ed., *Close To Home: Women Reconnect Ecology, Health and Development World-wide*, New Society Publishers, 1994.

Eco-cities/Sustainable Communities

Aldous, Tony, *Urban Villages: A Concept for Creating Mixed-Use Urban Developments on a Sustainable Scale*, Urban Villages Group, 1992.

Berg, Peter, et al., eds., *A Green City Program for the San Francisco Bay Area and Beyond*, Planet Drum/Wingbow, 1990.

Calthorpe, Peter, *The Next American Metropolis*, Princeton Architectural Press, 1993.

Canfield, Christopher, ed., *Report of the First International Eco-city Conference*, Urban Ecology, 1990.

Engwicht, David, *Reclaiming Our Cities and Towns: Better Living with Less Traffic*, New Society Publishers, 1993.

Girardet, Herbert, *The Gaia Atlas of Cities: New Directions for Sustainable Urban Living*, Anchor/Doubleday, 1992.

Gordon, D., ed., *Green Cities: Ecologically Sound Approaches to Urban Space*, Black Rose Books, 1990.

Moorehouse, Ward, ed., *Building Sustainable Communities: Tools and Concepts for Self-Reliant Economic Change*, Bootstrap Press, 1989.

Nozick, Marcia, *No Place Like Home: Building Sustainable Communities*, Canadian Council on Social Development, 1992.

Register, Richard, *Eco-city Berkeley: Building Cities for a Healthy Future*, North Atlantic Books, 1987.

Roseland, Mark, *Toward Sustainable Communities: A Resource Book for Municipal and Local Governments*, National Round Table on the Environment and the Economy (Canada), 1992.

Van der Ryn, Sim and Peter Calthorpe, eds., *Sustainable Communities: A New Design Synthesis for Cities, Suburbs, and Towns*, Sierra Club, 1991.

Walter, Bob, Lois Arkin and Richard Crenshaw, eds., *Sustainable Cities: Concepts and Strategies for Eco-City Development*, Eco-Home Media, 1992.

Ecofeminism

Biehl, Janet, *Rethinking Ecofeminist Politics*, South End Press, 1991.

Diamond, Irene and Gloria Orenstein, eds., *Reweaving the World: The Emergence of Ecofeminism*, Sierra Club Books, 1990.

Merchant, Carolyn, *The Death of Nature: Women, Ecology, and the Scientific Revolution*, Harper and Row, 1980.

Mies, Maria, and Vandana Shiva, *Ecofeminism*, Zed Books, 1993.

Plant, Judith, *Healing The Wounds: The Promise of Ecofeminism*, New Society Publishers, 1989.

Ecological Planning

Alexander, Christopher, et al., *A Pattern Language: Towns, Buildings, Construction*, Oxford University Press, 1977; *A Timeless Way of Building*, Oxford University Press, 1979; *The Oregon Experiment*, Oxford University Press, 1975; *A New Theory of Urban Design*, Oxford University Press, 1987.

McHarg, Ian L., *Design With Nature*, Doubleday/Natural History Press, 1969.

Steiner, Frederick, *The Living Landscape: An Ecological Approach to Landscape Planning*, McGraw-Hill, 1991.

van Dresser, Peter, *Landscape for Humans: A Case Study of the Potentials for Ecologically Guided Development in an Uplands Region*, Biotechnic Press, 1972.

Ecology and Environmental Systems

Krebs, Charles J., *Ecology: The Experimental Analysis of Distribution and Abundance*, Harper Collins, 1985; *The Message of Ecology*, Harper and Row, 1988.

Miller Jr., G. Tyler, *Living In The Environment*, Wadsworth, 1992.

Odum, Eugene P., *Ecology and Our Endangered Life-Support Systems*, Sinauer, 1989.

Odum, Howard T., *Environment, Power and Society*, Wiley-Interscience, 1971.

Real, Leslie A. and James H. Brown, *Foundations of Ecology: Classic Papers with Commentaries*, University of Chicago Press, 1991.

New Economics

Daly, Herman E., *Steady State Economics*, Island Press, 1991; with John B. Cobb, Jr., *For The Common Good: Redirecting the Economy Toward Community, the Environment, and a Sustainable Future*, Beacon Press, 1989.

Hawken, Paul, *The Next Economy*, Ballantine, 1983; *The Ecology of Commerce: A Declaration of Sustainability*, Random House, 1993.

Henderson, Hazel, *Politics of the Solar Age: The Alternatives To Economics*, Doubleday, 1981; *Paradigms in Progress: Life Beyond Economics*, Knowledge Systems, 1992.

MaxNeef, Manfred A., *Human Scale Development: Conception, Application and Further Reflections*, Apex Press, 1991; with Paul Ekins, eds., *Real Life Economics: Understanding Wealth Creation*, Routledge, 1992.

Meeker-Lowry, Susan, *Economics as if the Earth Really Mattered*, New Society Publishers, 1988.

History of Environmental/Ecological Change

Bilsky, Lester J., *Historical Ecology and Social Change*, Kennikat Press, 1980.
Crosby, Alfred W., *Ecological Imperialism: The Biological Expansion of Europe, 900-1900*, Cambridge University Press, 1986.
Polanyi, Karl, *The Great Transformation: The Political and Economic Origins of Our Time*, Octagon, 1980.
Ponting, Clive, *A Green History of the World*, Penguin, 1991.
Sale, Kirkpatrick, *The Conquest of Paradise: Christopher Columbus and the Columbian Legacy*, Knopf, 1991.

Environmental Crises

Carson, Rachel, *Silent Spring*, Houghton Mifflin, 1962.
Commoner, Barry, *The Closing Circle: Nature, Man and Technology*, Knopf, 1972; *The Poverty of Power: Energy and the Economic Crisis*, Knopf, 1976; *Making Peace with the Planet*, Pantheon Books, 1990.
Ehrlich, Paul and Anne H. Ehrlich, *The Population Explosion*, Simon and Schuster, 1990.
Meadows, Donella H., Dennis L. Meadows and Jorgen Randers, *The Limits To Growth*, Signet, 1972; *Beyond The Limits: Confronting Global Collapse, Envisioning a Sustainable Future*, McClelland and Stewart, 1992.
Suzuki, David and Anita Gordon, *It's a Matter of Survival*, Stoddart, 1991.

Forestry

Goodland, Robert, ed., *Race to Save the Tropics: Ecology and Economics for a Sustainable Future*, Island Press, 1990.
Hammond, Herb, *Seeing the Forest Among the Trees: The Case for Wholistic Forest Use*, Polestar/Raincoast, 1991.
Loomis, Ruth and Merv Wilkinson, *Wildwood: A Forest for the Future*, Reflections, 1990.
Maser, Chris, *The Redesigned Forest*, R. and E. Miles, 1988; *The Forest Primeval*, Sierra Club Books, 1990; *Global Imperative: Restoring Harmony With Nature*, Stillpoint Press, 1992.
Perlin, John, *A Forest Journey: The Role of Wood in the Development of Civilization*, Harvard University Press, 1991.

Green Politics

Bahro, Rudolph, *From Red To Green*. Verso, 1984; *Building The Green Movement*, New Society Publishers, 1986.
Kelly, Petra, *Fighting for Hope*, South End Press, 1984.
Porritt, Jonathon, *Seeing Green: The Politics of Ecology Explained*, Basil Blackwell, 1984; *Where On Earth Are We Going?* BBC Books, 1990.
Spretnak, Charlene, *The Spiritual Dimension of Green Politics*, Bear and Co., 1986; with Fritjof Capra, *Green Politics: The Global Promise*, Bear and

Co., 1986.

Tokar, Brian, *The Green Alternative: Creating An Ecological Future*, New Society Publishers, 1987.

Landscape Ecology

Forman, Richard T. T. and Michel Godron, *Landscape Ecology*, John Wiley, 1986.

Hudson, Wendy E., *Landscape Linkages and Biodiversity*, Island Press, 1991.

Naveh, Zeev and Arthur S. Lieberman, *Landscape Ecology: Theory and Application*, Springer-Verlag, 1984.

Zonneveld, I. S. and R. T. T. Forman, eds., *Changing Landscapes: An Ecological Perspective*, Springer-Verlag, 1990.

Landscape Planning

Davidson, Donald A., ed., *Land Evaluation*, Van Nostrand Reinhold, 1986.

Hansen, A. J. and F. di Castri, *Landscape Boundaries*, Springer, 1991.

Hough, Michael, *City Form and Natural Processes: Towards a New Urban Vernacular*, Croom Helm, 1984; *Out of Place: Restoring Identity to the Regional Landscape*, Yale University Press, 1990.

Jackson, John B., *Discovering the Vernacular Landscape*, Yale University Press, 1984.

Lyle, John Tillman, *Design For Human Ecosystems: Landscape, Land Use and Natural Resources*, Van Nostrand Reinhold, 1985.

Marsh, William M., *Landscape Planning: Environmental Applications*, John Wiley, 1991.

Pregill, Philip and Nancy Volkman, *Landscapes in History: Design and Planning in the Western Tradition*, Van Nostrand Reinhold, 1993.

Landscape/Ecosystem Restoration

Berger, John, *Restoring the Earth*, Knopf, 1986; ed., *Environmental Restoration: Science and Strategies For Restoring the Earth*, Island Press, 1990.

Bradshaw, Anthony David and M. J. Chadwick, *The Restoration of Land: The Ecology and Reclamation of Derelict and Degraded Lands*, University of California Press, 1980.

Jordan, William R., III, Michael Gilpin and John Aber, eds., *Restoration Ecology: A Synthetic Approach to Ecological Research*, Cambridge University Press, 1990.

Kusler, Jon and Mary Kentula, *Wetland Creation and Restoration: The Status of the Science*, Island Press, 1990.

Margolin, Malcolm, *The Earth Manual: How to Work Wild Land Without Taming It*, Heyday Books, 1985.

Nilsen, Richard, ed., *Helping Nature Heal: An Introduction to Environmental Restoration*, Ten Speed Press, 1991.

Permaculture

Berry, Wendell, *The Unsettling of America: Culture and Agriculture*, Sierra Club, 1977; *Home Economics; Fourteen Essays*, North Point Press, 1987; *What Are People For?* North Point Press, 1990.
Carroll, C. Ronald and John H. Vandermeer, Peter Rossett, eds., *Agroecology*, McGraw-Hill, 1990.
Fukuoka, Masanobu, *The One Straw Revolution*, Rodale Press, 1978; *The Natural Way of Farming*, Japan Publications, 1985.
Jackson, Wes, *Alters of Unhewn Stone: Science and the Earth*, North Point Press, 1987; with Wendell Berry and B. Coleman, *Meeting the Expectations of the Land: Essays on Sustainable Agriculture*, North Point Press, 1984
Mollison, Bill, *Permaculture: A Designer's Manual*, Tagari, 1990.

Perception of Place and Mapping

Aberley, Doug, ed., *Boundaries of Home: Mapping for Local Empowerment*, New Society Publishers, 1993.
Downs, Roger M. and David Stea, *Maps In Minds: Reflections on Cognitive Mapping*, Harper and Row, 1977.
Hiss, Tony, *The Experience of Place*, Knopf, 1990.
Tuan, YiFu, *Topophilia: A Study of Environmental Perception, Attitudes, and Values*, Prentice-Hall, 1974.
Wood, Denis, *The Power of Maps*, Routledge, 1992.

Planning History and Theory

Friedmann, John and Clyde Weaver, *Territory and Function: The Evolution of Regional Planning*, University of California Press, 1979.
Friedmann, John, *Planning in The Public Domain: From Knowledge To Action*, Princeton University Press, 1987; *Empowerment: The Politics of Alternative Development*, Basil Blackwell, 1992.
Hall, Peter, *Great Planning Disasters*, University of California Press, 1982; *Cities of Tomorrow: An Intellectual History of Urban Planning and Design in the Twentieth Century*, Basil Blackwell, 1988; *Urban and Regional Planning*, Routledge, 1992.
Weaver, Clyde, *Regional Development and the Local Community: Planning, Politics and Social Context*, John Wiley, 1984.

Post-industrial Society

Drengson, Alan, *Beyond Environmental Crisis: From Technocrat to Planetary Person*, Peter Lang Publishing, 1989.
Elgin, Duane, *Voluntary Simplicity: An Ecological Lifestyle that Promotes Personal and Social Renewal*, Bantam Books, 1982.
Johnson, Warren, *Muddling Toward Frugality*, Shambala, 1979.

Milbrath, Lester W., *Envisioning A Sustainable Society: Learning Our Way Out*, State University of New York Press, 1989.
Roszak, Theodore, *Where The Wasteland Ends: Politics and Transcendence in Post-industrial Society*, Anchor/Doubleday, 1973; *Person/Planet: The Creative Disintegration of Industrial Society*, Anchor/Doubleday, 1978; *The Voice of the Earth*, Simon and Schuster, 1992.

Radical Environmentalism

Chase, Steve, ed., *Defending the Earth: A Dialogue Between Murray Bookchin and Dave Foreman*, South End Press, 1991.
Davis, John and Dave Foreman; eds., *The Earth First! Reader: Ten Years of Radical Environmentalism*, Peregrine Smith, 1991.
Foreman, Dave and Dave Haywood, eds., *Ecodefense: A Field Guide to Monkey-wrenching*, Earth First! Books, 1987.
Manes, Christopher, *Green Rage: Radical Environmentalism and the Unmaking of Civilization*, Little Brown, 1990.
Scarce, Rik. *Eco-Warriors: Understanding the Radical Environmental Movement*, Noble Press, 1990.

Regionalism

Lubove, Roy, *Community Planning in the 1920s: The Contribution of the Regional Planning Association of America*, University of Pittsburgh Press, 1963.
MacKaye, Benton, *The New Exploration: A Philosophy of Regional Planning*, University of Illinois Press, 1962. Original 1928.
Mumford, Lewis. *Technics and Civilization*, Harcourt Brace and World, 1934; *The Culture of Cities*, Harcourt, Brace and World, 1938; *The Myth of the Machine*, 2 Volumes. Harcourt Brace Jovanovich, 1967, 1970.
Odum, Howard W. and Harry Estill Moore, *American Regionalism: A Cultural-Historical Approach to National Integration*, Henry Holt, 1938.
Sussman, Carl, ed., *Planning the Fourth Migration: The Neglected Vision of the Regional Planning Association of America*, MIT Press, 1976.

Critique of Science and Technology

Berman, Morris, *The Re-enchantment of the World*, Cornell University Press, 1981.
Capra, Fritjof, *The Turning Point: Science, Society, and the Rising Culture*, Flamingo, 1982.
Ehrenfeld, David, *The Arrogance of Humanism*, Oxford University Press, 1978; *Beginning Again: People and Nature in the New Millennium*, Oxford University Press, 1993.
Illich, Ivan, *Toward a History of Needs*, Pantheon, 1977; *Energy and Equity*,

Marion Boyers, 1979

Mander, Jerry, *In the Absence of the Sacred: The Failure of Technology and the Survival of the Indian Nations*, Sierra Club Books, 1991.

Zerzan, John and Alice Carnes, eds., *Questioning Technology: Tool, Toy, or Tyrant?* New Society Publishers, 1991.

Site Planning

De Chiara, Joseph and Lee Koppelman, *Urban Planning and Design Criteria*, Van Nostrand Reinhold, 1982.

Harris, Charles W. and Nicholas T. Dines, *Time Saver Standards for Landscape Architecture: Design and Construction Data*, McGraw-Hill, 1988.

Lowry, William P., *Atmospheric Ecology for Designers and Planners*, Peavine, 1988.

Lynch, Kevin, *What Time Is This Place?* MIT Press, 1972; *Good City Form*, MIT Press, 1984; with Gary Hack, *Site Planning*, MIT Press, 1984.

Robinette, Gary O., ed., *Energy Efficient Site Planning*, Van Nostrand Reinhold, 1983.

Soil

Brady, Nyle C., *The Nature and Properties of Soil*, Collier Macmillan, 1990.

Goldman, Steven, et al., *Erosion and Sediment Control Handbook*, McGraw-Hill, 1986.

Gray, Donald H. and Andrew Leiser, *Biotechnical Slope Protection and Erosion Control*, Van Nostrand Reinhold, 1982.

Hillel, Daniel, *Out of the Earth: Civilization and the Life of the Soil*, Free Press, 1990.

Sears, Paul Bigelow, *Deserts on the March*, Island Press, 1988. Original 1935.

Spiritual Ecology

Andrews, Valerie, *A Passion for this Earth: Exploring a New Partnership of Man, Woman, and Nature*, Harper Collins, 1992.

Macy, Joanna Rogers, *World as Lover, World as Self*, Parallax Press, 1991.

Nollman, Jim, *Spiritual Ecology: A Guide to Reconnecting with Nature*, Bantam, 1990.

Sjöö, Monica and Barbara Mor, *The Great Cosmic Mother: Rediscovering The Religion of the Earth*, Harper SF, 1991.

Willers, Bill, ed., *Learning to Listen to the Land*, Island Press, 1991.

Sustainability Manifestos

Goldsmith, Edward, ed., *Blueprint for Survival*, Penguin, 1972.

International Union for Conservation of Nature and Natural Resources (IUCN), et al., *World Conservation Strategy: Living Resource Conservation for Sustainable Development*, IUCN, 1980.

IUCN, et al., *Caring For The Earth: A Strategy For Sustainable Living*, IUCN, 1991.
The World Commission on Environment and Development, *Our Common Future*, Oxford University Press, 1987.
World Conservation Union, *Agenda 21, Working Toward A Global Partnership*, Oceana, 1993.

Systems Theory

Davidson, Mark, *Uncommon Sense: The Life and Thought of Ludwig von Bertalanffy, Father of General Systems Theory*, J. P. Tarcher, 1983
Gleick, James, *Chaos: The Making of a New Science*, Penguin, 1988.
Joseph, Lawrence, *Gaia: The Growth of an Idea*, St. Martins, 1990.
Lovelock, James E., *Gaia: A New Look at Life on Earth*, Oxford University Press, 1979; *The Ages of Gaia*, Bantam, 1988; *Healing Gaia: A New Prescription for the Living Planet*, Crown, 1991.
Waldrop, M. Mitchell, *Complexity: The Emerging Science at the Edge of Order and Chaos*, Touchstone, 1992.

Utopias

Callenbach, Ernest, *Ecotopia*, Banyan Tree Books, 1975; *Ecotopia Emerging*, Bantam Books, 1981.
Doxiadis, Constantinos, *Between Dystopia and Utopia*, Faber and Faber, 1966; *Ekistics: An Introduction to the Science of Human Settlements*, Hutchinson and Co., 1968.
Le Corbusier, *The Radiant City*, Faber and Faber, 1967.
Manuel, Frank E. and Fritzie Manuel, *Utopian Thought in the Western World*, Harvard University Press, 1979.
Soleri, Paulo, *The City in the Image of Man*, MIT Press, 1969.

Water

Black, Peter E., *Watershed Hydrology*, Prentice-Hall, 1991.
Dunne, Thomas and Luna B. Leopold, *Water in Environmental Planning*. Freeman, 1978.
Laws, Edward A., *Aquatic Pollution: An Introductory Text*, Wiley-Interscience, 1993.
Thorne-Miller, Boyce and John Catena, *The Living Ocean: Understanding and Protecting Marine Biodiversity*, Island Press, 1991.
Yates, Steven A., *Adopting A Stream: A Northwest Handbook*, Adopt A Stream Foundation/University of Washington Press, 1988.

Journals

Alternatives: Perspectives on Society, Technology and Environment. Faculty of Environmental Studies, University of Waterloo, Waterloo, ON,

N2L 3G1, Canada.

Ambio: A Journal of the Human Environment. Royal Swedish Academy of Sciences, Box 50005, S-104 05 Stockholm, Sweden. Eight issues/yr. 1972-

Journal of the American Planning Association. 1313 East 60th St., Chicago, Illinois, 60637, U.S.A. 1979-

Anthos. Verlag Graf-Neuhaus, Mohrlistr 69, 8033 Zurich, Switzerland. Yearly. 1962-

Antipode: A Radical Journal of Geography. Blackwell Scientific Publications, 238 Main Street, Cambridge, Massachusetts, 02142, U.S.A. Quarterly. 1969-

Journal of Biogeography. Blackwell Scientific Publications, 3 Cambridge Center, Suite 208, Cambridge, Massachusetts, 02142, USA. Three issues/yr. 1974-

Biological Conservation. Elsevier Science Publishers, Crown House, Linton Road, Barking, Essex, IG11 8JU, U.K. Monthly. 1968-

BioScience. American Institute of Biological Sciences, 730 11th Street NW, Washington DC, 20001-2584, U.S.A. Monthly. 1964-

City Magazine. 71 Cordova St., Winnipeg, Manitoba, R3N 0Z9, Canada.

CoHousing Newsletter. P.O. Box 2584, Berkeley, California, 94702, U.S.A. Quarterly.

Communities Magazine. 105 Sun St., Stelle, Illinois, 60919, U.S.A. Quarterly. 1972-

Conservation Biology. Blackwell Scientific Publications, 238 Main St., Cambridge, Mass., 02142, U.S.A. Quarterly. 1987-

Cultural Survival. 11 Divinity Ave., Cambridge, Mass., 02138, U.S.A. Quarterly. 1976-

Earth First! Journal. P.O. Box 1415, Eugene, Oregon, 97440, U.S.A. Eight issues/yr.

Earthword Magazine: The Journal of Environmental and Social Responsibility. EOS Institute, 1550 Bayside Drive, Corona Del Mar, California, 92625, U.S.A. Quarterly.

Eco-city Builders News. Eco-city Builders, 5427 Telegraph Avenue, Berkeley, California, 94609, U.S.A. Irregular.

Ecology. Ecological Society of America. Center for Environmental Studies, Arizona State University, Tempe, Arizona, 852873211, U.S.A. Eight issues/yr. 1920-

Ecology and Freedom. Social Ecology Network, Crouch Hill Recreation Centre, Hillrise Road, London, N19 3PT, U.K. Irregular. 1992-

The Ecologist. MIT Press Journals, 55 Hayward Street, Cambridge, Mass., 02142, U.S.A. Bimonthly. 1970-

Ekistics: The Problems and Science of Human Settlements. Athens Center for Ekistics. 24 Strat Syndesmou St., 10673 Athens, Greece. Bimonthly. 1957-

Environment and Urbanization. International Institute for Environment and Development, 3 Endsleigh Street, London, WC1H ODD, U.K. Semi-annual. 1989-

Environmental Conservation. Elsevier Sequoia SA, P.O. Box 564, CH-1001, Lausanne 1, Switzerland. Quarterly. 1974-

Environmental Ethics. Department of Philosophy, University of Georgia, Athens, Georgia, 30602, U.S.A. Quarterly. 1979-

Journal of Environmental Education. Heldref Publications, 4000 Albemarle Street NW, Suite 504, Washington DC, 20016, U.S.A. Quarterly. 1970-

Environmental Impact Assessment Review. Elsevier Science Publishing Co. Ltd., 655 Avenue of the Americas, New York, New York, 10010, U.S.A. Six issues/yr. 1980-

Journal of Environmental Planning and Management. Carfax Publishing Co., P.O. Box 25, Abingdon, Oxfordshire, OX14 3UE, U.K. Bi-monthly. 1980-

Environmental Values. The White Horse Press, 1 STROND, Isle of Harris, Scotland, PA83 3UD. Quarterly. 1992-

Environments: A Journal of Interdisciplinary Studies. Faculty of Environmental Studies, University of Waterloo, Ontario, N2L 3G1, Canada. Three issues/yr.

Fourth World Review: For Small Nations, Small Communities, and The Human Spirit. The Fourth World, 24 Abercorn Place, London, NW8 9XP, U.K. Bimonthly.

Garbage: The Practical Journal for the Environment. Old House Journal Corporation, 435 9th Street, Brooklyn, New York, 11215, U.S.A. Bimonthly. 1989-

In Context. P.O. Box 11470, Bainbridge Island, Washington, 98110, U.S.A. Quarterly. 1983-

Landscape. P.O. Box 7107, Berkeley, California, 94707, U.S.A. Three issues/yr. 1951-

Landscape Ecology. SPB Academic Publishing, P.O. Box 97747, 2509 GC, The Hague, The Netherlands. Quarterly. 1987-

Landscape Journal: Design, Planning, and Management of the Land. Journal Division, University of Wisconsin Press, 114 North Murray Street, Madison, Wisconsin, 53715, U.S.A. Semi-annual. 1982-

Landscape and Urban Planning. Elsevier Science Publishers, Journals Department, P.O. Box 211, 1000 AE, Amsterdam, The Netherlands. Eight issues/yr., 1986-

The New Catalyst. P.O. Box 189, Gabriola Island, BC V0R 1X0, Canada. Quarterly. 1985-. *The New Catalyst* Bioregional Series. Semi-annual. 1990-

The New Farm. Rodale Research Center, 400 South 10th Street, Emmaus, Penn., 18098-0099, U.S.A. Seven issues/yr. 1979-

The New Internationalist. P.O. Box 1143, Lewiston, New York, 14092, U.S.A. Monthly. 1973-

Our Generation. 3981 Boul. St Laurent, Suite 44, Montreal, Quebec, H2W 1Y5, Canada. Semi-annual.

Permaculture Activist. Route 1, Box 38, Primm Springs, Tenn., 38476, U.S.A. Quarterly. 1985-

Permaculture Magazine: Solutions For Sustainable Living. Permanent Publications, Little Hyden Lane, Clanfield, Hampshire, P08 0RU, U.K.

Places: A Quarterly Journal of Environmental Design. P.O. Box 1897, Lawrence, Kansas, 66044-8897, U.S.A. Quarterly. 1983-

Plan Canada. 541 Sussex Drive, 2nd Floor, Ottawa, K1N 6Z6, Canada. Bimonthly. 1959 -

Planning Perspectives: An International Journal of History, Planning, and the Environment. E. & F. N. Spon, 26 Boundary Row, London, SE1 8HN, UK. Quarterly. 1982-

Race, Poverty, and the Environment. Earth Island Institute, 300 Broadway, Suite 28, San Francisco, California, 94133-3312, U.S.A.

Rain. P.O. Box 30097, Eugene, Oregon, 97403-1097, U.S.A. Quarterly. 1973-

Raise The Stakes. Planet Drum Foundation. P.O. Box 31251, San Francisco, 94131, U.S.A. Semi-annual. 1978-

Real World: The Voice of Ecopolitics. 91 Nuns Moor Road, Newcastle upon Tyne, NE4 9BA, U.K. Quarterly. 1992-

Restoration and Management Notes. University of Wisconsin Arboretum, 1207 Seminole Highway, Madison, Wisconsin, 53711, U.S.A. Semi-annual. 1981-

Resurgence. Salem Cottage, Trelill, Bodmin, Cornwall, PL30 3H2, U.K. Bimonthly. 1966-

Transnational Institute for Appropriate Technology (TRANET). P.O. Box 567, Rangley, ME, O4970, U.S.A.

The Trumpeter Journal of Ecophilosophy. P.O. Box 5883, Station B, Victoria, British Columbia, V8R 6S8, Canada. Quarterly. 1983-

Upriver-Downriver. P.O. Box 103, Petrolia, California, 95558, U.S.A. Irregular.

Undercurrents. 355 Lumbers Bldg., Faculty of Environmental Studies, York University, 4700 Keele St., Downsview, Ontario, M3J 1P3, Canada.

Whole Earth Review. P.O. Box 38, Sausalito, California, 94966-9932, U.S.A. Quarterly. 1974-

Wild Earth. P.O. Box 455, Richmond, Vermont, 05477, U.S.A. Quarterly. 1991-

Wildlife Conservation. New York Zoological Society, 185th Street and Southern Blvd., Bronx, New York, 20006. Bimonthly. 1897-

♦

Author Biographies

Doug Aberley is a long-time proponent of bioregionalism as a balanced path to transformative social change. Trained as a community and regional planner, Doug worked for 15 years in the small community of Hazelton in northwest British Columbia. He is editor of the sixth in *The New Catalyst*'s Bioregional Series, *Boundaries of Home: Mapping for Local Empowerment*, and is active in exploring practical methods by which bioregionalism can be better understood and applied. He is currently completing doctoral research on the history and practice of bioregionalism at Heriot-Watt University in Edinburgh, Scotland, as well as being a Director of the David Suzuki Foundation in Vancouver, B.C.

Murray Bookchin is a founder and director of the Institute for Social Ecology in Vermont, and is perhaps best-known for his book *Toward an Ecological Society* (Black Rose, 1980). A historian, his view that human nature is essentially cooperative—what he terms "social ecology"— and that humankind, if freed from the tyranny of centralized, hierarchical power structures, can be self-organizing, has had considerable impact upon the alternative movement. A bioregional sympathizer, he is mainly active with the Social Ecology Project, PO Box 111, Burlington VT 05402, USA.

Christopher Canfield is a founder and community development coordinator of the Cerro Gordo Town Forum whose memebrs and supporters are planning and building an ecological village for up to 2500 people. An ecological community development consultant for 20 years, he was recently the recipient of a Sustainable Community Solutions award presented by the World Congress of Architects. Of 400 entries submitted in the competition, his description of Cerro Gordo's history and purpose was one of only 24 prize winners.

Raymond Dasmann has worked for the past forty and more years in the field of ecology and conservation with a particular interest in wildlife and wild country. His work with UNESCO, IUCN and the World Wildlife Fund has taken him to many countries and developed an awareness of the need to protect cultural diversity as well as biological diversity. He was instrumental in the founding of the bioregional movement, and has inspired generations of activists and ecologists with his many publications. At present he is Professor Emeritus at the University of California, Santa Cruz.

Suzy Hamilton is a journalist, environmentalist, and organizer with the Kootenay Barter Bank in Nelson, B.C. Like hundreds of other new residents in the West Kootenay, she is captured by the sense of community there, as well as the hope that there are enough like-minded people to restore local control. She has written for a number of magazines and newspapers, and is an avid bee-keeper and bridge player when she's not tracking stories or barterers for her Barter Bank Bulletin.

Jane Jacobs was born in Scranton, Pennsylvania, and now lives in Toronto, Canada, where she pursues her unrelenting analysis of the nature of cities. Her books include *Systems of Survival, The Death and Life of Great American Cities, The Economy of Cities,* and her classic, *Cities and the Wealth of Nations.*

David McCloskey originated near the confluence of the McKenzie and Willamette rivers in Oregon and now lives with his family in the Snoqualmie watershed, in Ish River country, Cascadia, on the northeast rim. He teaches sociology, anthropology, human ecology, and geography at Seattle University. Director of the Cascadia Institute, he has been writing on the significance of place and bioregionalism, specializing in the Cascadia bioregion, for over a decade.

Donella H. Meadows is a systems analyst, journalist, and college professor. She holds a Ph.D in biophysics from Harvard University, and is adjunct Professor at Dartmouth College in the Environmental Studies Program. She has authored, or co-authored, nine books, writes a nationally-syndicated column, "The Global Citizen," and lives in Plainfield, New Hampshire.

Bill Mollison coined the term "permaculture" (permanent agriculture) in the late 1970s and has written three best-selling books describing basic permaculture philosophy and practice. He has taught and consulted internationally on permaculture, and lives and works in Australia.

Helena Norberg-Hodge is Director of the International Society for Ecology and Culture and its daughter organization, the Ladakh Project. She has spent much of the last 17 years in Ladakh ("Little Tibet"), helping the Ladakhi people to maintain their cultural identity and ecological integrity in the face of rapid modernization. She is author of *Ancient Futures: Learning from Ladakh,* c/- I.S.E.C., 21 Victoria Square, Clifton, Bristol BS8 4ES, U.K.

Reed Noss is editor of *Conservation Biology,* the most widely cited journal in applied ecology, and is also the science editor for *Wild Earth* magazine. He has over 75 publications in ecology and conservation biology to his name, and his 21 years in the environmental field have included work as an ecologist for the Ohio Natural Heritage Program and the Florida Natural Areas Inventory, and as Biodiversity Project Leader for the U.S. Environmental Protection Agency. A research scientist at the University of Idaho, a research associate at Stanford University, and an assistant Professor at Oregon State University, he is also on the board of directors for both the Natural Areas Association and The Wildlands Project, P.O. Box 5365, Tucson, AZ 85703, USA.

Tony Pearse has worked for 15 years with some two dozen First Nations in B.C., the Yukon, and Alberta on land and resource issues, and has developed special expertise in resource data collection and mapping, land use research and planning, and the assessment of development impacts on natural and cultural environments of aboriginal communities. He also specializes in First Nations policy development relating to natural resources, particularly mining and wildlife, and is a founding director of the David Suzuki Foundation.

Dr. Janice E. Perlman, Founder and Director of Mega-Cities, is a senior research scholar at New York University. She is author of the award-winning book, *The Myth of Marginality: Urban Poverty and Politics in Rio de Janeiro*. Her 25 years of experience in urban development include serving as Coordinator of President Carter's Neighborhood Task Force, Special Advisor to the World Bank Urban Projects Department, Executive Director of Strategic Planning for the New York City Partnership, and consultant to various non-profit groups and local and national governments in the USA and abroad.

Richard Register is an artist, sculptor, designer, carpenter, and author of *Eco-city Berkeley—Building Cities for a Healthy Future* as well as other books and articles. A major organizer of the eco-cities movement, he has organized conferences on the topic, as well as having created the group Eco-City Builders who can be contacted at 5427 Telegraph Avenue, Berkeley, CA 94609, USA.

Mark Roseland is author of *Toward Sustainable Communities: A Resource Book for Municipal and Local Governments* (1992), and is currently research director and visiting Professor in the School of Resource and Environmental Management at Simon Fraser University, in British Columbia, Canada.

Susan Snetsinger is a conservation biologist with the Greater Ecosystem Alliance, based in Bellingham, Washington. She is currently conducting a landscape analysis of the Greater North Cascades Ecosystem, using GIS, and developing a scientifically-based reserve proposal for protecting biodiversity of the region. She is currently working toward the completion of an M.S. degree in Conservation Biology and Sustainable Development at the University of Wisconsin, Madison.

Gary Snyder walks and writes around the Pacific Rim. A long-time poet, Zen practitioner, and promoter of bioregionalism, he is the author of *Turtle Island, The Practice of the Wild* and, most recently, a volume of selected and new poems *No Nature* (Pantheon). His home base is in the northern Sierra where he is one of the founders of the Yuba Watershed Institute.

Frederick Steiner is professor and chair of the Department of Planning at Arizona State University. He has worked for city, county, state, federal and Indian agencies as well as private companies and nonprofit organizations. His projects and research include the areas of new community development, farmland protection, international planning, soil conservation policy, greenline planning, watershed planning, suitability analysis, environmental assessment, and landscape design.

David Suzuki, a Professor of genetics at the University of British Columbia and an internationally-known broadcaster, hosts the award-winning television series, "The Nature of Things." He has spoken out on environmental and human rights issues for more than twenty-five years through his television and radio shows, articles, columns, and public lectures. The author of several books, he is also Chairman of the David Suzuki Foundation in Vancouver, B.C.

Melanie Taylor is an architect, designer, and consultant as well as publisher of *The Home and Town Gazette*. She designed the community of Seaside in Florida, and Mashpee Commons on Cape Cod, transforming a strip shopping center into an urban plaza, and is a leader in the "new traditional," "small town" movement, New Haven, Connecticut.